LOUIS XIV

LOUIS XIV

An Informal Portrait

by

W. H. LEWIS

HARCOURT, BRACE AND COMPANY

NEW YORK

FIRST AMERICAN EDITION

Library of Congress Catalog Card Number:

PRINTED IN HOLLAND
BY DRUKKERIJ HOLLAND N.V., AMSTERDAM

TO
RUTH PARKER

ILLUSTRATIONS

*The above illustrations are reproduced by permission of the Trustees of
the British Museum*

FOREWORD

FOR his *Paris Sketchbook* Thackeray drew a black and white illustration which summarized his opinion of Louis XIV. To the left, on a tailor's dummy, are the huge wig, royal mantle, false calves, and high-heeled shoes, labelled 'The King'; in the centre, a little bald-headed man in a dark suit called 'Louis'; and on the right the two are combined into a caricature of Rigaud's famous portrait, captioned 'Louis the King'.

In this book we are concerned solely with the little man in the dark suit. It is not a biography of Louis XIV, still less is it a survey of French history during the period 1638–1715. We all have some idea of the 'Grand Monarque', but what, if anything, lay behind that magnificent façade? What were his ambitions, hopes, and fears? How did he make love, eat, drink, and dress? What were his personal tastes and prejudices? These are the questions which I have asked myself.

Of course Louis could not have existed *in vacuo*, and a certain amount of history is unavoidable, even in such a book as this. But I have restricted it to the bare minimum required to make the story intelligible, and must warn those who seek to understand the significance of the *Grand Siècle* that they must look elsewhere for their information. Nor do I apologize for the historical distortion inevitable in approaching Louis from the angle which I have chosen; for instance, the battle of Malplaquet in 1709 was of infinitely greater moment to Louis than was his failure to fight a battle at Heurtebise in 1676; but Heurtebise is treated more fully than Malplaquet because the former tells us much about Louis and the latter nothing.

This book, I repeat, is not a biography; but I venture to hope that it may some day provide notes for the definitive life of Louis XIV which is still lacking.

In writing this book I have been forced to consult so many authorities that I have decided to omit the bibliography; partly for reasons of space, partly lest I should seem to have promised more than I have performed. For those whose curiosity has been satisfied by what I have written, it would be otiose; and for readers who are tempted to delve more deeply in a fascinating subject I recommend the exhaustive bibliography given in Volume V (pp. 765–785) of the *Cambridge Modern History*.

W. H. LEWIS

AUTHOR'S NOTE

Money Values, pre-1914 rates

3 deniers, copper, equal	¼d	½cent
12 deniers, copper, equal 1 sol, equal	1d	2cents
20 sols, copper, equal 1 livre, silver, equal	1/8d	40cents
3 livres, silver, equal 1 crown, silver, equal	5 s	$1.25
11 livres, silver, equal 1 louis d'or, gold, equal 18/4d		$4.40

COURT TITLES

Contemporary writers almost invariably employ Court, and not legal titles. In addition to those detailed below, it should be noted that:

Archbishops and bishops are always referred to by the name of their sees; e.g., Fénelon is 'M. de Cambrai' and Bossuet 'M. de Meaux'.

Titles were never used by the nobility at Court; thus the Duc de Rohan was 'M. de Rohan', the Duchesse de Chevreuse 'Mme de Chevreuse', and so on.

When an unmarried woman is called 'Madame' it indicates that she was a canoness.

'Chevalier', a common junior title in the nobility, usually (but not invariably) means that the holder was a Knight of Malta.

Monseigneur   The Dauphin, the heir-apparent; but after the death of Louis XIV's son in 1710, subsequent heirs were called simply 'M. le Dauphin'.

Monsieur   The Duc d'Orléans, second son of the King. Until 1660 Gaston, brother of Louis XIII, bore this title, and the holder after that date was Philippe, brother of Louis XIV. But Philippe is often called 'the little Monsieur' during his uncle's lifetime.

Madame   The Duchesse d'Orléans. Philippe's first wife, Henrietta of England was 'Madame' from 1660 to 1670, and his second wife, Elizabeth Charlotte of Bavaria, held the title from 1671 to 1701.

Mademoiselle The eldest daughter of 'Monsieur'. Anne, Duchesse de Montpensier held the title until 1693, and was the daughter of Gaston, Duc d'Orléans; in 1693 Philippe's eldest daughter became 'Mademoiselle'.

M. le Prince The Prince de Condé, head of a collateral branch of the House of Bourbon. The title was dropped on the death of the fifth Prince in 1709.

Mme la Princesse The wife of 'M. le Prince'.

M. le Duc The Duc de Bourbon, eldest son of 'M. le Prince'. But Louis III, who succeeded as Prince de Condé in 1709, continued to be known as M. le Duc.

Mme la Duchesse The wife of 'M. le Duc'; from 1685 the holder of this title was a daughter of Louis XIV by Mme de Montespan.

M. le Comte The Comte de Soissons, head of the French branch of the House of Savoy.

Mme la Comtesse Wife of 'M. le Comte', after 1657 Mazarin's niece, Olympe Mancini.

M. le Grand The Grand Equerry of France.

M. le Premier The First Equerry of France.

I

MIDNIGHT 4 September 1638, Queen Anne of France groaning in protracted labour with her first child; delightful sounds to Louis XIII in the adjoining room, who began to show some animation as he discussed his chances of being a widower before sunrise. But he was to be disappointed. At two o'clock on the morning of the 5th Anne bore the boy who as Louis XIV was to dominate his century; who before the day was out was called *Le Dieudonné*; and of whom within a week legends that he was something more than human were to circulate; as for instance that he had been born with a full set of teeth.

To the love-starved Queen her little Dauphin was a treasure from whom she could not bear to be separated, a marvel to be proudly exhibited to the Court, and her sole topic of conversation; with the result that before the child was a year old, the Louis cult which was to warp the future King's character was already established among the courtiers.

In his first portrait he lies on the lap of his bare-breasted nurse, head, arms, and the ribbon of the St Esprit projecting from the cylinder of linen in which he spent his days swaddled in his own excrement. Legends of the miraculous Dauphin were circulating unceasingly, but some people were sceptical; whispering of Anne's twenty-three child-less married years, of the King's lack of virility, and asking if it was credible that *le Dieudonné* was his son. And such suspicions continued to thrive as late as 1702, when a pamphlet was published in which it was stated that Louis XIV's father was Louis XIII's favourite, Cinq-Mars. But no convincing case has ever been made out against Louis XIV's legitimacy, and such tales are mere scandal-mongering.

The Royal Astrologer was present at Anne's accouchement, but as the horoscope has been lost we must endeavour to cast it for ourselves by seeing what sort of parents Louis had. His father we may dismiss briefly, for the boy inherited nothing from him but the Crown, and the thirteenth Louis died before he could exert any influence on the Dauphin's formative years. Bullied in childhood by his Italian mother and her favourite, Concini, Louis XIII had been a furtive, timid child who became an awkward, jealous, suspicious man, coldly cruel, and diffusing his own boredom over his Court; hating his Spanish wife who despised him. And when he died in 1643, his widow led the rejoicings of the Court.

Anne's first gift to her son was the physique which withstood his own abuse of it and the care of his physicians for nearly eighty years; and to her he owed much of his character, notably the deep but narrow Spanish piety which was its foundation. For though Louis was to see himself as the typical Frenchman, he was not really French at all, but was predominantly a Spaniard—grave, taciturn, with immense natural dignity and a strong sense of the divine sanction of his own autocracy.

Until 1643 most of Anne's life had been passed in the shadows; married at fifteen, her pride both as a beautiful girl and a Hapsburg had been cruelly hurt by the coldness of her husband, who, though not actually impotent, showed a marked lack of virility; and when Anne consoled herself with 'honest gallantry' after the Spanish fashion, Louis' dislike of her turned to hatred. A hatred fomented by Richelieu for political reasons, with the result that Anne was relegated to semi-disgrace. Until 1643 she was a cypher, but as Regent of France she showed that she was not negligible; though lazy, she had the dogged pride and endurance of her House, coupled with an innate common-sense and a shrewd knowledge of men and their motives; and when aroused, she could show both energy and decision. Though sometimes an injudicious, she was always a loving mother, who never forgot her duty of handing over the Kingdom to her son with the prerogatives of the Crown unimpaired. Louis not only recognized his debt to his mother, but loved her 'in a manner unusual in persons of his quality'; and to the end of his life kept the anniversary of her death as a day of mourning. And perhaps the best thing that can be said of Anne's second son Philippe, born 21 September 1640, is that he was an affectionate and grateful son.

Had his father's life been prolonged Louis XIV would probably have had a miserable childhood, for as early as 1641 Louis XIII was already jealous of his heir; resenting the adulation offered to him, accusing Anne of teaching the boy to hate his father, and threatening to deprive her of the custody of her children. But already in 1641 the Court saw with thankfulness that the thirteenth Louis had not much longer to live. Seeing what Louis XIV was to become, it is amusing to find his Governess, Mme de Senécé, reporting in 1642 that whilst her pupil's conduct is satisfactory, he is 'too humble and submissive' for his station. And it was perhaps to arouse his pride that Senécé one day showed the boy a portrait of Richelieu, saying, 'There he is, the cur!' 'Give me my arquebus,' said the Dauphin, 'and I will shoot him'; possibly it was this incident which sowed in Louis the seeds of that dislike for Prime Ministers and contempt for idle Kings which was to distinguish him.

But if Louis was humble and submissive, his intelligence was expanding rapidly; already at five he was beginning to learn that art of saying and doing the right thing which later became second nature to him. 'Do you want to reign?', said a courtier to him on 13 May 1643. 'No', replied Louis in tears, 'I do not want my good Papa to die'. However, to everyone's satisfaction his good papa died the next day, and on the 18th Louis made his first appearance as King; at a *Lit de Justice* where he was assured by the Advocate-General that he was 'a visible Divinity' and 'the symbol of God'.

On the following day Louis de Bourbon, Duc d'Enghien, better known by his subsequent title of Prince de Condé, won the battle of Rocroi; the most complete victory gained by France over Spain in the Thirty Years War. And flatterers told the little King that his father, seeing a vision of the glories destined for Louis XIV, had been divinely inspired to appoint the twenty-two year old Enghien 'the instrument to wreathe his cradle with laurels'.

Absurdities which naturally had their effect on the 'visible Divinity'. who was already developing that 'imposing majesty' which was to be his most characteristic trait. A majesty apparent as early as 1644 to the critical eye of a foreign ambassador—'The King', he wrote to his Court, 'has a noble air which breathes grandeur; he is robust, with rather a severe glance, but it is a severity full of charm. He laughs rarely in his childish games, and stands for long periods without moving. He knows he is the King, and wishes everyone else to know it too'.

But behind the scenes Louis was less imposing; his tutor complained that he could teach him nothing, and that the King was adept at sheltering behind his mother, who spoilt him; and he hinted that Anne's familiarity with her servants was setting the child a bad example. However, the tutor's warning came too late, for Louis had already acquired the habit of making friends of his domestics, and continued to do so for the rest of his life.

But if Louis' formal education was neglected, he was beginning to understand his world; and the better he understood it the less he liked it. Mazarin was now firmly established as Prime Minister, and was probably already married to the Queen, in whose eyes he was perfection; even a child saw that Mazarin was the master, and Louis resented, without understanding, the relations which existed between his mother and this foreigner who behaved so differently from anyone else at Court. Useless for the King to complain to Anne of the familiarity with which the Cardinal treated him, for this merely called Mazarin's attention to Louis' resentment; and the child, surrounded by Mazarin's spies, developed a reticence which Society labelled stupidity. But Society erred. What had happened was that an intelligent little boy was applying the Spanish proverb learnt from his mother—'No flies enter a shut mouth'. Instead of talking he listened and bided his time.

One result of Louis' reflections was that he determined to be a Henri IV, not a Louis XIII. The former he often heard spoken of, the latter never, for Anne so hated the memory of Louis XIII that his name could not be mentioned in her presence; a conspiracy of silence hung over the late reign, and all that the young Louis could discover about his father was that he had reigned and was now dead. It is significant that in his memoirs Louis XIV mentions Louis XIII only once, and Richelieu never. In 1645, when Louis was eight years old, Mazarin appointed himself Superintendent of the King's education. But his supervision was limited to isolating the King from contacts hostile to himself; the spy net about the child was tightened up, and Mazarin made it obvious that no mercy was to be expected by those who should attempt to waken Louis to the fact that he was the master only in so far as he made himself worthy of being so. Good books were as suspect in the royal suite as were visitors of merit, and Louis, who was not blind to what was happening, became increasingly resentful of the Cardinal's dominance.

In one respect however the little King was fortunate; Mazarin attached no importance to his religious education, which remained in the Queen's hands, and she, being a woman of sincere piety, stood no nonsense where religion was in question; in 1646 for instance, we find Louis imprisoned for forty-eight hours for swearing. And he was lucky too in having for his valet the upright and kindly La Porte, who, next to his mother, exercised the strongest influence over his formative years.

Louis had begun by disliking him when in 1645 he was taken out of the hands of the women and given a Governor. He was horrified to discover that La Porte was to share his bedroom, and distressed to find the valet completely ignorant of fairy tales for the bedtime story. But soon, says La Porte,

> he showed no aversion to me; on the contrary, when he was going to sleep he would make me put my head on his pillow, and if he woke in the night he would creep into my bed . . . I have often carried him back asleep to his own. He was a docile child, and would always listen to reason. He had brains, seeing and understanding what went on around him, but talking little. He was naturally good and humane, with the promise of becoming a great Prince. But insufficient care was taken in fostering his good qualities.

And small wonder. We have seen how Mazarin regarded his responsibilities towards the young King, and the Governor was worse than the Superintendent. That official, who had taken office in 1645, was the Maréchal-Duc de Villeroi, a man of forty-seven, a careerist to his fingertips, who is still remembered for his summary of the duties of a courtier—'Hold the chamber pot for a great man so long as he stands firm, and the mimute he begins to slip, empty it over his head'. To Villeroi the only problem in his new post was how to ingratiate himself with the King without giving offence to Mazarin, and he solved it by letting both King and Cardinal do exactly what they pleased; Mazarin was satisfied, and Louis, with precocious cynicism, gave his verdict on the Governor within six months; he nicknamed him 'Maréchal Ouisire'.

By 1646 Louis' education was causing anxiety; 'dull and listless', said his school report, and he was more than ever in the Queen's room, where everyone praised and no one contradicted him; or bathing in the Seine; or tiring out his companions in the riding and fencing schools; or paying calls, and enchanting his subjects by riding freely about Paris in gold-embroidered clothes on his white pony.

But if he shirked school, Louis eagerly assimilated his mother's lessons. And had Anne's instructions been limited to religion, all would have been well, for Louis never forgot her precepts, even in the midst of his subsequent debaucheries. But unfortunately he acquired much from the Queen besides religion; a deep hatred of liberal ideas, driven home by her constant warning that the slightest resistance to the Royal will was a sin against God as well as against the King; and an almost pathological detestation of heresy—'he sucked it in with his mother's milk', said his Confessor triumphantly. And that same Confessor was afterwards to boast that he had convinced the King that Jansenist was a synonym for heretic.

At nine Louis was rather childish for his age, still indulging in his favourite game of pretending to be a valet—for preference the valet of a little peasant girl. For he had no companions of his own rank, because Mazarin, in order to keep him in ignorance of his true position, had refused him any Children-of-Honour. So Louis valetted his servants' daughters with that gravity which already so well became him.

In this summer the King began the exploration of his realm with a visit to Dieppe; an exciting adventure, during which a sham naval battle was staged for his benefit, and better still, some fireships were burnt. But Louis' interest in his navy was short-lived, for probably even then he realized that the sea was not the element on which a King could win that personal glory for which Louis thirsted; 'I always feel,' he confessed in later years, 'that a French victory at which I am not present, detracts from rather than adds to the glory of my reign'.

From Dieppe the Court proceeded to Fontainebleau, where Louis entertained the Prince of Wales. But neither he nor the future Charles II shone at the meeting; which is hardly surprising, for what could a youth of seventeen find to say to a child of nine? Especially a child who 'was prudent enough to say nothing for fear of not speaking well'? But if nothing of Louis the perfect host had yet appeared, the sick Louis in November was father to the man who was to die so magnificently in 1715. On the 10th he was attacked by smallpox, and during the worst of his illness he talked kindly to those who served him and was docile in the hands of his doctors; and to his mother he showed a tenderness which was obvious in spite of the characteristically stately language in which it was expressed—'he constantly called her

18

and begged her to sit beside him, assuring her that her presence sensibly diminished his sufferings'.

We hear a good deal about Louis' education in 1648; he studied Latin, Italian, drawing, mathematics, strategy, music, and physical accomplishments in all of which he was reported to be a docile pupil. It sounds an imposing curriculum, but it was mere window-dressing —'I am an ignorant fellow who learnt nothing,' he told the girls of St Cyr in 1694.

This is about the last we see of the royal schoolroom, for the outbreak of the Civil War on 13 May really ended Louis' education; though attempts were made to resume it after the rebellion ended in 1653. This war, the first Fronde, was an attempt by the Parlement to restore the constitution destroyed by Richelieu, and was supported by the rentiers whom Mazarin had cheated by manipulating Government Stock for his own profit. We are here concerned with the struggle only as regards its impact on Louis, and unfortunately its first result was to give him a lifelong hatred of the rentier, whom he classified as a new species of rebel. So that when he came to govern France, he was a man committed to raising revenue by direct taxation rather than by loan; a policy which was to have disastrous consequences in years to come.

France was now engaged both in the Thirty Years War abroad and in a civil war at home; and so long as the army was tied down in Flanders, not much could be attempted on the domestic front. But on 20 August Enghien, now Prince de Condé, routed the enemy at Lens and Mazarin was able to recall him and his troops for offensive measures against the capital. Louis, fast acquiring a political sense, summed up the consequences of Lens neatly—'How angry the Parlement will be!' he observed.

In 1649 Condé was ready to take drastic action against Paris, and his first move was to arrange for the evacuation of the Royal family to St Germain, thus leaving him free to blockade the city. At three on the morning of 6 January the King and his brother were awakened, hustled into a plain coach at the garden gate of the Palais-Royal, and driven out to St Germain. An exciting adventure for any ordinary boy of ten, but Louis was incapable of any emotion except rage that he was leaving Paris under duress; and when he learnt that the mob had refused permission for his baggage to follow him, he doubtless decided that some day he would settle accounts with his Parisians.

In the capital the news of the Royal flight was greeted with consternation and anger, the militia was put under arms, the gates guarded, and serious preparations for civil war were begun. But neither side had the strength necessary to ensure victory, and after much negotiation, aided by bribery, peace was signed at St Germain on 1 April.

On 18 August the Court returned to Paris amidst scenes of frantic enthusiasm, the King behaving with perfect self-possession during the slow drive to the Palace. As the Royal carriage passed through the crowded streets at a walking pace it was rushed by workmen who insisted on shaking hands with the King and assuring him of their affection; also mentioning, no doubt by way of a hint, that they were about to drink his health; whilst the women loudly expressed their admiration of the King's beauty.

The Court noticed that it was a changed Louis who came back to Paris, for psychologically the first Fronde had ended his childhood; more secretive, more silent, more adroit at learning by listening, he was becoming a King. His Grand Chamberlain was sharply reprimanded for unpunctuality; his cousin the Duchesse de Montpensier, known at Court as 'Mademoiselle', having refused him the entry to her suite, received a lecture on the respect she owed her King; and to Mazarin he spoke in such a tone about the state of his worn-out coach that the Premier ordered him five new ones on the spot.

In one way only did the new Louis resemble the old, namely in his inability to conceal his dislike for Mazarin, whom he nicknamed 'The Grand Turk'; and one night this year, hearing that the Cardinal was waiting in the anteroom to attend the royal *coucher*, he refused to leave his dressing room until Mazarin, tired of waiting for him, had returned to his own rooms—an incident which left Mazarin in a very thoughtful mood.

But if Louis had ceased to be child, he was still a boy when he was with La Porte, who tells us how about this time he read the King a lecture on the complaisance shown to the great, after which the following conversation took place:

Louis: Do you scold your own children as you do me?

La Porte: Sire, if I had children who behave as you do, I should not scold them but whip them severely, because people of our sort

20

cannot afford to be fools; if they are, they die of hunger, but a King, however great a fool he may be, can rest assured that he will never lack for anything, and that is why so many little Kings show neither application nor desire to improve. Are you annoyed at my frankness, Sire?

LOUIS: No.

In January 1650 Condé, whose pretentions and greed had become intolerable, was arrested and imprisoned at Vincennes; a move which, whilst it temporarily raised the credit of Anne and her Premier, was to lead to the outbreak of the second Fronde, and which instantly led to attempts by Condé's partisans to raise the provinces against the Government. To counter this Mazarin sent Louis and the Queen on an extended tour of the disaffected areas, which proved a brilliant success. The 'innocence and beauty' of the King delighted the people of Rouen, where he was received with great rejoicings; and in April he had his baptism of fire at the siege of Bellegarde, encouraging his unpaid troops by the calmness which he showed when one of his staff had an arm torn off by a cannon ball. But for Louis himself the experience had unfortunate results; he came home with the conviction that sieges were the 'kingly' form of warfare, and thus, when he came to command armies, a siege had always to be arranged for him, often to the grave detriment of French overall strategy.

October found Louis, his mother, and his brother in Bordeaux, a Frondeur stronghold which had surrendered to the Crown at the beginning of the month. But the spirit of revolt still lingered, and here the magic of the King's presence failed to achieve the same results as at Rouen; the applause at his entry was feeble, and the magistrates perfunctorily offered him 'a very bad collation, accompanied by a firework display of little beauty'.

In 1651 Louis, though not yet thirteen, began to be dimly aware that girls were intended for some other purpose than playfellows; during a ball in January his attentions to Elizabeth Tarneau, the daughter of a Paris lawyer, were so conspicuous and so ardent that her father had to take her home; to the intense annoyance of Louis, who was with difficulty prevented from sending for his arquebus to put a bullet through Tarneau's window. And in the summer he took to riding frequently with 'Mademoiselle', the attraction being one of her Ladies,

Mme de Frontenac, for whom he showed so violent and public a calf love that Anne had to forbid the outings. 'When I am master', said the King, furiously, 'I shall go where I wish; and I shall be master very soon.'

But such outbursts were rare, and for the most part Louis played the role of puppet King with a gracefulness which imperfectly hid his growing ennui; 'a bird singing in a cage', is the verdict on Louis at this time; but already there were far-sighted courtiers who prophesied that 'he would long remember what was being wrought against him now'.

1651 marks the lowest ebb of Louis' fortunes; in Paris the revived Fronde was triumphant and the royal family was imprisoned in the Palais-Royal, so strictly guarded that there could be no chance of repeating the coup of 1649. And on one February night 'Monsieur', the King's uncle, had the insolence to send a servant to the palace with orders to satisfy himself by personal inspection that the King was really in bed. Worse still, the mob, refusing to accept the man's assurance, burst into the royal bedroom to see for itself. True, when Anne had shown them Louis they retreated on tiptoe, 'showering a million whispered benedictions on his head'; but this denouement did nothing to quench the fire of Louis' rage, which was to burn for the rest of his life. And though he never afterwards referred to the incident, we may be certain that for sixty or more years to come, a week never passed without his recalling it. We can see the lessons of that night in all Louis' subsequent policy; his exclusion of his own family from the slightest share in Government; the reduction of the nobility to the status of domestic pets and their replacement in positions of trust by the bourgeoisie; the crushing of the Parlement; and the removal to Versailles which ensured that never again need a King of France be trapped in Paris. The pitiless severity with which Louis treated Fouquet in 1664 was not primarily because Fouquet had robbed him, but because he had fortified and garrisoned his island home of Belleisle, and the King saw there the headquarters of a new Fronde. Even in trifles he could not rid his mind of the civil war; when at the height of his splendour he would intervene patiently to compose a quarrel between two nobles, he did so not in the interests of domestic peace, but because he knew that a small spark can start a great fire; he remembered what had so often been the result in his young days of allowing a discontented noble to retire from Court. His distrust of nobles who preferred the country to Versailles, his constant watchfulness to prevent the formation of cliques, the marked disfavour shown to those who attempted to talk politics, all stem from the Fronde.

But even as a boy Louis had the useful faculty of being able to pigeonhole without forgetting a problem which was not ripe for solution, and he seems to have spent an agreeable summer; trying out new methods of attack and defence on his model fortress in the palace gardens; taking country walks; hunting and dancing; and swimming to and fro across the Marne. 'And already', writes the Maréchal de Clérembault, 'his powers of mind would not disgrace a man of twenty five'.

On 7 September Louis attended Parlement in state to declare his own majority, and at the sitting Anne formally resigned the Regency; but in fact things continued as before, and Louis remained in Mazarin's leading strings for another ten years. But the political consequences of the formality were of considerable importance.

On 13 February 1651 Mazarin, yielding to irresistible pressure, had gone in person to Hâvre and there released Condé; afterwards escaping himself to the neighbourhood of Cologne because he feared for his life in France, where the Parlement had put a price on his head. But from his place of exile he maintained constant touch with the Queen, and in fact continued to govern France as absolutely as if he was in Paris. Condé, most inept of politicians, had spent his time since his release in hesitations, in making enemies, and in changing sides; but on 15 September he finally plunged into open rebellion and placed himself under the protection of the King of Spain. But Condé had fatally mistimed his rising. The declaration of Louis' majority had automatically deprived 'Monsieur' of the Lieutenant-Generalcy of the Kingdom, dissolved the weak Council of Regency, and left Mazarin in autocratic control of the Royal power. Worse still, many great nobles and skilled officers who would have seen nothing blameworthy in making war on a Regent, refused absolutely to fight the King; and finally, had Condé timed his rebellion for even a month earlier he might easily have forced Anne to summon the States-General, which would certainly have met in a mood hostile to the Crown.

Nevertheless Condé won the first move, thanks to the audacity of his wife who, taking with her their little son, escaped from Montrond where she was in house arrest and threw herself into Bordeaux, forty-eight hours before the King's attempt to do so—and persuaded the city to shut its gates in the King's face. Rarely had Louis been more angry; in tears of rage he sobbed to his entourage, 'I shall not always be a child; this Bordelais scum shall not lay down the law to me much longer'.

1652 was for Louis a year of wandering up and down France, showing himself wherever Mazarin, now returned from exile, thought that his presence might be useful; trailing behind him a penurious Court, often under conditions of much hardship. But to comfort Louis was all his life indifferent, and this year was invaluable to him. In the comparatively humble role to which he was now reduced, the King was acquiring what was far more profitable than any book-learning; he was getting to know his own people, questioning chance-met innkeepers, ostlers, tradesmen, all the busy folk of the roads. To 1652 he owed it that with the single exception of Charles II of England, he understood his subjects as did no other European monarch. And also he was fast developing character; he had already conquered a hot temper, and was now admired for his extraordinary self-possession. Already he loved keenness, intelligence and wit, hated gossip, disparagement, jealousy and scepticism. 'The most candid and sincere soul in France,' reports his Confessor, 'respectful to the Queen, loving her deeply, and also the little "Monsieur", his brother. Judicious, brave, truthful, gay, agreeable, prudent, and pious'. And if the Confessor is over-enthusiastic, he at least tells us that Louis already possessed that charm of manner which, when he saw fit to exercise it, few men and no women were ever able to resist.

Already shrewd judges saw that he would go far; Fourilles, Inspector-General of cavalry, writing to a friend in this year says:

People do not know the King; many think that he is fit for nothing and knows nothing. But remember in years to come what I say to you today; in his own time the King will show that in brains and courage he need fear no comparison with the Kings his predecessors.

But Louis could still be a child at times, and by our standards a very nasty one. During 1652 the Court was lodged so poorly at Corbeil that the King and his brother had to share a room which was just big enough to hold two beds. On awaking Louis accidentally spat on Philippe's bed; Philippe retaliated by deliberately spitting on the King's; Louis' retort was to spit in Philippe's face; Philippe, not to be outdone, jumped up and urinated over the Royal bed, a compliment which the King returned; and a free fight ensued. 'Monsieur', we are told, was much angrier than the King, but the King was much more difficult to appease. It is a typical illustration of the paradox of the *Grand Siècle*, the astonishing conjunction of exquisite politeness and an elaborate code of manners with a grossness which would be unbelievable if it were not so well attested. And there was to be little improvement. Move on thirty years and we find 'Madame', the King's sister-in-law, and 'Monseigneur', the heir to the Crown, engaging in public contests as to which could make the greatest number of embarrassing noises during a given period; advance another twenty years and we can enjoy the spectacle of the adored Duchess of Burgundy taking an enema whilst laughing and chatting with the King and his circle.

Louis' Odyssey continued. In February he was at Saumur where the inhabitants thought to please him by a miserable lampoon vilifying Condé; but they had failed to reckon on the Bourbon pride of race; the King stopped the performance at once, for Condé bore the King's name. May found him at Etampes, swallowing with who knows what inward bitterness a fresh mortification put upon him by Mazarin; the Superintendent of Finance had given Louis a hundred pounds to distribute in 'gratifications' to his wounded soldiers. But Mazarin had got wind of the gift and insisted upon Louis handing the money over to him, with the result that the King could offer his ragged army nothing but smiles and compliments. He had not at this time, we are told, enough influence to dispose of a lieutenancy in a line regiment without Mazarin's leave.

On 2 July Condé was trapped by Turenne under the walls of Paris at the Porte St Antoine, and there turned at bay to fight for his life as in the arena; for the city ramparts were black with spectators, and the King and his courtiers thronged the high ground behind the Royal army. It would have gone ill with Condé had not 'Mademoiselle' bullied the watch into opening the gate for the beaten Frondeurs and covered their retreat by firing on the Royalists with the cannon of the Bastille; 'she has killed her husband,' said Mazarin; meaning thereby that he would see to it that 'Mademoiselle' should never realize her ambition of marrying Louis XIV.

Throughout the summer and early autumn anarchy reigned in Paris whilst the Court hovered about its environs awaiting the inevitable surrender. On 14 October Condé slunk out of the city to join the Spanish army in the Netherlands, and a week later the King entered his capital, where he was given a rapturous welcome, the ranks of the escort being constantly broken by frenzied citizens who fought to get near enough to the King to kiss his boots. Louis behaved with his usual stately grace, but not for a single moment did he forget that this scum that now slobbered over him was the same that had flowed into his bedroom less than two years earlier. And it was to the Louvre that he returned, not to the Palais-Royal; for the latter was an open house whilst the Louvre had a moat and a drawbridge.

Once in Paris, Louis wasted no time in setting his house in order; the leading Frondeurs were banished on 21 October, the small fry fled or submitted, and on the 22nd the King addressed his Parlement in a speech in which he made no attempt to conceal his bitter anger. 'Everybody knows', he said, 'how dangerous your assemblies have been to my realm. I have learnt that you are presumptuous enough to propose their continuance. And, M. le Premier President,' pointing at him with his riding whip, 'I am here to forbid it'; and before the terrified magistrate could stutter out a word, Louis turned on his heel and left the building. The political and financial role of the Parlement was finished.

In 1653 Mazarin dismissed La Porte, whose hostility to him had always been marked; and the valet probably brought about his own disgrace by circulating the horrible story which he has preserved in his memoirs, namely that Mazarin was a homosexual who had corrupted the young King. La Porte's accusation is supported by no contemporary, and we may dismiss it as a libel. Any corruption with which Mazarin tainted Louis was intellectual, not physical, and was such as is inevitable when an elderly cynic lives in close association with a boy of fifteen; it was Mazarin for example who taught Louis to regard the religious orders as parasites, and to label the devout as visionaries whose aspirations were a danger to the State. But luckily Father Paulin, who died on 12 April, had done his work so well that Mazarin was unable to turn Louis XIV into a Frederick the Great.

This winter Mazarin began Louis' real education, and thenceforward King and Cardinal were generally closeted together for two hours a day, Mazarin talking whilst the King listened. Keep your family down, said Mazarin; avoid familiarity with courtiers; adopt a severe attitude to those who beg; distrust everybody, especially ministers, for they will deceive you if they can; keep your affairs an impenetrable secret; take your subject's money but spare their blood. Cynical maxims perhaps, but not without their value.

In 1654 Louis began to attend meetings of the Council of State where he was encouraged to volunteer solutions of the problems on the agenda; and Mazarin was unperturbed by the Royal tutor's report that the King was lazy, and averse to learning anything. 'Do not worry', said the Cardinal, 'leave him to me; he never attends a Council without asking a hundred questions'. But some attempt was made to resume Louis' formal education, though in fact such work as he now did was done in bed in the mornings, and he showed much dexterity in transforming these working hours into conversations; for by the Tutor's admission, Louis' dislike of books was now ineradicable.

But Louis' day was not an idle one; prayers and toilet followed his lessons in bed, then a ride, then fencing and dancing, then a talk with Mazarin. Next, a visit to his mother, with whom he always dined; then a drive, and home to the Council which closed his official day. But already he was by choice the open-air man he was to remain until the end, a quality which he inherited from his grandfather. Probably he was at this time happiest when he was on active service —'Oh, if only I could be a private gentleman for eight hours!', he exclaimed whilst watching the preparations for the battle of Arras in 1654. And already he had begun to show that indefatigable interest in military detail and contempt for discomfort which were to characterise him throughout his life; he marched all day with the troops, and on getting into camp rode out to inspect the advance guard, returning untired after fifteen hours in the saddle; and when he got back to find that the supply wagons had not arrived, he merely laughed.

It is at Court functions that we see the last traces of the vanishing boy in Louis. At a ball in 1655 he committed the faux pas of selecting Mazarin's niece, the Duchesse de Mercœur, as his partner for the first dance, despite the fact that the Princess Royal of England, his future sister-in-law, was present; and Queen Anne had to separate the pair, though the exiled Queen of England endeavoured to smooth matters over by saying that her daughter was tired and did not wish to dance. 'And', adds our informant, 'after the ball the King was well scolded by his mother, which he thoroughly deserved'. He however showed to better advantage when later in the same year he met at Chantilly another ex-royalty, the proud, erudite, Lesbian Christina of Sweden, who was greatly struck by his conversational gifts, and formed a high opinion of his abilities.

This Chantilly party was Louis' real debut in society; the ladies, astonished at the ease of the hitherto timid boy, so shy with women, awoke to the fact that if Louis was not yet a King, he had at least become a man, and a prize for someone. But for whom? At first it looked like being the seventeen year old Olympe, second of Mazarin's nieces, 'the nymph Mancini' as her flatterers called her. Judging from her portraits it is hard to believe that Olympe had any physical attractions, and as for her other qualities, 'Mademoiselle' found her gauche and ill-mannered, and wondered how the King could love her. Mme de Lafayette says that while no one could call her good-looking, she was 'capable of pleasing', and that whilst her wit was neither remarkable nor very polite, it was natural and agreeable. 'Ugly and wicked', was 'Madame's' verdict, and we feel that 'Madame' was right; for this cold, vindictive, spiteful schemer was a thoroughly bad woman, a bad sister, a bad wife, a bad mistress, a bad friend, and in all probability a poisoner. But Louis loved 'the Goose', as she was so inappropriately nicknamed, and this made her the fashion. Not that the King's love went beyond mere flirtation, for Olympe was frigid, and ambitious of a great marriage, whilst this was the Louis who could still tell his friends that he could not understand the recklessness of a man who dared to go to sleep at night with a mortal sin on his conscience.

II

BY 1656 Mazarin had imported his sister, Mme Mancini, and her five daughters into France with the prudent intention of dowering the girls at Louis XIV's expense instead of his own. Laure, the eldest and the only respectable one of the quintette, he had married in 1651 to the Duc de Mercœur, a bastard grandson of Henri IV by Gabrielle d'Estrées; Olympe, the second girl, we have just met; and there remained Marie, Hortense, and Marianne, now aged sixteen, twelve, and eleven respectively, all three living with their widowed mother. Marie was the Cinderella of the family. Whilst every indulgence was shown to her sisters, who, she says, 'amused themselves to their heart's content', she remained at home in the charge of 'a sour old chambermaid' , with the comforting knowledge that she was on the eve of being forced into a nunnery.

Then in 1656 Mme Mancini fell ill, Louis was ordered to call on her daily, and it was not long before Marie attracted his attention; he began to look forward to his daily calls on the widow, for in her anteroom he was sure to find Marie, whose 'fire, vivacity, and playfulness' (the description is her own), he found strangely disturbing and delightful.

But Marie's hour had not yet come, for early in 1657 Louis took a sudden passion for one of his mother's Maids-of-Honour, Mlle de la Motte-Argencourt, a blue-eyed blonde, not strikingly beautiful nor very clever, but who talked pleasingly and was a lovely dancer. Marazin was alarmed, and so too was Anne, who gave Louis a scolding which Louis endured without amending his ways; on the contrary he began to talk to the girl like a man who had lost all control. But La Motte proved difficult, and though the mother did her best to sell her daughter to Louis, she rejected his proposals. Then Mazarin intervened; pointing out crudely that La Motte was a grown woman who wanted a man, not a boy whose hands trembled whenever he touched her; and he went on to say that the King's wooing was a subject of ridicule to La Motte and her companions. All his life ridicule was the only thing which Louis feared, and he was both hurt and horrified by the disclosure; the La Motte episode ended as abruptly as it had begun, and once more Louis turned his thoughts to Marie Mancini. Olympe had married the Comte de Soissons, 'M le Comte' at Court, on 20 February, and on 19 December 1656 Mme Mancini had died, thus liberating Cinderella; and Louis, who still had some sense of what was decorous, had given up flirting with Olympe since her marriage; so the stage was set for his most serious love affair.

Throughout February the pair met daily, and when the Court moved to Fontainebleau in the spring it was obvious to everybody that they were deeply in love. To Louis, intoxicated at having won a girl's heart, Marie was of course perfection, but viewed dispassionately she was not an attractive young woman. In appearance she was very thin, with a brownish-yellow complexion, hard eyes, a mean mouth, and nothing of the appearance of a woman of quality; and according to Mazarin, who knew his niece much better than Louis ever did, she had a fantastic mind, boundless ambition, a contempt for everyone, and a genius for extravagant conduct. But she was generally agreed to be witty, gay, and challenging. In short, one of those girls who make the utmost of every asset, and whose cleverness persuades a man to endow her with charms which do not exist outside his own imagination.

Marie's real trouble was that, like so many neglected children, she had grown up in a dream world of her own creation; she was a voracious reader of romances and persuaded Louis to share her taste for them; dragons, ogres, wicked fairies, were made to be vanquished by her lover's magic sword, and as her own romance, like those of her favourite heroines, was bound to end in wedding bells, the more difficulties to be overcome on the road to the Church the better the romance. Hence her brusque impetuosity, her refusal, perhaps inability, to face facts, and her utter lack of foresight. And she made Louis as blind and inconsequent as she was herself.

The King, though deeply in love, did not slip easily into the role of wooer, being hampered not only by the timidity of youth but by his temperament. Marianne, the youngest sister, tells us that although he lived among them with wonderful kindness, he had about him something so serious and so solid, not to say majestic, in all his manners that he could not help instilling respect, though that was far from being his intention; and only Marie did not feel the constraint of his presence. Absorbed in love, Louis began to neglect business; at Council meetings he was distrait, and took to slipping out of the room half way through the session until Mazarin expostulated; which did nothing to endear him to Louis, and it must have been a relief to both master and pupil when the King set out for the front on 7 May to besiege Montmédy. Throughout the siege he frankly showed off for Marie's benefit, and when the place surrendered Louis was far enough forward to receive the surrender in person. And judging from what Marie had to say, he had his reward:—

> The King showed prodigious bravery . . . and when I was told of it I could not hide the joy I felt . . . and the King had the kindness to say to me that to see that light in my eyes he would have done far more than he had.

No wonder Louis returned to Paris in high spirits, for he had acquired some personal reputation and believed that Anne and Mazarin smiled on his courtship. A supposition in which he was woefully astray; neither Queen nor Cardinal dreamt that Louis was any more in earnest than he had been with Olympe or La Motte-Argencourt, and they encouraged this new intimacy only because they thought it was drawing the King out, and accustoming him to behave easily in women's society.

We have a glimpse of Louis in his exuberant mood of that winter; at the supper table there was of course only one armchair, that set for the King:

LOUIS: Cousin, the armchair is yours.
MADEMOISELLE: No, Sire, no.
LOUIS: Well, who will take it?
OLYMPE: I will. (Does so).

After which Louis, having forced all to sit down, said, 'As there is only one place left, I suppose I must take it'. And when driving Marie home in his coach afterwards, he cried out, 'How I wish we could be attacked by robbers!'

It is interesting to observe that Louis at nineteen was already mastering his part as 'the greatest actor of royalty the world has ever seen'. We have just met him off-stage; here in this same winter is a snapshot of him playing the King:

> Serious, grave, and affable. His majesty imprinted respect in the

hearts of those who approached him. He spoke little and well; his words had an astonishing power of implanting love or fear in the recipient, according as they were kindly or severe.

In May 1658 at the siege of Dunkirk Louis acquired that thirst for glory which was to make him the curse of Europe; but showed too a praiseworthy capacity for hard work, sweltering on the hot sands by day, shivering by night in the marsh mists of a country foul with the stench of last year's unburied dead. The result was that on June 29 he contracted typhus fever, and on 1 August had to be taken to Calais, where he became so ill that by the 7th his life was despaired of. Mazarin was panic-stricken, and had good reason to be; for if Louis died and 'Monsieur' succeeded him it spelt disaster for France and ruin for Mazarin; Philippe with his rouge pot and his female clothing was not the stuff of which Kings were made; and the greedy homosexuals surrounding him would proceed to banish the Cardinal and divide his enormous wealth between them. But in the middle of the month, and against all probability, Louis began to mend, and by the 22nd he was able to leave for Compiègne in an improvised ambulance.

At Court such attention as could be spared from events at Calais was concentrated on the violent and unconcealed grief which the impulsive Marie had displayed during the crisis of Louis' illness; and when the invalid returned, what more agreeable tonic could he find than this news? Gratitude stimulated his passion, and Marie's kindness convinced him that in her he had found the woman who would protect him from the loneliness which was to afflict him all his life.

From Compiègne the Court moved to Fontainebleau, loveliest of all the royal seats, and there began for Louis and Marie a period of enchantment; they floated in cushioned barges to the music of violins, went rock climbing, or wandered through the forest together; feasted, made love, and danced until two in the morning. Halcyon weather, especially for Marie, who already knew Louis well enough to understand what she described as 'his eloquent silence, more persuasive than any rhetoric'. And when on top of everything, the courtiers began to show her the honours due to a Queen, her cup of happiness was filled to the brim. Fortunately for her she was unaware of the real sentiments of these so deferential gentlemen; which were that she was a stubborn, proud, conceited girl, with no warmth in her charm, and lacking both manners and courtesy.

32

By the autumn Anne had realized that the affair was serious, and began to press Mazarin to hasten on her son's marriage; a problem to which the Cardinal had been giving leisurely consideration for some time past. Anne's dream was that Louis should wed her niece, Marie Thérèse of Spain, and thus end the Franco-Spanish war which had already lasted twenty-four years. Louis was the Infanta's only eligible *parti*, and in addition it was becoming clear that Spain must shortly sue for peace. Mazarin dealt with the problem by looking ostentatiously elsewhere for a Queen of France. An invitation was sent to Louis XIV's aunt, the Dowager-Duchess of Savoy, to bring her daughter Marguérite to visit her French relations at Lyons; and the invitation was eagerly accepted. The original intention was that Louis and his gentlemen only should meet the Savoyards at Lyons, but Marie understood her Louis too well to trust him alone on any such dangerous adventure. She briefed the King to tell his mother that he felt himself too inexperienced to enter upon a negotiation of such delicacy without her guidance, and Anne swallowed the bait; whilst Mazarin raised no objection, thinking that Marie's presence at Lyons would prevent Louis from taking any inconvenient fancy for Marguérite.

The King's conduct on the journey intensified Anne's anxieties; Louis, pleading headache, refused to travel in the coach, and so, 'like some romance of chivalry', as 'Mademoiselle' sourly remarked, he and Marie rode side by side through the autumn country. A long, slow journey, but all too short for both of them, though it was not until 28 November that they reached Lyons. On 2 December the Savoyards arrived, twenty-four hours after a Spanish diplomat had entered the town to offer the hand of the Infanta to Louis. Mazarin's ruse had worked perfectly, and the negotiations with Savoy became a comedy played at poor Marguérite's expense; for Louis was not let into the secret. On the 2nd he galloped out to meet Marguérite, then galloped back to his mother. 'Well, my son?' said Anne. 'She has the easiest bearing in the world; her complexion is olive, but suits her well; she has beautiful eyes; she pleases me and is quite to my taste', replied Louis. And the courtiers, who knew that she was one of the plainest Princesses in Europe, had some difficulty in hiding their amusement at Louis' eagerness to possess a wife.

When the Savoy coach met the French cortège, the King entered it, 'and began at once to chat with Marguérite as familiarly as if he had known her all his life; which surprised everyone very much, for he was as a rule cold, and not inclined to be sociable'.

Marie viewed her lover's behaviour with indignation, and wondered if Louis could really be attracted by the creature; and the same evening she adroitly attacked him on his weakest side, his vanity and his fear of ridicule—'Are you not ashamed of letting them force such a hideous bride on you?', she said, and much more to the same effect.

It worked. Next day everyone saw that Louis' attentions to Marguérite were cooler than they had been at the first meeting; and Mazarin chose this moment to break the news of the Spanish offer to Louis. The King, who had momentarily desired Marguérite only because he was thrilled at the idea of possessing a woman, was pleased; and nothing remained but to get rid of the Savoy party without provoking a diplomatic rupture. Somehow this was accomplished without an open quarrel, but the parting between the two Courts was very cold.

At twenty time moves slowly; and Louis, having got rid of Marguérite, dismissed the Spanish marriage as something which would happen in a future too remote for present consideration. He lingered on at Lyons, where he and Marie were inseparable, not parting until late at night when he would himself drive her back to her lodgings in the Place Bellecour—ground floor lodgings with windows low enough to be entered without difficulty from the Place, a circumstance which gave sleepless nights to Marie's governess, Mme Venel. One night, says Marie, old Venel, patrolling half asleep, came into her room to see that she was alone in bed, and in feeling, accidentally put her finger in Marie's mouth. Marie, waking in a panic, promptly bit it to the bone; 'and the King told the whole story next day, to the great amusement of the Court'.

In January 1659 the Court left Lyons, and the homeward journey was a repetition of the outward one, Louis and Marie riding hand in hand, the girl warmed by the ardour of the boy's love, and confident that she had won the hearts of the Queen and Mazarin. But poor Marie was lamentably mistaken; in fact she had made an enemy of Anne by her arrogance, and her proprietary attitude towards the King—'she followed the King everywhere and was always whispering in his ear, even in the presence of the Queen, unhindered by what respect and good manners should have prompted her to do'. And as for Mazarin, he had determined to end a comedy whose usefulness had ceased with the departure of Marguérite from Lyons; especially as it was now evident that Marie was doing everything in her power to disgust Louis with the Spanish marriage. For a moment perhaps he had toyed with the idea of making his niece Queen of France, but when he sounded Anne she received the hint with such disgust that he dismissed the thought from his mind and set to work in earnest to separate the lovers. Marie acted with her usual indiscretion by inflaming Louis against Queen and Cardinal; and when Louis waited on his Premier with a formal request for Marie's hand, Mazarin decided that the time for drastic action had come. He sent Marie with her sisters Hortense and Marianne off to Rochelle in the custody of Mme Venel. Louis' rage at the news was so terrible that his mother dared not see him for three days on end; and she even appealed to Mazarin to rescind his order. But he was inflexible. And Louis had to content himself with swearing to Marie that come what might she should be his wife. 'You are the master; you weep; but I go', answered Marie bitterly.

Louis' anger against his mother was short-lived; for he loved her, found the estrangement intolerable, and moreover Anne handled the business with skill, persuading her son that so far from their being enemies, Louis' love for Marie was a misfortune which they must endure together for the honour of France—'and the King began to complain, not of his mother, but with her'.

On 22 June the Mancini girls left for Rochelle, escorted for the first part of the journey by Mazarin, en route for the frontier to lead for France in the peace negotiations with Spain. His position was an unenviable one; he was leaving behind him a King who asked for nothing better than to see the negotiations fail; and Anne, deprived of his guidance, might weaken about Marie's exile. Things became worse when the girls reached their place of banishment; Mazarin had reluctantly been compelled to sanction a correspondence between Louis and his niece in order to prevent the King from making a sudden dash to Rochelle. But he had assumed that it would be limited to a weekly letter, sent through the post, which he could either forward or destroy, according to its tenour. Louis, however, did not fall into such an obvious trap; he organized his own courier service of life Guards, carrying, as Mazarin complained, 'whole volumes rather than letters'.

The Premier expostulated with his master:

35

I entreat you by your glory, by your honour, by your duty to God, by the interest of your realm, by anything that can move you, to force yourself into a state of mind in which your journey to Bayonne (for your marriage) will not be made with displeasure.

But for sole response he received a curt acknowledgement stating that when His Majesty felt himself in need of M. le Cardinal's advice, he would not fail to ask for it.

On 11 July when the Mancinis reached Rochelle, there began a duel between Marie and her governess, Mme Venel doing her utmost to see the girl's letters whilst Marie, helped by Louis who sent her Mazarin's letters to himself, counter-spied on the governess. On the 12th, for instance, Venel excuses herself to Mazarin for her failure to see a letter which Marie had written to Louis, and offers the plaintive explanation that her charge seals her letters the moment they are written, and does it so thoroughly that it is impossible to hit upon any method of opening the packet which would be undetected by the King; and the report closes with the complaint that there are so many doors in the lodgings which they occupy that she cannot possibly guard them all, especially after dark. Nor was Venel successful in her endeavours to use little Marianne as a spy, for Marie soon learnt that her private conversations with Hortense were reaching the Cardinal, and forbade Marianne the room. Then came Mazarin's final exasperation, an apologetic letter from Anne saying that she was so alarmed for the King's health that she had consented to his inviting Marie to meet the court at St Jean d'Angély. And this was followed hot-foot by a despairing letter from Venel, who had been told of the invitation by Marie—'For the love of God, tell me, Your Eminence, what I am to do?' Small wonder that Mazarin could no longer conceal his irritation in writing to the King:

You do me the honour to say that you are more than ever resolved to follow my advice, and at the same time you do the exact opposite . . . in fact I must conclude that you will have the goodness to follow it when it is in conformity with your inclinations . . . You are the master, but not to the extent of extorting my approval of conduct which is prejudicial to your reputation, and if I do not see signs of your mastering yourself, the only course left to me will be to retire from your service, taking with me the person who is the cause of all these misfortunes.

On 13 August Venel and her charges reached St Jean d'Angély, where they were welcomed by the King alone. He had outridden his Court, no doubt by previous arrangement with Marie, and after the first greetings he went into the salon where he and Marie remained tête-à-tête until the Queen arrived. The result was of course a renewal of their vows, followed by much skilful advice from Louis on the methods which Marie should employ in order to smooth down Mazarin; and then Louis went off to supper, returning immediately afterwards for another private talk with Marie which lasted until two in the morning. It must have been an agonizing night for governess Venel, and it was probably her report which prompted Mazarin to write again to the King:

> Since that last meeting, which I thought would be fatal, you have recommenced writing every day ... telling her everything, and taking her into your entire confidence ... and, what is incomprehensible, you adopt every possible method to heat your passions when you are on the eve of marrying. In fact you work to make yourself the most unhappy of men ... And what role does this girl intend to play when you are married? Does she think I shall be so infamous as to agree to her adoption of a métier which will dishonour her?

But finally the King looked reality in the face; in a despairing letter to Marie he explained that destiny had been too strong for them, and that it was his fate to marry the Infanta. It was a stunning blow for Marie, but injured pride came to her support; she replied forbidding Louis to write to her again, and then informed Mazarin that she placed herself at his disposal, requesting only that she should be married before the King. The storm was over, but it left a disquieting groundswell; the King looked ill and listless, refused to attend entertainments, and when his ambassador, just back from Madrid, gave him a glowing account of the Infanta's charms, Louis stared with lack-lustre eyes and dismissed him without a single question.

But Spanish sloth brought Louis a respite; the diplomats agreed that the marriage could not take place until the spring, so the French Court decided to winter in Provence; and on 7 October moved to Toulouse where Louis could get the hunting which was unobtainable at Bayonne. We can sense the King's apathy from his conduct on the journey; he spent the whole time in his coach, where a table had been fitted so that the company could gamble from morning to night, and Louis did not get out even for his meals.

Mazarin had conquered his King, but now something had to be done about Marie. In November the Bishop of Fréjus was sent to persuade the girl that a dazzling future awaited her if she would marry the Constable Colonna, Viceroy of Aragon; a proposition vehemently rejected by Marie for precisely the same reason that it was passionately advocated by Mazarin, namely that it would entail exile from France. If she must marry, said his niece, why not Prince Charles of Lorraine? And Venel, at her wit's end, wrote to Mazarin urging that the important thing was to get the girl married at once, never mind to whom.

For Louis, dragging his sorrow from town to town, a listless spectator of the preparations for his own marriage, and struggling to wear a mask of tranquillity, it was quite as dreary a winter as it was for Marie. And Louis in addition was feeling acutely the humiliation of hanging about the gates of Spain until it should please Philip IV to hand over his bride.

In December the Mancinis returned to Paris, and on getting home Marie's first care was to examine her wardrobe; and whilst doing so the poor girl broke down completely—'The last time I wore that dress, she sobbed, 'the King said "It suits you to perfection, *my Queen*" '. And she found little consolation, either in the attentions of Prince Charles or in the visit of an astrologer, bribed by Anne to predict a glorious future for her as the wife of Colonna.

On 4 June 1660 Louis saw his bride incognito; he was introduced to Philip IV in the presence of Anne and the Infanta as a French gentleman desirous of the honour of kissing his Catholic Majesty's hand. On the 6th the two Kings swore peace, and on the 7th Marie Thérèse crossed the frontier to spend the night with the Queen-Mother of France; and in the evening Anne and the betrothed couple had supper in private, 'all as much at home as if they had spent their whole lives together'. The wedding was celebrated on the 9th with all possible pomp in a shimmer of costly stuffs and the sparkle of innumerable gems; the little bride almost fainting under her load of jewelry and brocade. But it was the King, with his perfect sense of theatre, who held all eyes, dressed in black from head to foot, and without a single ornament. In the evening Marie Thérèse was escorted from Anne's lodgings to those of the King, where the royal family supped together, and as soon as the meal was over Louis announced that he was going to bed; 'it is too soon', whispered Marie Thérèse to her mother-in-law. But when the news arrived that the King was in bed, she sat down on a couple of cushions and undressed without making any fuss, saying, 'Quick, quick, the King is waiting for me!' And then the two were bedded 'with the blessing of the Queen, their common mother'. On the following morning a deeply interested Court noticed 'the great tenderness which the King showed towards the Queen, and she to him'. Marie Thérèse indeed made it blatantly obvious that she was passionately in love with her husband; as she continued to be always, in spite of the mortification which Louis' infidelities inflicted upon her. And Louis, if not exactly in love with his wife, was at any rate touched by her passion and treated her better than either his mother or the Cardinal had anticipated. Their married life was in fact as successful as the average *ménage* of the period; and Marie Thérèse filled her difficult part blamelessly, giving Louis no reasons for complaint and many for remorse.

Anne had thought it a promising honeymoon, and her shock and disappointment were therefore all the greater when Louis left Court abruptly on 28 June for Brouage, the place where Marie Mancini had spent the last days of her exile. Mazarin was horrified; Marie was at Paris, Louis and she were bound to meet there, and in what mood would the King be after his trip? Deciding that his niece must be married out of France forthwith, he set to work unscrupulously to organize a campaign of defamation against Marie. He himself wrote sarcastic letters to Louis explaining just how ridiculous his subjects found the spectacle of their king weeping at the seaside over a girl whose 'goings on' with Prince Charles of Lorraine were the talk of Paris; Anne wrote in a similar strain; so did venal courtiers; and so did Olympe, whose sisterly animosity made her letters the most telling of all. The result was that Louis arrived at Fontainebleau on 13 July in a fury of injured vanity; and when ten days later Marie came to pay her respects, the King greeted her with a freezing politeness which stung like a blow. Marie returned abruptly to Paris, and there on 26 August, was with her own consent, betrothed to Colonna.

It was not until after Mazarin's death that Louis discovered the trick of which he and Marie had been the victims; there was a tender reconciliation, many tears, and a passionate appeal from Louis that even now Marie should break with Colonna. But she stood firm, holding herself bound in honour to the Constable, and on 11 April 1661 she was married to him by proxy. Shortly afterwards she left for Italy, Louis being with her until the last. As he handed her into her coach he sighed deeply without saying a word, then bowed as low as to the door; Marie burst into tears, and the coach drove off. It was their last meeting, but the memory of Marie lingered with Louis as did that of few other women; and when in 1672 she revisited France, he did not trust himself to see her. He would never love again in exactly the same way. His other loves might be better or worse, nobler or baser; and perhaps in either case a little less human.

In 1660 Mazarin gave the final polish to Louis' political education; the two hours a day formerly allotted to the task imperceptibly lengthened until most of Mazarin's leisure was devoted to secret conversations with Louis. The Venetian Ambassador reported to his Government at this time that there must be some deep, hidden sympathy between King and Cardinal to account for the subordination of mind and will on the part of a great Prince to a private individual; and went on to give his impressions of Louis, who was, he said, a very religious man with great purity of morals and an honest temperament; secret as the tomb, and skilled in dissimulation. No one, he added, had ever heard him speak ill of anyone, or could boast that the King had shown him either partiality or confidence. And he concluded by praising Louis' keen, unaffected curiosity, and his readiness to listen to advice.

By January 1661 it was obvious to everyone except Mazarin himzelf that he was dying, and by 22 February he too had recognized the fact; and, thrifty to the last, was resenting the good money poured out to his doctors for their purgings, bleedings, asses' milk, and partridge soup; making himself extremely unpleasant on the subject of men who accepted fees without doing anything in return for them.

Almost until the end the long conversations with Louis continued, and it was no doubt then that Mazarin recommended Colbert, who was to become the King's greatest administrator; and it is certain that in these last days he warned Louis against the dishonesty and overweening ambition of Fouquet, the Superintendent of Finance.

On 7 March Mazarin said goodbye to the King, Queen-Mother, 'Monsieur', the royal family, and the end came on the 9th. He was not greatly missed in the palace, for with advancing years he had grown so avaricious, ill-tempered, and autocratic that even to Anne his death came as a relief; and no doubt that of Louis was even greater, though he allowed Mazarin to play himself off the stage with a self-effacement which verged on the hypocritical. From his visits to the dying Premier he had always emerged in tears, and to his courtiers he affected to be overwhelmed at the thought of the burden which was so soon to crush his own shoulders; but can anyone believe that Louis' plans for the time when Mazarin disappeared were not even then cut and dried, or that he wished the Cardinal's life to be prolonged? Mme de Motteville, Anne's most intimate friend, gives an account of the behaviour of the royal family on learning of Mazarin's death which rings truer than Louis' affectation of incapacity. The King, Queen and 'Monsieur', she says, finding themselves in private, began to breathe more freely; the pleasures of liberty came to console them in their affliction; and the Queen-Mother was the first to say to those who kept on offering eulogies of the dead man, that the subject might now be dropped, as they could turn their time to better account than in listening to speeches which had become useless.

On 10 March Louis announced his intention of being his own Prime Minister and the personal reign began.

He started on his huge task with much in his favour; superabundant energy, self-confidence, and no misgivings. For what apprehensions could be entertained by the Eldest Son of the Church, God's lieutenant on earth? And France joyfully endorsed his own view of his position; all classes were in disgusted reaction from the miseries of the Fronde and the long reigns of Richelieu and Mazarin; all were vociferous in demanding to be ruled by youth with absolutism. To paraphrase Voltaire, if Louis XIV had not existed it would have been necessary to invent him. As an immediate consequence, the young King was nearly drowned in the tidal wave of flattery which broke over him, the universal assurance that if he was not himself God, he was at least super-human. And the Church led the chorus; when Marie Thérèse produced an heir on 1 November, Father Sénault, the famous preacher, in the dedication of his congratulatory sermon to Louis, assured the King that he was not afraid to offer His Majesty his only son in the same way that every day at the altar he offered the Son to the Father.

Sometimes this universal flattery 'however' provokes not our indignation but our laughter; as for instance in this excerpt from Louis' medical diary, an official document kept by the First Physician:

41

The King, having devoted himself assiduously and with much prudence to acquiring a complete grasp of all that appertained to the good of the State, took a purgative and passed a quantity of bile.

Small wonder that Louis began to ask himself seriously if he had shirked his responsibilities by not assuming his Kingly duties at the age of fourteen when he attained his legal majority. But his common-sense answered his own question. He remembered his inexperience in 1652, realized the difficulty which he would have had in ridding himself of Mazarin, and decided that he had acted rightly. For there was in Louis a common-sense which he was never to lose, and he himself recognized its value; 'the chief function of a King', he said, 'is to give free play to his common-sense'. And as Sainte Beuve remarked, if in Louis we find little more than common-sense, it is common-sense raised to its supreme degree. Louis kept his head, in spite of the adulation lavished upon him. 'Kings', he said, 'are but men dealing with other men; and to attain that degree of perfection which they make their aim in life, is an impossible task for feeble human nature'.

And he was quick to grasp the fundamental difficulties of his office, particularly the terrible loneliness of the Throne; 'the hard and rigorous condition of Kings', he called it, 'who owe a public explanation of their every action to the whole world and to posterity, and yet cannot give it to a single contemporary without betraying the secret motives of their actions and thus stultifying their most important decisions'.

On the first day of his reign Louis wrote out what he remembered of Mazarin's precepts. Especially his advice to exclude from the Council all Churchmen, soldiers, and nobles; Churchmen because they have one eye on their sovereign and the other on the Pope; soldiers because their solution of any diplomatic problem is a declaration of war; and nobles because with noble ministers a King becomes *primus inter pares*, whereas with bourgeois advisers he is publicly recognized as the only begetter of national policy.

Good resolutions bubbled out of Louis during the first weeks of his reign, and he determined to disappoint those who thought his decision to rule was a passing whim; holding 'that a King who cannot govern is unfit to reign'. And he realized that, having once begun to rule, there could be no slackening; 'no King is more dangerous than the one who, generally asleep, wakes with a start every now and then and begins to blame everyone for some failure for which he has only himself to thank'. But though the final decision must always be the King's, it would be absurd to suppose that he can rule unaided; in talking over matters of business, he said, a King not only learns much from others but draws much out of himself. And because his grandeur puts him out of touch with his subjects he must talk to those who stand nearer to them and are therefore able to see a thousand things which are unperceived by the King.

Much has been written about Louis' indifference to the welfare of his people; yet on this subject he himself says that the obedience and respect which a King receives from his subjects are not free gifts but are offered in exchange for the justice and protection which they receive from him. They ought to honour the King, he ought to save and defend them; and a King's debt to his people is greater than is their debt to him. Louis' desire to improve the lot of his subjects is in fact apparent throughout the reign, and if he was unsucessful in so doing it was because he was a man of his time, incapable of appreciating the fact that neither his own nor his subject's positions could be bettered under a fundamentally vicious economic system.

Nor was he hypocritical in saying that war is unjust when the objective can be attained by diplomacy; his fault was to think in all good faith that he had exhausted peaceful means when with a little more patience he could often have gained his ends without war; and when, perhaps subconsciously, his longing for glory led him to mistake an opponent's dilatoriness for defiance. For war fascinated him, and already he was burning for personal military fame. This year we get a significant glimpse into his mind:

LOUIS: If ever I have a war I would wish to take the field myself.

A COURTIER: It is almost a fault for a King to risk his life in battle; how much did not France suffer from the imprudent valour of François I?

LOUIS: Imprudent as much as you like; but that imprudence placed him in the class of great Kings.

Louis' ministers were disconcerted not only by the energy but also by the informality of the King; he would descend unexpectedly upon a ministry at odd moments and demand to know every detail of the office work; 'knowledge of these little things', he said, 'gave me a thousand facts which were not without value when I came to make big decisions'. In Colbert's office he was fired with a new enthusiasm; France should be not only the greatest military power in the world, but also the foremost commercial one. New factories were opened, subsidies given to new industries, and before the end of the year courtiers realized that there was no surer way to Louis' favour than to persuade a foreign technician to settle in France.

From commerce he turned to the publication of edicts which made swearing, blasphemy, and duelling punishable; and, as avid for pleasure as for reform, he turned from edicts to the state of his theatre. Here is a letter of 1661 to the Duke of Parma:

> My cousin, I want to complete my Italian Company. I have no Harlequin, and beg you to send me one without delay, assuring him that he will be as favourably treated as any other member of the company.

And he even found time to suggest to Molière, now in high favour, that the well-known hunting bore, Soyecourt, should be taken off on the stage.

Already Louis' famous politeness was becoming apparent; in July he wrote this in answer to a lady who had begged his help in a lawsuit:

> When one knows how to ask what is reasonable with such a grace as you do, one is never importunate. Bear in mind that your respect will offend me if you do not, when occasion demands, have recourse to me with the confidence which your esteem merits.

Apparent also is the gracious kindliness for which he was to be celebrated. Hearing that a noble who had bought the post of Chevalier d'Honneur to the Queen was having difficulty in raising the purchase money, Louis sent him £5,000, with a note to the effect that having heard that the gentleman was calling on his friends' purses, he was mortified to find that the King had not been included in their number.

III

ON 31 March 1661 Louis' brother 'Monsieur' married his first cousin, Henriette of England, daughter of the late King Charles I. Anne seems to have been the only person who really desired a match which they had all inherited from Mazarin, and even Anne's satisfaction was to be short-lived; whilst Louis' consent was noticeably half-hearted. But 'Monsieur' was momentarily thrilled; as a wedding present Louis had given him their late uncle's appanage of Orléans, and on top of that he had all the excitement of preparing his trousseau.

'Monsieur', now twenty-one, was a very different man from Louis. His mother's pet and plaything, a toy for her women, he had developed an effeminacy which had degenerated into homosexuality; though, unlike most perverts, he enjoyed female society, loved to be allowed to play lady's maid at a girl's toilet, and was never happier than when gossiping with half a dozen young women of his own age. But these were his relaxations. The business of this unfortunate creature who, said contemporaries, would have made a lovely Princess, was to entice the men with his excellent figure, his delicious complexion, and his languishing airs. For the rest, Philippe was a spiteful, jealous young man, over-dressed, heavily rouged and scented; charming on a superficial acquaintance, constantly committing the gravest breaches of etiquette; by no means brainless, but incapable of making any use of his abilities; and unable to keep a secret. The best that can be said of 'Monsieur' is that both his mother and his brother loved him; which in Louis' case is rather surprising, for of all vices there was none which the King so detested as Philippe's. Yet he did more than tolerate 'Monsieur', he admitted him into his intimacy. In private Philippe was allowed an armchair, all distinction of rank were dropped between them, and the brothers always remained on affectionate terms; 'Madame' was to write many years later that nothing could be freer or more amusing than the two brothers' chaffing of each other. But Louis never gave Philippe his confidence, and 'Monsieur' was often the last courtier to hear important news.

The bride had had an upbringing so different from that of her husband that she almost belonged to another class of society, the shabby-genteel. During the Fronde, when the Court of France had no money for poor relations, she and her mother had suffered actual want. Henriette had known what it meant to leave the table hungry, had learnt that stockings do not darn themselves, and had suffered as only a girl can from the knowledge that her best clothes would have been rejected by a lady's maid in a good house. Small blame to her that she grasped at marriage, even marriage with 'Monsieur'. She did not of course love him, no woman could; but to her this drawback was more than outweighted by the prospect of wealth and the certainty that there could now be no question of her ever returning to England.

In six years the girl whom Louis had thought unworthy of the honour of dancing with him had changed into a radiant woman who from the moment of her arrival at Court had all the men swarming around her. Many of them have described Henriette, but in terms so eulogistic that we get only a vague impression of perfection; it is to the women that we must turn to discover what she was really like. She was apparently a tall girl who was by no means a beauty, but whose whole person was rendered loveable by her charm—'she had in her that something which engenders love, she had no difficulty in arousing it, and she enjoyed doing so'. Her best features were her roses and cream complexion, good teeth, bright eyes, and red lips, but she was too thin for her height, and had she lived, she might have turned scraggy in her thirties. For the rest, she did her chestnut hair admirably, dressed with taste, and managed to conceal from everyone except Louis XIV that she had nearly as good a brain as her brother, Charles II. In short, no great beauty, but a high-spirited, clever, vivacious girl with considerable sex appeal, which she had every intention of exploiting to its utmost to make herself the idol of Louis' Court. It is hardly surprising that the marriage was a failure. Philippe, by his own confession, took just a fortnight to tire of being a husband; and then was horrifed to find that in Henriette he had a rival, not an admirer; and that the young men of the Court praised her beauty more than they did his own.

'Madame's' debut at Court was brilliant, and when it became apparent that the King was not insensible to her charms, Henriette's triumph was assured. Not that Louis deliberately fell in love with his brother's wife; he only found her the most delightful lady at his Court, and felt bored when he could not spend several hours a day with her.

46

After all, he was not only head of the family, but also 'Madame's' host, and civility demanded that he should exert himself to make his guest feel at home; so he used all his own charm to ingratiate himself with 'Madame'.

And Henriette? No one knows whether she became Louis' first mistress or not; but personally I doubt if she ever surrendered to him. She had a cooler head than the King; she was an accomplished coquette; and she had a considerable score against Louis. There was that business of the public snub he had administered to her at the ball of 1655, and within the last few months it had reached her ears that the King, in allusion to her figure, had nicknamed her 'the bones of the Holy Innocents'. Henriette was a young lady who always paid her debts, and my impression is that she took her revenge on Louis for his former indifference towards her by tantalizing him with hopes of a favour which she never had any intention of granting.

When the Court migrated to Fontainebleau, it was plain to the least observant that 'Madame' had made a conquest of Louis; and also that Louis was very willing to be her captive. For the first time in his life he had plenty of money, he was at the hottest period of young manhood, and the gay, informal, picnic life of Fontainebleau gave opportunities for love-making which did not exist in the crowded Louvre. Louis threw discretion to the winds and settled down to a siege of Henriette which he conducted with considerable adroitness; 'she arranged all the entertainments, and the King cared only for those which she enjoyed'. Every day she and Louis went bathing together, returning to rehearse a ballet or to stroll in the woods; then came supper on the canal, with the band playing Lully's provocative music on the bank; then an open-air ball; then a drive through the dim rides of the forest in an unlit coach, from which the two often did not get back until three in the morning. 'It seemed to everyone that there existed between them the kind of feeling that leads up to a great passion'.

But Louis behaved with a recklessness which made his conduct a matter of common knowledge, and kind souls hastened to offer Marie Thérèse and 'Monsieur' their condolences on the royal indiscretion. The little Queen was furious. She had in her that blend of piety and passion which was her Hapsburg heritage, she detested the French way of life, and she was shocked at the effrontery of Frenchwomen. If she had had her way, the palace would have been a desert in which Louis oscillated, not between Paris and Fontainebleau, but between the chapel and the conjugal bedroom. From the outset she had been insanely jealous, and being a stupid woman had shown it. Love and gallantry were the breath of life to this youthful Court, but so far most of it had been very innocent; even so, Louis had only to pay a compliment to a lady to make her the object of the Queen's hatred. Then there was 'Monsieur', bored, jealous, taking no part in the ballets because Louis got more applause than he did, and now showing every sign of becoming troublesome. He began to play the injured husband, first for the novelty of it, and secondly to let his brother see that Philippe was a husband who knew how to assert his own rights. Last there was Anne, who would gladly have ignored a situation whose existence she did not care to admit. But that became out of the question, for her niece would talk of nothing all day but the King's infidelity; and if Anne succeeded for a moment in avoiding Marie Thérèse, it was only to run into Philippe, whose sole topic of conversation was his brother's outrageous behaviour. Of the two, the young Queen was the bigger nuissance; she was stupider than Philippe, and was threatening to make a scene; though Anne tried hard to make her understand that she could do nothing which would be more certain to alienate Louis, who, like all egoists, had a horror of scenes and rarely forgave their perpetrators.

In July Anne was exasperated into taking action. To Louis she spoke severely about the effects of his ill-conduct on the Queen, who might worry herself into a miscarriage; and she invited the Queen of England over from Colombes to scold Henriette. Both the culprits seem to have been sobered by some very plain speaking; 'the eyes of the King and "Madame" were at last opened, and they decided to put an end to these rumours at any cost'. They had a conference of the sort usual on such occasions; each emphasized the purity which characterised their friendship, each bewailed the stupidity of the family; but what was to be done? Then Henriette had an inspiration. Why should not Louis pretend to be in love with one of her Maids-of-Honour, and as ostentatiously as possible? This would be noticed by everyone, and no surprise would be expressed at Louis' frequent visits to 'Madame's' apartments; when he came, the dummy mistress would be turned out of the room; and if 'Monsieur' surprised Louis with Henriette, why, Louis was trying to enlist 'Madame's' help in overcoming the girl's scruples. Louis thought the scheme a brilliant one, and it only remained to fix upon the dummy;

little La Vallière, suggested Henriette, naming the one she considered the least attractive of her household. So be it, said Louis; and he forthwith began to pay his court to her.

La Vallière—Louise Le Blanc La Baume, Demoiselle de La Vallière, to give her her full style—now in her seventeenth year, was a typical representative of a class with which Louis was unfamiliar, the poor provincial nobility. Her father, a retired cavalryman, had died penniless when she was seven, and her mother had remarried beneath her, one St Rémi, steward to the old 'Monsieur', Louis XIV's uncle, to whose Duchess Louise had been a Maid-of-Honour. When 'Monsieur' died in 1660, Louise and her mother migrated to Paris, where the girl was taken up by a busybody, Mme de Choisy, who in April 1661 had secured for La Vallière the same post in the household of the new 'Madame' as she had held in that of the old one.

Louise was the very antithesis of Henriette; a lovely platinum blonde, with an exquisite complexion, whose chief attraction was a low and extraordinarily sweet voice, whose fascination was never forgotten by anyone who had heard it; and though she was slightly lame, she danced well, and her limp was not unbecoming to her. She was not as clever as Henriette, but she had a good deal of common-sense, and was better educated than her rival; and, unlike her mistress, she was open, faithful, and entirely lacking in coquetry.

Louis was now visiting 'Madame' every day in her rooms, and every day he there saw La Vallière in the anteroom; and she attracted him more and more. From smiles they got to exchanging remarks, and from remarks to conversations which grew in length as the days passed. It was La Vallière's novelty as much as her charm which conquered Louis. Marie Mancini, and 'Madame' in a better-bred way, were both of the dashing, challenging type that looks a man straight in the eyes even when he is at his most amorous; whereas shy, gentle Louise could scarcely be persuaded to take her eyes off the ground when addressing this Apollo who had come down from Olympus to do her the supreme honour.

'Madame' had that confidence in her own charms which only a successful rival can overthrow, coupled with a more than ordinary feminine blindness to a beauty in which she herself could see no appeal; and it was some time before she realized that so far from Louise being the pretext for the King's visits to her, she had become the excuse for

49

his visits to Louise. Hell had no fury like Henriette's when she was at last forced to recognize this humiliating fact, but, being a woman, it was upon the unfortunate La Vallière, not the faithless Louis, that she emptied the vials of her wrath. Then in her extreme anger she began an ostentatious affair with another of her admirers, the twenty-four year old Comte de Guiche, who had been rash enough to set up as the King's rival for the leadership of the smart set at Court. It was probably the best revenge which 'Madame' could have taken; for Louis, though absorbed in La Vallière, found time to be both shocked and annoyed that a Princess who had been honoured with his notice should condescend to a mere noble.

History has been more indulgent to La Vallière than to almost any other royal mistress. And with good reason, for not only was she swept off her feet by a genuine passion, but even at the height of her favour she refused to ask Louis anything for her own or anyone else's benefit; and she repelled with horror the suggestion that she should use her influence to bring about anyone's disgrace. But to represent her as the unwilling victim of the King's lust is to falsify the picture; by all accounts she was in love with Louis before he fell in love with her, yielded to his first entreaty, and went with joy to the little room which an obliging courtier had placed at his master's disposal. By July she had become Louis' mistress, and the fête which he gave on the 20th for Louise was a tacit announcement of the fact.

Now as always Louis had the enviable gift of being able to clear his mind in an instant of any thoughts not relevant to the matter in hand, and as soon as he sat down at his desk, La Vallière ceased to exist for him; and when he returned to his mistress, the business he had just left vanished from his consciousness as he crossed her threshold; indeed throughout this intrigue he was working harder than ever at his *métier du roi*.

It was the Finance Department which now engaged his attention, and already he had insisted that a detailed weekly balance sheet of the national income and expenditure should be presented to him; and the more deeply he entered into the matter the more clearly he began to realize that though Mazarin was dead, there were still two Kings of France and that he was the lesser one.

The greater was Nicolas Fouquet, the suave, charming, brilliant Don Juan who held the post of Superintendent of Finances; and the King could hardly take up a document which did not illuminate Fouquet's grip on the national economy; even to discover what enterprises he did not control was difficult. And soon Colbert began to produce evidence of the financier's wholesale bribery; for Fouquet was a typical product of a corrupt age, and the magic of Dumas must not blind us to his dishonesty. Being a clever man, he at first outwitted his bewildered King; when Louis demanded explanations, Fouquet gave them freely; but somehow in retrospect he did not seem to have explained very much. So as a first step towards checkmating his ingenious Superintendent, Louis gave him Colbert as a coadjutor. The latter soon collected indisputable evidence of Fouquet's dishonesty, but Louis determined to give the Superintendent another chance. He sent for him, confronted him with proofs of his guilt, and promised to forget the past if Fouquet would undertake to deal honestly with him in the future. But, as Louis himself tells us, the financier, 'so far from becoming wiser, merely tried to become more skilful in fraud'. Every day he continued to swindle the King, and every evening Colbert exposed his fresh rascalities to Louis. Then on 17 August Fouquet entertained Louis at Vaux, his country seat, with a magnificence which made the King's own entertainments look like village fêtes. He could hardly have behaved more ineptly; so far from being flattered, Louis felt humiliated, and was indignant at the outpouring of millions on the pleasures of a single night. 'After this', he said with an irony which escaped his host, 'I shall not dare to invite you to visit me'. But the popular legend that he decided there and then to arrest Fouquet is untrue; Louis had already made his decision before he went to Vaux, and had postponed the arrest only because it was necessary that Fouquet should first complete his contracts with the tax-farmers for 1662.

The meeting of the Estates of Brittany gave Louis the opportunity to isolate Fouquet; the King announced that he would visit Nantes in person for their meeting, and commanded the attendance of the Superintendent also, on the grounds of his great influence in the province; perhaps another touch of irony on Louis' part, for he was even angrier with Fouquet for buying and fortifying the island of Belleisle off the Breton coast than he was over his swindles. On 29 August Louis left Paris for Nantes.

Before doing so he took an affectionate farewell of his wife, to whom he was still tenderly attached; 'his new passion,' we are told, 'had not effaced the legitimate one which he entertained for her'. It was obvious to all beholders that the separation gave him genuine pain, and his tears, which he endeavoured to hide, went far to console Marie Thérèse for her numerous grievances. There is no need to accuse Louis of playing a part; he was still living with the Queen, and continued to do so for the rest of her life. But he refused to accept the convention that a man can love only one woman at a time.

On 5 September Fouquet was arrested at Nantes, and his downfall was the signal for a financial witch-hunt. 'At the start everyone rejoiced to see the tax-farmers humiliated, but they were treated so severely that folk ended by pitying them.' In 1664 Fouquet was sentenced to banishment, but Louis altered the sentence to life imprisonment. For which he has been much blamed; but he was really frightened of Fouquet, and with some justification, for if the Superintendent had not envisaged the possibilities of starting a civil war, why had he turned Belleisle into a private fortress? Furthermore, Louis knew that France swarmed with people who had been Fouquet's pensioners, and rightly or wrongly he felt that to leave the fallen man at liberty would be to allow him to keep alive a subversive faction in France from across the frontier.

But much more than a financial revolution was needed before Louis could regard his own acts with any degree of satisfaction. So far his triumphs had all been domestic, and it was on the European stage that he burned to distinguish himself. As he said, he passionately desired to let the world see that there was still a King in Christendom; and it is significant that after his return from Brittany the Court began to notice that he hated to be eulogized for victories won during the lifetime of Mazarin. 'They wounded him to the depths of his heart', as he himself candidly admitted. Then in October came the Vatteville incident, which gave the world its first insight into the Louis Quatorze style of diplomacy.

Vatteville was a native of Franche-Comté, who had been a thorn in Louis side throughout the Fronde. In 1661 he was posted as Spanish Ambassador to Whitehall, and in September of that year Sweden changed her English Ambassador; and according to custom, the coaches of all the other Ambassadors were to meet that of the incoming Swede and follow it to Whitehall in the traditional order of precedence of their masters. Vatteville determined to take this opportunity to assert the precedence of the King of Spain over the King of France, by force if necessary. To oppose this, d'Estrades, representing France, brought a picked detachment of his own regiment over from Dunkirk and prepared to fight, but with misgivings, for France was very unpopular in England at the moment, and the mob would probably side with Spain. D'Estrades' fears were justified; the mob joined the Spaniards, there was a pitched battle in the streets, and France lost it with six men killed and thirty-three wounded.

The news reached Louis as he was sitting down to supper, and, pushing back his chair violently, he left the room, in spite of the entreaties of the two Queens that he would do nothing rash. The Spanish Ambassador Extraordinary was ordered to leave France instantly; the new ordinary Ambassador was turned back at the frontier; and Louis' own Ambassador was recalled from Madrid. The affair was finally settled by Philip IV's apology in writing, and his agreement that the Ambassadors of France would in all circumstances and at every Court, take precedence over those of Spain.

It was a storm in a teacup, but this one would not gather from Louis' own account of the business—'I do not know', he wrote, 'if since the foundation of the Monarchy anything has happened by which it has acquired more glory'. It would be hard to make a more fantastic claim, but thus Louis consoled himself for the abject Spanish surrender which had robbed him of a war; and he admits as much:

> It was not difficult to let everyone see by these demonstrations what was in my heart. For it is true that I would have carried to the last extremities an indignation so righteous as mine; and I should have regarded the evil as a good if it had led to a legitimate war in which I could have acquired honour by putting myself at the head of my armies'.

In the following year it was the turn of the Pope.

Louis and Alexander VII had been quarrelling almost continuously since Alexander's election in 1655, and in 1662 Louis sent the arrogant Duc de Créqui to Rome with secret orders to make himself intolerable; which Créqui, a rough, overbearing sort of man, at once succeeded in doing; as indeed he would have done without any orders at all. The inevitable explosion occurred on 20 August when the Papal Corsican Guard fired on Créqui's coach, killing a page and wounding some of the servants. Créqui at once left Papal territory and reported to Louis, who instantly mobilized for a punitive expedition against Rome. But again the King was defrauded of a war; Alexander surrendered unconditionally and was pardoned; the terms being the cession of Avignon, the disbanding of the Corsican Guard, and the erection of a column in Rome, on which was to be cut the story of the outrage and the nature of its expiation. Lastly Cardinal Chigi, the Pope's nephew, was made to come to Fontainebleau and was there compelled to read an apology for the Holy Father's crime before the assembled Court of France.

It was for every cabinet in Europe an ominous glimpse of the shape of things to come.

The dawn of 1 November 1661 found Louis by the bedside of his Queen, who since midnight had been in agonizing labour; throughout the night Louis had held her hand, 'suffering with her and giving her at each moment marks of his tenderness', whilst the poor woman screamed at intervals, 'I don't want a child, I want to die!' But all went well, and at eleven fifty-three the Queen was delivered. Louis himself opened the window and shouted down to the mob, 'The Queen has just given me a boy'. And at the end of the month he made a pilgrimage to Chârtres to return thanks for his wife's recovery.

But when he re-entered Paris on 10 December, it was to La Vallière and not to the Queen that he hastened; for he had not seen Louise for a fortnight. Ostensibly his visit was to 'Madame', but his interviews with her had become a formality, and after a short, strained conversation he would withdraw into the anteroom where Louise awaited him. 'All the doors were left open; but people were less likely to interrupt them than if they had been triple barred'.

January 1662 found Louis and Charles II at loggerheads. Louis was still irritated by Charles's refusal to punish those of his subjects who had supported Vatteville in the London battle of the previous year; an irritation in no wise allayed by Charles's bland explanation that there were administrative difficulties in the way of hanging the six thousand odd Londoners who had assisted at d'Estrades' discomfiture. And now Charles had curtly refused to waive the salute due from French ships to English in the Channel; for Charles, who was prepared to sell most things, drew the line at selling the honour of the English Navy:

My ships must do their dutys let what will happen of it, and I should be very unworthy if I quit a right and goe lower than ever any of my predessesours, which is all I have to say.

Whereupon the indignant Louis wrote to d'Estrades:

What I have noticed is that the King my brother takes an air which hints at a threat. I know no power under heaven which can make me advance a step by this method. I thought the world had a slightly better impression of me. I desire that for all reply to such a haughty declaration he learns from you that I neither demand nor ask any accomodation of this affair, because I know very well how to uphold my rights.

Neither King would give way, neither wanted war, and the problem was solved by each giving secret orders to his ships to steer clear of the rival fleet.

On top of his dispute with Charles, Louis had a violent quarrel with La Vallière in February. When Louise had become a Maid-of-Honour to the new 'Madame', an old colleague from Blois had secured a similar appointment; an intriguing, managing girl called Montalais, who ran about the Court acting as go-between in other people's love affairs. Louis, who disliked her, had forbidden La Vallière her company, but had been disobeyed—'she obeyed in public, but Montalais would sometimes spend whole nights with her'. And to Louise, Montalais had confided all the ins and outs of 'Madame's' intrigue with the Comte de Guiche. Poor Louise would gladly have remained in ignorance of this affair, for when anything weighed on her mind she was unable to conceal the fact. Louis, who was both sharp-witted and suspicious, soon discovered that she was hiding something from him, and taxed her with it. Louise foolishly admitted that she had been told certain things about a member of the Royal family which she could not communicate to the King. Louis pleaded, stormed, threatened fruitlessly and finally left the room in a fury. The two, during their honeymoon, had sworn that whenever they quarrelled they would never go to sleep without making it up, and through the night Louise waited vainly for her lover's forgiveness; and when dawn came without the longed-for message, she thought that all was over. In panic and despair she fled on foot to Chaillot, where she begged for admission to the convent. But the nuns were not quite so unworldly as to admit the King's mistress without the King's consent. The day was 24 February, and Louis had just concluded a farewell audience to the Spanish Ambassador when a courtier entered and whispered something in his ear. All noticed that the King betrayed great agitation, left the room immediately, and within a few minutes was seen galloping through the palace gates with his face muffled in a grey cloak. Bound, of course, for Chaillot, where he found Louise in tears on the floor of the parlour; and after such a scene as we can imagine, the two returned to the Tuileries, 'Monsieur's' official residence. But here a fresh difficulty arose. Everyone understood La Vallière's position at Court, but in the Household Directory she was merely one of 'Madame's' Maids-of-Honour; and 'Madame' had scores to settle with Louis. She played the virtuous housewife; no, certainly not, she could not readmit to her service a lady who had been guilty of such misconduct; she neither knew, nor desired to know, what had prompted this shameless escapade . . . and so on and so forth. And it was not until she had reduced Louis to tears that she allowed poor La Vallière to slink back to her attic.

But Louis was only at the beginning of troubles which were to show him that polygamy, like all other amusements, must be paid for. On 26 February the Court preacher was Bossuet, and in his own Chapel the King had to stomach a sermon preached directly at him, in which he was exhorted to listen to his conscience and renounce 'those delicate pleasures which in ordinary people are called vices.'

Then a week or so later the Spanish Letter Plot broke.

Its instigator was 'Mme La Comtesse'; she had never been Louis' mistress, but as his social guide in the 'fifties she had enjoyed a pre-eminent position, and she still resented her relegation to the background. She detested La Vallière, feared her honesty, yet was incapable of believing that the favourite was other than a sly, greedy girl who was making a fortune out of Louis; and she thought that if Louise could be replaced by a tool of the Soissons clique, the new mistress could be made a conduit to divert the wealth of France to the Hôtel de Soissons. A letter purporting to be from the King of Spain to his daughter, Marie Thérèse, was prepared, and in it the Queen was told that La Vallière was her husband's mistress. This was smuggled into the palace, and the conspirators hoped thus to raise such a scandal that Louis would be compelled to dismiss Louise; after which they would catch him on the rebound with their own nominee. But unfortunately it was to Louis, not to Marie Thérèse, that the letter was delivered, and he naturally took very good care that no hint of its existence reached the ears of his wife. And the sole result of the plot was that Louis decided to add the conspirator's candidate to the Royal harem. This was Mlle de La Motte-Houdancourt, a young and pretty girl, but a natural courtesan; she cared nothing for the King, was cold and greedy, and refused absolutely to sell herself to Louis if she had to share him with La Vallière; not out of distaste, but because she wanted the whole of La Vallière's supposed emoluments for herself.

Whether she would ultimately have yielded or not we cannot say, for almost at once Louis found himself—literally and metaphorically—up against a brick wall. La Motte-Houdancourt was a Maid-of-Honour to the Queen, and Mme de Navailles, who was in charge of these girls, held the odd view that Maids should be such both in fact and in name. With rare courage she told Louis bluntly that it was nothing to her how he amused himself, so long as he did not attempt to seduce the Queen's Maids; but that if he did, she would defend their virtue by every means in her power. Louis, whilst complimenting Mme de Navailles on her spirit, took her warning as a challenge to his ingenuity, and had a secret door contrived into one of the Maids' bedrooms, which during the day was hidden by the bed curtains. But Mme de Navailles was as sharp-eyed as she was honest; she discovered the door, and during Louis' next absence from Court, had it bricked up; to the great annoyance of Louis, who then started climbing along the roof to the windows of the Maids' attics; but once again he had to leave Paris and when he returned he found that every window now had iron bars; and he was only prevented from committing the final indiscretion of climbing down the chimney by Houdancourt's giggling assurance that the chimney too was barred.

At this stage Anne took a hand in the game. She speedily discovered that Houdancourt was the tool of 'Mme La Comtesse', and that her tender billets to the King were dictated to her at the Hôtel de Soissons. And so well informed was Anne that she was able to tell Louis the contents of Houdancourt's next letter before he received it. Anne's version was correct, word for word; Louis was furious; the girl had nearly succeeded in making him ridiculous, and from that moment for him she ceased to exist.

And La Vallière? She was perfectly aware of what had been going on, and when Louis crept back, she gave him such a talking to as he had never yet had from any woman. Louis was thunderstruck, but the 'shy little violet' meant business, and it was only after the King had made humble and repeated apologies that she forgave him. The reconciliation was followed by a second honeymoon, during which the lovers were often at Versailles, which Louis thought might make a week-end box where he could escape with Louise from the formality of the Louvre; and at Versailles the two 'played together like children'.

When we remember that the Louis who had his wife and Louise to attend to, and who rarely went to bed before two in the morning, was also the man who ruled France, we are not surprised to learn that in this year his health was causing anxiety. Already he suffered from stomach trouble brought on by over-eating and bad teeth; and the intensity with which he lived produced headaches, dizziness, palpitations, and depression; as Dr Vallot put it with courtly tact, his Majesty took insufficient sleep.

But in spite of all this, Louis carried on unflinchingly with his routine—Council of Finance from ten o'clock to half past one, dinner, then an afternoon meeting of the Council; two hours at his Latin, 'I finding it shameful to be ignorant of what all others knew'; evening Council at ten o'clock; then supper and then Louise.

All the time Louis was making discoveries:

How can a King govern instead of being governed, if he does not know his own financial position? He is at the mercy of some Superintendent, or even some obscure clerk, whom he is obliged to consult as if he were an oracle, and he cannot undertake anything without explaining it all to these people, and he can only act with their permission.

And he realized that delegation of work without delegation of authority is impossible—'Never leave to another anything which you can do yourself'. A dangerous maxim, and Louis' adoption of it showed his limitations; for the enormous mass of work with which he saddled himself meant that in many cases his decisions were based upon a superficial view of the matter before him. Had he not been so jealous of delegating authority, the machine of government would have run more efficiently. He had already discovered that everyone who approached a King did so to ask a favour, and he had established rules for his own guidance:

One must not judge the fairness of a pretention by the eagerness with which it is supported; on the contrary, the least reasonable claims are the most warmly pressed; for passion and interest are naturally more impetuous than reason. The wise King will always consider the results of granting a petition, and not the merit of the person who tenders it.

Whilst pondering upon this subject, Louis hit upon an ingenious method of rewarding the importunate at no expense to the State. He instituted the *habit-à-brevet*. This was simply a gold-embroidered cloak of watered silk, which could be worn only by those courtiers to whom the King gave a *brevet* or patent to do so, and from Louis' point of view the innovation was a brilliant success; the patent cost a few sous only, the favoured men had to buy the cloak themselves, and Louis was deluged with appeals for patents.

1662 was a difficult year for France, there being a corn shortage which caused widespread distress. Louis tackled the problem manfully; foreign corn was bought in large quantities, sold at a loss to those who could afford to buy it, and distributed free to the poor. And here again we have evidence which contradicts the customary picture of a Louis XIV careless of the welfare of his people. 'I never spent money to better purpose', he wrote, 'for my subjects are my true wealth, and the only wealth worth saving, other kinds being worth nothing at all unless one understands how to use them'.

But his 'lifting a burden of four millions off the shoulders of his people' in the same year was a much less popular move. What he in fact did was to write off that amount of gilt-edged stock. And as such manipulation was not then so well understood as it is today, the stock-holders regarded as a theft of their savings what we are conditioned now to accept as a conversion operation.

If a full treasury, a strong army, a loving mistress, and the adulation of twenty million people could combine to produce happiness, Louis would indeed have been a happy man in 1663. But he was not, for he was, after his own lights, a Christian; if he had been a worse man he would have been a happier one, for always his conscience came between him and the full enjoyment of his disorderly life. For the next twenty years the knowledge that he was living in mortal sin was to be an intermittent torment to him. It is significant of his state of mind that at Whitsuntide 1664 he refused to confess or communicate, and he was reproached for this backsliding; but surely the omission was in the circumstances rather creditable to him than otherwise?

Though the Spanish Letter Plot had failed, Louis can hardly have been so optimistic as to suppose that he could keep his wife in ignorance of his liaison with La Vallière indefinitely. And during 1663 the facts at last reached her.

Marie Thérèse was stupid; but even a stupid woman's wits are wonderfully sharpened by any doubts of her husband's fidelity, and the Queen had had her suspicions before the end of 1662. 'That girl with the diamond earrings', she said one evening, pointing to La Vallière, 'is the one the King loves'. It was an awkward moment for Mme de Motteville, to whom the remark was addressed; she was thrown into confusion, and finally stammered out that all husbands, without ceasing to love their wives, were unfaithful, or rather pretended that they were so in order to be in the fashion.

Then 'Mme La Comtesse' told Marie Thérèse everything there was to know about La Vallière; and like the serpent she was, then begged a private audience of Louis, to whom she reported that he had been betrayed by Mme de Navailles. The King, still smarting under his defeat in the matter of the Maids-of-Honour, seems to have accepted the Soissons woman's information uncritically; and when Mme de Navailles chose this inopportune moment to appeal to Louis to show more consideration for the Queen, he thought that she was now adding hypocrisy to treachery and his anger boiled over. The Navailles lingered in semi-disgrace until 1664 when the King ordered both husband and wife to sell their posts and leave the Court. It was one of the meanest acts of Louis' life, and even the prevalent King-worship did not prevent every honest man and woman at Court from expressing the warmest sympathy for the victims.

All pretences between Louis and Marie Thérèse were now at an end, and the King not only admitted to her that La Vallière was his mistress, but behaved with that brutality which is a man's only defence against the knowledge that he is thoroughly in the wrong. A bitter little scene this year shows the terms on which husband and wife were now living. Louis had returned from La Vallière at four in the morning to find the Queen sitting by the fire with Mme de Chevreuse:

LOUIS (coldly): Madame, why are you not in bed?

QUEEN: I was waiting for you.

LOUIS: You seem to imply that you wait for me often.

QUEEN: And so I do, for you no longer care for me; you seem to care more for my enemies.

LOUIS (mockingly): Alas, Madame, that you should have learnt so many things! Go to bed, and do not argue so much.

QUEEN: I want to tell you that I love you always, whatever you do to me.

LOUIS: And I will manage that you shall no longer be troubled; but if you wish to please me you must cease from all communications with Mme de Navailles.

But very different was Louis' behaviour to his mother when she had a severe attack of fever in April; he sat up with her for several nights, having had a mattress placed at the foot of her bed on which he occasionally dozed, fully dressed; and he nursed her with wonderful care, changing her sheets himself, and in fact waited on her with more skill and tenderness than any of her women showed.

Hardly had Anne recovered when Marie Thérèse caught the measles, and then Louis showed a sympathetic attention to his wife which contrasted pleasantly with his recent cruelty—'He never left her bedside, but was always with her'. The result was that he himself caught the disease, and so badly that for twenty-four hours his life was in danger; during which time he alternately implored La Vallière's presence, and forbade her to approach him for fear of infection.

It was perhaps La Vallière's tales of country life which prompted Louis this year to enquire into the doings of his provincial nobility; which he did with his usual thoroughness, sending out a long questionnaire to all Intendants. What were the marriages and connections of each family in his district? Their morals? Their property? How did they treat their peasants? Did they farm their own land? Were they warlike? Did they prefer provincial to Court life?

Next he turned to the problem of the rentier class, whose liquidation he was now considering seriously; writing on 24 October, Condé said that the King had expressed a hope of buying up the whole of the Paris Municipal Loans; adding that this would be a big undertaking, even if practicable, and that it looked as if the King would find himself faced with serious difficulties. Difficulties which in fact proved insuperable, and Louis had to content himself with half-measures; on 10 December he bought in eight million livres of New Loan at a low and arbitary price, whilst holders of the Old Loan were offered their choice between a twenty per cent reduction in the value of their holdings or of being bought out completely—at Louis' price. It is evident that both Louis and his advisers had failed completely to grasp the point that the existence of a rentier class was a guarantee of the stability of the Throne and an insurance policy against a new Fronde. For the majority of the Loans were held in Paris, and by the class which could make or mar a popular rising.

Simultaneously with this rigging of the gilt-edged market Louis was making every effort to direct capital into Colbert's nationalized industries, and also pressing on with a measure for expropriating the colonial landowners. For Colbert, whose economics were almost as naif as Louis' own, had persuaded him that State ownership of the means of production spelt increased efficiency at a lower cost.

These activities bred considerable discontent in Parisian moneyed circles, and it was no doubt with a view to allaying it that in December Louis took the unprecedented step of inviting a number of the leading merchants to dinner; and whilst they were dining he sent them a polite message of regret that the state of his health debarred him from the pleasure of drinking a glass of wine with them.

In August Louis at last managed to engineer a war, or at least what his flatterers described as such; he invaded Lorraine and took the citadel of Marsal. An affair of no interest except for the disclosure of the unexpected fact that Colbert was now Louis' confidant in his liaison with La Vallière. From Lorraine Louis wrote frequently to La Vallière through Colbert—'Those letters in blank envelopes you will forward to the person I mentioned to you on leaving. You understand.' And again—'I address the letters for the Queens to you; and you know what to do about those which have no address'.

The 'war' ended, Louis returned in triumph to Paris, and on 19 October the winter season opened with the first performance of Molière's *Impromptu de Versailles*, commissioned for the occasion by the King himself. On 19 December La Vallière bore the King her first child. 'We have a boy', wrote the accoucheur to Louis, 'at three thirty this morning, who is very strong. The mother and child are doing well, thank God'. This event took place secretly at the Palais Brion, where Louis had installed Louise on his return from Lorraine; and indeed so cautious was the King that he defeated his own purpose. Romantic tales circulated about the birth, and have done so ever since; such as that Louise was masked during her labour. There seems to be no truth in this, but what is both true and astonishing is the discovery that Colbert, the great minister of state, made all the arrangements, even down to buying the baby-linen and selecting a confidential maid; and it was Mme Colbert who brought up the child.

IV

1664 opened with Anne and Louis more seriously estranged than they had ever been; for a variety of reasons, but the fundamental trouble was that Louis was a man of twenty-five and Anne would not realize the fact. Scenes between the two were frequent. One day at the height of their quarrel, the King entered Anne's private room where she was chatting with 'Monsieur' and 'Mademoiselle'; both of whom left the room in the hope that if mother and son found themselves alone together there would be a reconciliation. But Louis, after remaining for some time leaning against the window, made a low bow to the Queen-Mother and left her without a word. However, he loved his mother too much to risk a permanent breach; next day he sought her in her oratory and fell on his knees in tears to ask her pardon, saying that he had not slept all night for thinking of his conduct. Anne met his advances half way, but was ungenerous enough to make his surrender the occasion for a severe lecture on his general behaviour. He was, she said, drunk with his own grandeur, put no limits to the satisfaction of his desires, and was daily endangering his salvation. Louis, still in tears, replied that he knew it; that there were times when he was sorry and ashamed; but that his passions were too strong for his reason and that he could not truly say that he even desired to resist them. To which Anne replied sadly that his recognition of his sins showed that God had not entirely abandoned him. And Louis was sufficiently disturbed by the conversation to promise his wife that he intended to give up the role of gallant at the age of thirty and assume that of a good husband. After recording which, it would be unfair not to remember that when in the winter Marie Thérèse bore a child which lived for only a month, Louis 'was in a furious fear', sat up several nights with her, and spent much of his time in tears. Within a couple of months his tears were again in request at a similar ceremony, when his second child by La Vallière was born.

For Louis it was a year of intense activity. The Emperor was fighting the Turk, and in April Louis, who was now posing as a Crusader, pressed on him a French contingent of six thousand men, which was unwillingly accepted; but which won the victory of St Gothard on 1 August. Charles II had acquired Tangier, therefore France must also have an African colony; so in July Beaufort, the former Frondeur, who had been Admiral of France since 1658, was sent to Algeria where he and Vivonne, brother of Mme de Montespan, established a bridge-head at Gigeri.

Some of Louis' orders to Beaufort read curiously as part of the briefing of a Commander-in-Chief. In August for instance he gave him orders to buy specimens of any rare fauna to be found in Algeria, and especially to send as many birds as he could collect. Also orange trees, 'those with good strong trunks', for the Royal hot-house and the State apartments.

On 5 May Louis gave one of his gorgeous fêtes, *Les Plaisirs de l'Ile Enchantée*, but this was an oasis in a Sahara of such incessant hard work as annoyed the courtiers greatly. On 27 June when the Court was at Fontainebleau, one of them wrote to a friend complaining of his boredom; the King, he said, was shut up practically from dinner time onwards, the Queens gambled, and the rest of the house party was hard put to it to kill time.

La Vallière's position at this period was a curious one; she had resigned her post in 'Madame's' household, everyone knew what she now was, and yet she lived as secluded from the Court as if her liaison with the King was still a secret. It was a state of affairs which was becoming inconvenient to the King, who could no longer spare the time for visits to the Hôtel de Brion; so he decided to recognize Louise as his mistress and force her on his wife and his mother. Without any warning he brought her into Anne's room one evening, and set her down to make a fourth at cards with 'Madame', 'Monsieur', and himself. Anne was furious, Marie Thérèse more angry still. But there was nothing to be done; the intrusion counted as a presentation, and the girl's birth entitled her to appear at Court; and the Court ladies, who had hitherto ignored her existence, rushed to fawn upon her.

In later years we hear a good deal about the boredom which underlay the magnificence of Court life at its zenith, but few historians seem to have remarked that ennui was already apparent in 'the beautiful years' between 1661 and 1678. In the early part of 1665 for example, we find the Duc d'Enghien, Condé's eldest son, complaining bitterly of a courtier's lot; 'we were all very bored with the big ball on 23

January at the Palais-Royal'. In February things were worse; throughout the month there was a Ballet three nights a week, in which the same dancers had to appear, Enghien among them, and on the other nights there was a ball—'you may imagine how sick of it all we get'.

But not Louis who, as 'Mademoiselle' complains, worked his Court to a stand-still. The higher in favour you were, the more gruelling your day; on 28 May for instance, Louis and his cronies hunted before dinner, played tennis all afternoon, and of course attended the routine Court ball in the evening. An astonishing performance for a man who had also managed six or more hours office work during the day. And for the women, Court 'pleasures' were scarcely less exhausting than they were for the men. On 14 June, to give one instance, Louis gave a fête at Versailles, which meant that the ladies had to leave Paris at six in the evening in full Court dress. On their arrival a collation was ready for them, after which there was a comedy, a ballet, the inevitable ball, and a long supper; and the first of the revellers got back to Paris about eight o'clock on the following morning.

While this treadmill of pleasure continued, by August Louis had stepped up his working day from six to eight hours; small wonder that he found himself rather unwell, and had fits of giddiness.

And upon him was about to fall one of the greatest sorrows of his life. The trouble had begun in February, when Anne was suffering from an acute pain in the breast; and when she was examined, even the doctors had no difficulty in diagnosing a neglected cancer which had become inoperable. As the alternative treatment to the knife was to bathe the place in hemlock water, it is hardly surprising that by November Anne was worse and not better; and by the summer of 1665 all hope had been abandoned, though some pretence at treatment still continued, Vallot having now substituted cabbage water for hemlock. At least it is consoling to learn that as the pain increased, the sufferer was kept heavily dosed with opium. All accounts agree that Louis was overhelmed with grief, and until the end he was constantly with his mother, showing her all those little attentions which he knew so well how to render.

But even under this burden 'the show must go on', and Louis continued to behave as his world expected him to do; seducing Mme de Monaco, the Duc de Gramont's restless, dissipated daughter; imprisoning Lauzun, Mme de Monaco's lover, for attempting to interfere;

and hunting with Louise, whom he admired more than ever since he had discovered that she rode well to hounds. In September, after the first night of *L'Amour Medicin*, he gave Molière a pension and promised to stand god-father to his first child; and on 24 December he celebrated Christmas Eve by reducing the interest on Government Stock from six to five per cent.

Throughout January 1666 Anne's sufferings were terrible, and 'were augmented by the stink of her cancer'. But she uttered no complaints; 'God', she said, 'puts me in this disgusting state to punish me for having loved the beauty of my own body too much'. On the last evening of her life she gave some final admonition to Louis, who was crying by her bedside; regarding him fixedly with the majesty of a Queen and the authority of a mother, she said, 'Do what I have told you; I repeat it with God on my lips' (she had just received Communion). Louis bowed and said that he would not fail to carry out her order—'and to this day no one knows what it was'.

She died on the morning of 20 January; and Louis, on the evidence of his valet, spent the whole of the following night in tears and groans. He never forgot his mother, or the great debt he owed her for her services during his minority. Writing of her death more than ten years later, he said:

> After this blow I could no longer endure the sight of the place where it had fallen, so I left Paris instantly . . . The obligation to notify all the Princes of Europe of my loss cost me more than you might think; particularly the letters to the Emperor, the King of Spain, and the King of England, which etiquette compelled me to write with my own hand . . . it is difficult, whilst one's grief is still fresh, to write of it to others without increasing it by the recollection of incidents hitherto unnoticed.

Of the depth and sincerity of Louis' grief there is no doubt; mother and son had loved each other, and had lived together with a familiarity which was then unusual in royal, or indeed in any families. Yet to Louis Anne's death must have been a relief; a feeling no doubt repelled with horror, but growing in strength nevertheless. As long as Anne lived, there was someone whose criticism Louis dreaded, and in whose presence he ceased to be the King; and with her death the last brake on his conduct was removed. It was on 21 January 1666 that the 'Grand Monarque' was born.

Something which proved irrecoverable vanished with Anne; Marie Thérèse lacked her aunt's charm and talent for holding a Court. And rank ceased to have the importance accorded to it by the Queen-Mother. For two reasons; first, Louis dreaded another Fronde, and secondly he had in his character a curiously Oriental streak; and both his phobia about civil war and his penchant for the role of benevolent Asiatic despot led to his obliterating as far as possible all distinctions of rank. His politeness was perfect, but he made little distinction between a Duke and a private gentleman; both were merely subjects in the new France where only Marshals and bourgeois Viziers stood out at all clearly against the colossal figure of the Great King. And the position of women altered for the same reasons; there were to be no more female politicians whispering to the men, for Louis had seen what came of that; and as regards their manners, let them live as they pleased in secret, provided that they observed the strictest decorum in public. As an old courtier complained, meritorious conduct now meant showing an abject deference to the King; urbanity and politeness vanished from a Court in which the King did not make those nice distinctions which he should have done between men of different ranks. And as for putting the women in a position in which they hardly dared to speak to a man in public, what the King accomplished by this was not to make women more virtuous, but merely less polite, and finally more brazen. But one must admit that this particular courtier exaggerated; he was one of those people whose life was spent in looking back over his shoulder at 'the good old times'.

After Anne's death Louis recaptured something of the ebullience which had followed on his release from Mazarin's dominance, and plans, theories of government, reforms flowed from his pen; perhaps the best of the latter being the abolition of the absurd system whereby the provinces in which troops were billeted had to bear the whole cost of their maintenance. Not only was this charge transferred to the central Government, but henceforward when units were on the move they were preceded by purchasing agents who bought for them supplies in the towns and villages at market rates; which was a vast improvement on the system of letting the Colonels requisition from an impoverished peasantry on notes which might or might not ultimately be honoured by the Army Intendant. This was a part only of a real attempt to infuse some discipline into the army; for, as Louis himself said, more battles are won by discipline than by sword thrusts and musket balls—'The advance of well-drilled troops shows a self-assurance which frightens the enemy; and generally it is sufficient that troops should appear brave, because the enemy, convinced that they are so, will not wait long enough to put the assumption to the test'.

It is revealing to see the order in which Louis at this time placed his duties as a sovereign; firstly, to augment his own glory, secondly to expand his frontiers, and thirdly to ameliorate the lot of his people. A policy of naked selfishness had Louis' practice followed his theory; but in fact he knew that no King is so absolute that he can afford to flout public opinion, and in reality he avoided *ex cathedra* decisions as carefully as did the Popes:

> I was reduced to settling this matter by my own authority, a thing which rarely happens to me; for though my decisions need no man's endorsement, I am always pleased when I can execute my plans by a majority vote [of the council of State].

The self-restraint imposed by Kingship had not yet become second nature to Louis and in his memoirs he more than once complains of how irksome he found the discipline which he imposed upon himself. Particularly the constant watch he had to keep upon his tongue, not only in matters of business, but in familiar conversation. 'What a queer thing it is', he wrote, 'that a sovereign, who is free to do what he pleases, is denied the right of free speech, and is reduced to listening instead of talking. But there is no doubt that loquacity is one of the most dangerous habits into which a Prince can fall'.

In 1662 Louis had made a defensive alliance with Holland to calm the well-founded Dutch suspicion that he intended to attack the Republic in the near future. And he was greatly annoyed when in 1666 he found himself at war with England as the unwilling ally of Holland; a maddening interruption to his plans for the Spanish Netherlands, and a danger to his scheme for making England a satellite of France. But Louis handled the situation with remarkable skill, showing himself a friendly enemy to Charles II and an ineffectual ally to Holland without making an irreparable breach with either. A small contingent was sent to help the Dutch, and Louis, who could not without making himself ridiculous have appeared in the field at the head of it, consoled himself for his enforced inactivity by writing a eulogy of the straightforward conduct of Kings by Divine Right as contrasted with the baseness and treachery of Republics; and massed troops on his north-eastern frontier, ostensibly to aid the Dutch, but actually for a surprise attack on the Spanish Netherlands in 1667.

These were busy times for Louis. His mornings, he tells us, were allotted to matters of justice, commerce, financial affairs, and despatches; the afternoons to current business. In the evenings he returned to his office to work on military affairs with his War Minister, Louvois, a genius who forged the instrument with which Louis was almost to conquer Europe; a man described as 'the greatest clerk and the greatest brute that ever lived'. 'And after that', concludes the King, 'when I had any time to spare, I worked on these memoirs which you are now reading'. Even then he had not mentioned all his activities, for he was now taking time out of his scanty leisure to improve his neglected education. And let us remember that many of what he called his leisure hours were in fact devoted to keeping the social machinery running in one of the most touchy and quarrelsome Courts on record. Largely by the force of his own personality. Voltaire, who knew Louis XIV in the King's last years, said that his dignified, charming voice, coupled with his known dislike of hurting anyone's feelings, won the hearts of those whom his presence would otherwise have intimidated; and that though Louis' bearing would have been ridiculous in any one else, it befitted both the man and his rank.

On the other hand it was Louis himself who was responsible for the coarsening and deterioration of society which so many observers noticed in 'the beautiful years'. Where the King led the Court followed, and it was in vain that Louis urged decorum as long as he ostentatiously exempted himself and his mistresses from obedience to his own rules. So long as his mother was alive he had maintained some show of decorum in his affair with Louise; but now his behaviour towards her in public was that of an Oriental ruler towards his favourite wife. And too, it was Louis' own passion for heavy gambling which produced such incidents as that in January 1666 when a young noble of good family, a Clermont, was caught cheating at cards in the King's own room, where by palming cards he had swindled the Duc de Gramont out of some seven or eight hundred pounds. 1666 was for

Louis an uncomfortable year. After Anne's death he had been generous in his promises of love and care for 'Monsieur', and he had kept his word; but Philippe was finding the purely ornamental role of Son of France irksome. He viewed his brother's increasing stature with envy, and in March there was an explosion; 'Monsieur' demanded an arm-chair for 'Madame' when she visited the Queen, instead of the armless chair to which Court etiquette entitled her. This was to attack Louis on his most tender spot, but he replied kindly that he could not grant a request which would place 'Monsieur' and 'Madame' on an equal footing with himself. And for once all Louis' charm was exercised in vain; like the spoilt child he was, 'Monsieur' proceeded from entreaties to complaints, from complaints to tears, and from tears to rage. But Louis was adamant, though in recalling the incident afterwards he described it as a trifle; but he went on to say that to a King who wished to retain his prestige, even the most trifling distinctions of his rank were 'infinitely precious'.

Nor was 'Monsieur' more successful in his attempt to secure the vacant government of Languedoc; 'to give a province to a Son of France', said Louis curtly, 'is to show oneself utterly lacking in fore-sight and common-sense'. And when Philippe, with his usual tactless-ness, protested that their uncle Gaston had been a provincial Governor, the King replied dryly that it was his recollection of that fact which had prompted his remark.

By 1666 La Vallière was no longer the shy violet who had captured Louis' heart; so utterly had she given herself to him that there was no mystery, no challenge to Louis left in her. The lovely complexion was gone, and her face was beginning to show the lines of sadness and anxiety. But it was not entirely, or even mainly the dimming of her beauty which lost Louise her only lover. She was one of those women born to live apart, to be loved in secret, and it was the excite-ment of a secret shared, the perilous joy of a liaison conducted under the unsuspecting eyes of his wife and his mother, which had aroused and maintained Louis' passion. And now Louise, the secret lover, had settled down into a fading beauty publicly filling the role of official mistress to the King of France; and Louis, seeing her at last in the full sunlight of the Court, noted her wrinkles and found his passion cooling rapidly.

Though many had envied Louise in her hour of triumph, her lot was not in fact a happy one, for she was very lonely; she was the mortal whom the god she idolized visited only in darkness, vanishing with the daylight, and leaving her to fill in the long solitary hours with dreams of his return. And even if she had been of the companionable type, she would have been unable to gratify her tastes; for Louis disapproved of any friendships between those of his inner circle and the common herd; he had hinted as much to Louise, and to her a hint from the King was a command. One clever woman had however managed to force the doors of Louise's apartments, and once inside had rapidly established herself as La Vallière's confidante and dearest friend. Her name was Athénaïs de Rochechouart-Mortemart, formerly Mlle de Tonnay-Charente, and since 1662 Marquise de Montespan. Athénaïs was very beautiful, very witty, and when she set herself to please, quite irresistible; and poor La Vallière, the girl from the country manor, was first dazzled then delighted with the attentions and delicate flattery lavished upon her by this lovely daughter of one of the greatest Houses in France—all unaware that Athénaïs, who regarded her with unmitigated contempt, was using her merely as a stalking horse in her plans to capture Louis.

Life had, though in a very different way, treated Athénaïs as hardly as Louise. Though she was lovely, a Duke's daughter, and had six hundred years of pedigree behind her, she was drowned in debt, unhappily married, and if she could not ensnare the King—quickly—she foresaw the day drawing near when there would be nothing for it but flight from her creditors to the dreariness of some provincial château. But she had audacity and no scruples of any kind, and was prepared to move hell and earth to supplant La Vallière; she knew that if she could once attract the King's notice, she could amuse him —which Louise could not—and the first step taken, she trusted to 'the most lovely body in all France' and the aid of the Devil to bring Louis speedily to book. For she was a regular attendant at the Black Mass, and surely her devotion to the Powers of Darkness must sooner or later win her their support?

Perhaps it did. On the first occasion when Louis surprised Athénaïs in his mistress's quarters, the intruder was reduced to modest confusion and left the room without a word; on the second, Louis noticed that she was a remarkably pretty woman; and on the third, Athénaïs provoked more than one of the King's rare laughs by her original and piquant conversation. And then she took care not to meet Louis again for several days. Her tactics were completely successful, and we can imagine her delight when poor naive Louise reproached her friend for her absence and told her how much it had disappointed the King. The cosy little parties *à trois* were resumed, and it was not long before even La Vallière realized the significance of Louis' unconcealed chagrin if by any chance he failed to meet Mme de Montespan in her rooms. It could now only be a question of time until Louise got her dismissal.

Louis the ardent lover was also, let us remind ourselves, Louis the husband, and he was far too punctilious a man to neglect his duties to Marie Thérèse, who on 2 January 1667 presented him with a daughter. We must let the King announce the fact in his own words:

> This year opened with the accouchement of the Queen . . . which caused me some anxiety; for I may say that she was worthy of the attentions which I showed her, and that perhaps heaven never assembled on one woman more virtue, beauty, birth, love for her children, and respect for her husband.

Only Louis could have written this, but we must not dismiss it as humbug; he was, as we have said before, a polygamist, and his affection for the Queen was perfectly genuine. But the revealing words in his eulogy are 'love for her children'; for Louis' most amiable characteristic was his love for all children and his unvarying kindness to them. Even now he was hesitating about giving himself to Montespan whenever he thought of the children La Vallière had borne him.

Louis in 1667 was feverishly completing his preparations for the first of those aggressions which were to make him the best hated man in Europe; and now as always, his plans were masked by an increase in the tempo of Court festivities. Towards the end of February he gave a *Carrousel*, or mock tournament at Versailles, where everyone was dressed magnificently, and followed this up with two balls and a masque; apparently with more satisfaction to himself than to his courtiers, for our informant adds, 'we have had so many balls this Carnival that everyone will be delighted when Lent begins'.

France was still nominally at war with England, though the plenipotentiaries were assembling at Breda. And their impending meeting offered a good illustration of Louis' belief in the extreme importance of trifles to a King who was determined to go forward and not backwards. To his own representative he wrote that if the meetings were to be held in public, he was to consent to this only on the understanding that he was given his choice of the two apartments opening into the Great Hall of Breda—'and you are to chuse that which is next the chimney which in all likelihood is the most noble and capacious'.

Mid-May found France in the last stages of preparation for the attack on the Spanish Netherlands; and every effort was being made to give what was really a *blitzkrieg* the air of a holiday jaunt. Paris on 15 May, we are told, outshone the magnificence of Solomon and dimmed the splendour of the Emperor of China. Every street was a sea of plumes, gold-laced uniforms, carriages, mules superbly harnessed, parade chargers, saddles embroidered with gold, and excited officers running into each other as they dashed to and fro to make last minute additions to their outfits. Nine days later the King launched his invasion, on the pretext that he was entitled to territorial compensation in the Netherlands for his wife's unpaid dowry, but actually to push his northeastern frontier further away from Paris, which the decrepitude of the Spanish Empire offered him a chance of doing without any danger, and at a small cost. To Europe Louis explained that he was not at war with Spain; he was merely crossing the frontier with an escort—of thirty-five thousand troops—to receive his Queen's property from its Spanish caretakers. And to support this impudent fiction, Marie Thérèse and her ladies, including Montespan, were ordered to accompany the army.

The war was a farce; except at Lille there was no resistance worth mentioning, and in under two months Louis had conquered the Spanish Netherlands. This so-called 'War of Devolution' is interesting only because it is Louis' debut as a Generalissimo, and because easy victory stimulated the growth of latent defects in his character. As a mere soldier he behaved creditably; he often stood fire to satisfy himself that he could do so without flinching, and his presence encouraged the troops, who saw with satisfaction that their King slept on straw as they did, was in the saddle most of the day, and spent his nights in the trenches. 'He looks haughty', said the Savoy Ambassador who was with Louis' Headquarters, 'but he gives his orders mildly. He has not yet slept under a roof, in spite of the fact that he has had the toothache for a fortnight'.

But we note that all observers are silent as to the abilities of Louis the General; for the very good reason that Louis the General existed only in Louis' imagination, and such as he was in 1667 he was to remain for the rest of his military career—courageous, energetic, efficient in matters of detail, but without any real tactical or strategic flair, and an embarrassment to his nominal subordinates upon whom whom devolved the realities of command.

Of his own true standing as a General, Louis remained sublimely unaware; who, reading his Memoirs, would imagine that the success of the campaign was entirely due to Turenne's ability, and the tact with which he concealed it from the King? 'I persuaded M. de Turenne to follow me . . . and marched straight on Lille with that happy genius which has never yet been lacking in me . . .' And to Pellisson, his historiographer, who accompanied the expedition, he explained that love of his own glory came before all else in his soul. He was, he said, pleased that a just grievance had opened the gates of glory to him, and given rise to the opportunity to show the whole earth that there was still one King in the world. And a day or two later he drew Pellisson aside again, remarking that it would ill become a King to speak of his own glory before those who had been witnesses of it; and that was why he left it to History—in other words Pellisson—to evaluate it fully.

In only one branch of a Commander-in-Chief's duties was Louis really praiseworthy; Louvois did not yet feel himself secure enough to give free rein to his brutality, and consequently Louis behaved in conquered territory with that humanity which came naturally to him when he followed his own instincts. He paid for everything taken from the Flemings, hanged soldiers guilty of rape, and cashiered a Guards officer for striking a peasant. If we tire of the mass of pettifogging detail from which these facts have been unearthed, we note that Louis' absorption in small things often had happy consequences; for instance when before Lille, he could remember to write to Colbert at Paris, telling him to see that something was done for the widow and family of the potter who had just died at Versailles.

Louis the statesman showed courage and breadth of vision when peace came to be signed in 1668; for it was with a full knowledge of the loss of prestige and popularity which he was about to incur, that he not only agreed to make peace but to surrender most of his conquests except the frontier fortresses; realizing, as his people did not, the wisdom of lulling Europe's suspicions of his long-term designs. It was not an easy decision to make, for as Louis tells us himself, there were powerful arguments on either side, and there was no one whom he could consult freely. Finally he decided that he would gain more by a generous peace than by prolonging the war, on the cynical ground that 'it seemed desirable to build up a reputation for integrity and moderation with his smaller neighbours'.

On 13 May 1667 Parlement had registered Letters-Patent which set everyone talking; Letters whereby 'our dear and well-beloved and very loyal Louise de La Vallière' received the estate of Vaujours, which was erected into a Duchy for her benefit, with reversion to 'Marie Anne, Our natural daughter'; Marie Anne, who was to grow into the most beautiful girl of her day, who was to become Princesse de Conti, and who in adolescence was to show that she was indeed her father's daughter; for someone who was in a position to know has told us that 'she was all love, and they were afraid to let her have any Pages more than ten or twelve years old'. This favour to La Vallière society rightly interpreted as a polite dismissal, though Louise still strove desperately to believe that the man whom she loved so deeply, and by whom she was again pregnant, would not treat her with such cruelty. But a few days later she got a stunning blow; the list of ladies 'commanded' for the Netherlands journey appeared; her name was omitted, that of Montespan was included. By mid-June Louise had found the loneliness of Versailles intolerable, and she took the unprecedented step of leaving to join the Queen's household without an invitation; on the 20th, to the fury of Marie Thérèse, she arrived at La Fère where the ladies had halted; a fury kept white hot by Montespan, who next day on the road kept saying in the Queen's coach, 'I wonder at her audacity in presenting herself before the Queen. Heaven preserve me from ever being the King's mistress; but if I was, I should feel shame in the Queen's presence'.

At Avesnes the ladies caught up with the King, and Louise, frantic with misery and suspense, committed the further outrage of pulling her coach out of the column and galloping across country to the spot where she saw Louis. And when she met him, all hope died in her; for she was greeted with that icy politeness which the King reserved for presumptuous strangers. Though characteristically enough he was very angry with the Queen for snubbing his discarded mistress, insisted on her giving Louise a seat in her own coach, and invited her to dine with the Royal family; his wife needed to be taught a lesson in what was due to a Duchess of France who had enjoyed the supreme honour of bearing children to her King. But all this meant nothing to Louise, who on the following day was sent back to Paris; and on some night between 9 and 14 July, Montespan sold herself to Louis at Avesnes. It is to 'Mademoiselle' that we owe this information, which she has given us with her usual dry discretion. Montespan, she said, was lodged in the room next the King's; and it was noticed that the sentry on the step between the two chambers was suddenly withdrawn. After that had been done, the King spent much time alone in his own room whenever Montespan did not appear in the Queen's train. The Duc de Mortemart's reaction to the news that his daughter Athénaïs had become the Royal mistress casts a revealing light on what must have been the moral climate in which the girl had grown up. 'Thank God', he exclaimed, 'a stroke of luck has come our way at last!'

And so Louis became possessed of a great lady whose wit and loveliness were as undeniable as is the tedium with which we read of them. For the better we get to know Athénaïs, the less we like her; with all her wit, her gaiety, her sparkle, she was a vile woman; there was in her a rottenness of soul which made her cold-blooded sexual immorality a mere venial sin; we sicken of her Black Masses, her poisons, her disgusting associates in the underworld of Paris, of the horror of her secret life which was for so long to remain unsuspected by Louis. Though he was the victim of her abominable practices almost from the beginning of their liaison; for there appears to be little doubt that the head-aches, dizziness, and fits of depression from which he suffered for the next ten years were produced by the poisonous love philtres with which Athénaïs began to drug him in 1667.

But leaving the darker side apart, it is difficult to feel any indulgence for either partner in this sordid business; Louis and La Vallière had been young lovers who came together under the influence of an overwhelming passion, and we can still enjoy their romance at second hand. Whereas the Montespan affair, in spite of its duration, reminds us not of love but of the casual encounter of a roué and a street-walker. Lust and boredom actuated Louis, greed and debt Athénaïs. For in spite of her birth, she had the instincts of a courtesan. Even the behaviour

77

of one; her appetite for money, jewelry, clothes, rich food and wine, was insatiable, and if any of them were denied her, she could be as shrilly vituperative as a defrauded prostitute. Though she could turn herself out magnificently when the occasion demanded it, she was slovenly and dirty in private life; one feels that Louis, when it was too late, must often have regretted his lost La Vallière, who was as dainty as she was disinterested.

It was as much Athénaïs' hard, arrogant air of triumph as Louis' marked attentions which betrayed the new liaison to his intimates, and soon the Queen was the only member of the family who did not know that Louis had a new mistress; and her naive efforts to discover what was happening afforded much amusement:

> THE QUEEN: The King does not come to bed until four o'clock, when it is broad daylight. I am sure I do not know what he finds to amuse him.
>
> LOUIS: I read and answer despatches.
>
> THE QUEEN: But could not you do that at some other time?

'I', says 'Mademoiselle', 'kept my eyes on my plate, and the King made no answer'. But he perhaps felt some twinges of conscience, for shortly afterwards he volunteered to provide his wife with a company of Spanish comedians, on the strict understanding that he was never to be expected to witness their performance.

This year Louis pondered a domestic reform which he certainly would not have ventured to suggest in Anne's lifetime, and which was a belated fruit of Mazarin's teaching. He seriously considered taking steps to reduce the number of religious in the Kingdom. Many, he wrote, are useless to the Church and a burden to the State; but, always sensitive to public opinion, he finally decided against any drastic action and contented himself with raising the age at which vows could be taken, forbidding the establishment of new religious houses, and suppressing those which had been irregularly opened.

Then from Church matters Louis turned a fresh page in his note book to give his successor some advice on the ever fascinating topic of women; and as on this subject he can claim to have been an expert, we quote him verbatim:

> Once you allow a woman to talk to you on business you are done

for. The tenderness which we have for them makes us unconsciously adopt their views ... which are almost invariably wrong. They are eloquent, pressing, obstinate, and generally only because they dislike one man, or want you to advance another. And they cannot keep a secret ... Your only assurance of safety is to forbid them to talk of anything but pleasures.

On 23 January 1668 England, Holland, and Sweden entered into the Triple Alliance to curb Louis' aggressions. Louis, though taking this as a personal insult, realized that he was in no condition to embark on a general war. He salved his wounded pride with the easy conquest of Franche-Comté, from which he returned more than ever convinced of his own military genius; and a month later he again showed Europe that 'there was still a King in the world' by despatching a force to Candia to assist the Venetians against the Turk.

Louis had anticipated a certain loss of popularity after his moderation in the Netherlands, but he was much concerned when he discovered how deeply the whole of France resented the peace terms. Even the canaille seemed to have lost that 'esteem and affection' for him, 'to the retention of which a Prince should direct all his acts and thoughts'. In June the widow of a workman told Louis in his own palace that he was a tyrant and a whoremonger; and a man was arrested about the same time for saying, in allusion to the murder of Henri IV, that 'there were still Ravaillacs in France'. And Louis also sensed a tone in society which hurt him more than he cared to admit; his nobles, exasperated at being robbed of a long war, were whispering that the King was a mere parade soldier whose thoughts turned to peace whenever he heard the whistle of a cannon ball. And the great bourgeois families were beginning to murmur about the King's disorderly life and his contempt for common decency.

In view of his damaged prestige Louis decided that every possible means must be adopted to conceal from his subjects the fact that he was now committing the sin of double adultery; for Montespan still had a husband, a troublesome man 'who made a desperate fuss about the King's liking for his wife'. So having considered the matter, Louis moved his Court to the comparative solitude of Chambord.

And then began for the wretched La Vallière six years of martyrdom. She gently complained to Louis, who told her that he would not deceive her, and that it was true that he loved Mme de Montespan; but that for herself he still had a genuine affection; that she would have every reason to be satisfied with what he was doing for her, but that it was his wish that she should continue to live with Mme de Montespan on the same terms as heretofore. But if she showed the slightest hostility to the Marquise, he would adopt a very different line of conduct towards Louise to that on which he was at present decided.

It is Louis at his worst; he knew that Louise still loved him, but he insisted that she should remain his nominal mistress and the dearest friend of Montespan. The two women were forced to share a suite; and when Louis visited them, his orders were that Louise was to sit in the anteroom whilst he passed into Athénaïs' bedroom next door. The King's coarseness revolts us nearly as much as does his brutality; and his cold-blooded scheme had not even the merit of success. For the courtiers, especially the women, seeing La Vallière's ravaged face and Athénaïs' air of triumph, were left in no doubt as to the real facts. On Louise's anguish it would be painful to dwell, nor do we wonder that when at last she entered religion, the Carmelites said that she had done much to expiate her sin in the previous six years.

Louis was now working harder than ever, and 'his hours were as strictly apportioned as those in a monastery'. From Saturday to Monday midday he worked with Lyonne, his brilliant Foreign Secretary; on Monday afternoon the Council of State assembled and was in session until Wednesday, when Colbert appeared and stayed until Friday morning. The rest of Friday morning the King spent with his confessor, and in the afternoon he gave himself a half-holiday, spent usually in playing tennis, hunting, or inspecting the progress of his building operations at Versailles. And we notice that whatever diminution of popularity he may have suffered with the nobility and the people, Louis' reputation in official circles stood as high as ever. Pomponne, who was to succeed Lyonne in 1671, remarked in 1668, 'with a sort of ecstasy' that those who did not know the King, could not imagine the grandeur, the penetration, and the enlightenment of his mind, the justness of his remarks, and the charm of his manner when he laid aside the proud mien with which he clothed himself in public. And this is a testimonial of the first importance, for as it happened there was no chance of its ever reaching Louis' ears.

V

1669 was for Louis a year of intense diplomatic activity as a preliminary to his impending attack upon Holland; and he showed his habitual skill in isolating his chosen victim. Domestically, however, the year was not so successful. Lauzun, released from the Bastille in 1666, and now higher in favour than ever, craved the vacant post of Grand Master of the Artillery. And Louis, against his better judgement, and in spite of the objections of Louvois, nominated him for the position, stipulating however that Lauzun should keep his promotion secret until it was officially announced. But Lauzun, being a Gascon, could not deny himself the satisfaction of boasting, and Louis, reproached by Louvois, was extremely annoyed. The Artillery remained vacant, and when Lauzun reminded Louis of his promise, the King answered dryly that his promise had been conditional. Whereupon Lauzun appealed to Mme de Montespan, who promised to do her best to overcome the King's opposition. Time passed, nothing happened, and Lauzun, at the end of his patience, took a resolution which seems incredible but is nevertheless well attested by his contemporaries. He was on intimate terms with Mme de Montespan's chamber-maid, and persuaded her to let him hide under the bed in the room where Louis and Montespan met in the afternoons. To us today it is difficult to realize the full extent of the risk he ran; a sneeze, even an unguarded movement, and Lauzun would have vanished for ever from the eyes of men into the living death of the Bastille. But luck was with him, and he overheard the whole conversation of the lovers; which revealed the interesting fact that Montespan, so far from helping him, was doing all she could to injure him with the King.

When Lauzun, choking with rage and dust, could safely emerge, he hurriedly changed his clothes and stationed himself at Athénaïs' door; and when she appeared he offered himself as her escort to the evening reception, asking her 'in a gentle, respectful voice', whether he might flatter himself that she had remembered her promise to speak to the King on his behalf? Montespan fell into the trap, and assured him that she had done her utmost. They were now entering the great salon, and Lauzun, with bent back and the obsequious smile of a man who had on his arm the Mistress of France, whispered in her ear what everyone assumed to be a string of compliments; actually he was repeating word for word what she had really said to the King, and as they neared the Royal circle he overwhelmed her with a torrent of filthy abuse in the language of the brothel—always with the same deferential smile. And the favourite dropped fainting at Louis' feet, where she was with some difficulty restored to consciousness. It was terror, not rage which had overcome Montespan; intensely superstitious, she assumed that Lauzun had obtained his disconcertingly accurate knowledge by supernatural means, and that her master the Devil was betraying her.

Indeed Athénaïs at this time can hardly have been happier than was La Vallière; for the Paris police had begun those investigations which were ultimately to overthrow her. Already two of the worst scoundrels with whom she had had criminal dealings were in prison, and at any moment they might make confessions which would damn her in Louis' eyes. And as a refinement of torture, she dare not display the least uneasiness; when Louis was in her arms she must play the ecstatic lover, and at other times she must always be the gay, witty Marquise without a care in the world, adapting herself to the King's every mood, maintaining that endless and exhausting stream of bright conversation which alone could keep Louis from relapsing into boredom. And this too at a time when she, who disliked children, was about to bear the first of her bastards, a boy born on 6 November.

Louis, unlike his mistress, loved children, but when he heard that Athénaïs was pregnant, the extreme awkwardness of the situation overcame his pleasure at the thought that he was again about to become a father. How was the child to be disposed of? Somehow the evidence of his latest debauchery must be hidden from the inquisitive eyes of his people. And then Athénaïs thought of a needy protegée who would be thankful to take the child, one Mme Scarron, widow of a comic poet who had died in 1660.

It was with misgiving that Louis consented to the widow's appointment; for he intended to see much of his children, and necessarily of their governess also; and he understood that the lady was a *précieuse*, a type of woman he detested. However, Montespan revealed the position to Mme Scarron and proposed that she should take charge of a child which had a King for its father. But the young widow, proud of her own gentle birth, refused to undertake the education of a child of Mme de Montespan's; and when pressed, finally answered that she would not burden herself with such a charge unless the King in person asked her to do so. Louis heard with amazement that Mme Scarron, so far from jumping at a position which even Mme Colbert had not thought beneath her, was making difficulties. But there was no help for it, he was forced to interview the widow, who at last consented, solely to oblige His Majesty. And Louis, when he realized that instead of conferring a favour he had been manoeuvered into accepting one, began to think that there was more in Mme Scarron than he had imagined. And so the problem of the third royal nursery was solved.

The winter of 1669–70 saw the birth of the Grand Design. If the isolation of Holland was to be complete, the assistance or at worst the neutrality of England was essential; and the Grand Design was simply a conspiracy hatched between Charles and Louis behind the backs of their respective ministers, first to bring England into the war, and secondly to enable Charles, with Louis' support, to win over or force his subjects into the Roman Church.

Louis found this his toughest piece of bargaining, for Charles, a cleverer man than his cousin, realized that here at last was a deal which if handled properly would secure him a nearly adequate income; not an adequate one, for to a man of Charles's tastes and habits there was no such thing as an adequate income. Charles was playing with fire and knew it; but he had no intention of executing the religious part of the plot, and felt tolerably sure that he could commit his country to war with the Dutch without endangering his own safety.

Louis was urgent, Charles hung back. He talked to the French Ambassador of his affection for Louis, of gentlemen's agreements, of his duty to the true faith; but he must have time and money—lots of time and lots of money. And when at last pinned down to concrete proposals, his terms dumbfounded Louis—£200,000 for Charles's declaration of his conversion, cash in advance, but the declaration to be at Charles's convenience; £800,000 a year subsidy during the war; and various overseas and continental pickings.

Here a touch of comic relief entered into the haggle in the person of the Abbé Pregnani, a well-known Paris astrologer whom Louis sent to Whitehall early in 1670, bribed to tell Charles that he foresaw terrible misfortunes threatening him if he failed to put himself under the protection of Louis. Charles made no objection to Pregnani's visit; he listened to his predictions with his usual airy disillusionment, then put the Italian oracle in his coach and carried him to the Newmarket spring meeting, where the prophet tipped him a loser for the first three races on the card. Charles told the story in a letter to 'Madame', intended for Louis' eye, and this is the last we hear of the French King's curious attempt to produce a supernatural intervention in his favour at Whitehall.

In spite of Louis' views on women in general, he made an exception in favour of 'Madame', who was one of the few people who knew all the ins and outs of the Grand Design; and who in 1670 was practically one of Louis' Secretaries of State. Through her hands passed all the correspondence between the two Kings, and she proved worthy of their trust.

Much had happened to 'Madame' since she and Louis had flirted at Fontainebleau in 1661, and she had had ample opportunity to regret her marriage to 'Monsieur', who had recently passed through an emotional crisis which had had repercussions on 'Madame's' comfort. The vilest of 'Monsieur's' favourites was the Chevalier de Lorraine, now in his late twenties, 'beautiful as an angel', and reputed to be the most depraved man in France; an engaging person who, though not a pervert, practised homosexuality to keep his hold on 'Monsieur'. Then in 1669 'Monsieur' made the horrifying discovery that not only was the Chevalier unfaithful to him, but that he was also keeping one of 'Madame's' Maids-of-Honour; instead of dismissing the Chevalier, 'Monsieur' dismissed the Maid, to the great indignation of Henriette. Then in 1670 Louis arrested Lorraine for insolence, and 'Monsieur's' rage knew no bounds. He dragged 'Madame' to Villers-Cotterets, and solemly announced that he would not sleep with her until the Chevalier was released; the scandal was enormous, for to the XVIIth Century 'Monsieur's' act was tantamount to a legal separation.

But things were too serious for Louis to tolerate any nonsense from 'Monsieur'; 'Madame's' presence at Court was essential, and the King insisted on it. Henriette was given an office on the same floor as the King's and there the finishing touches were put to the Grand Design.

Then came more trouble. Charles had set his heart on Henriette's coming to Dover to conclude the Design, or Treaty of Dover, and 'Monsieur' saw a chance of disappointing his wife; he absolutely declined to let her leave France. Then suddenly changing front, he said that he himself would conduct 'Madame' to England; a *volte face* which embarrassed Louis, for he had already told 'Monsieur' that the trip was purely a family reunion which had no political significance; and how then was he to forbid Philippe to take 'Madame' to meet a brother who was 'Monsieur's' first cousin? In his perplexity he appealed to Charles, and Charles found the answer. In a formal letter to Louis he replied how delighted he would be to welcome 'Monsieur', but that it would be most unseemly if he allowed Louis' brother to visit him unless the Duke of York simultaneously visited the King of France; and unfortunately the Duke of York was not available. Therefore to his infinite regret . . . Charles must have enjoyed writing that letter.

Armed with it, Louis spoke to 'Monsieur' as his King; 'Madame' was travelling to England alone, and Philippe could please himself whether he sulked at St Cloud or accompanied Henriette to the Coast. 'Monsieur' collapsed, and on 28 April joined the party leaving for Dunkirk. He would have done better to have stayed at St Cloud. Every day, usually in shocking weather, the Court was on the road by seven; at St Quentin, which was reached on a fast day, there was no fish, butter, or eggs, and the bread was half baked; on the following day the convoy struggled through roads deep in mud, and strewn with dead horses, mules, and bogged wagons until even Louis began to complain of the length of the journey. At Landrecies the floods were out, the river was unfordable, and at ten at night the King found 'a miserable house on a heath' for shelter. 'Mademoiselle', who was carrying the Queen's train, dropped up to her knees in a mud-hole, and was rebuked by Marie Thérèse for her lack of decorum—'Cousin, don't *pull* at me like that!' Then it was found that the house contained no food whatsoever, so the party once more stumbled out into the night, and this time was lucky enough to strike another dwelling where a supper of sorts was procured. The soup, said 'Mademoiselle', was so cold that it would have congealed if it had been properly boiled; there was a plate of very nasty cold meat; and a fowl which could be dismembered only by the King and herself each taking a leg and pulling with all their might. After supper the whole royal family had to sleep on the floor in one room, and at four in the morning they took the road again.

No wonder that when they reached Dunkirk even Louis felt indisposed, whilst Henriette was exhausted. She was in fact already fatally ill, and had only another six weeks to live; but she had before her a brief sunset of unalloyed happiness. On 16 May she reached Dover where her much loved Charles met her, and they remained together until 2 June when Henriette returned to France with the Secret Treaty, signed on the previous day. At half past two on the morning of 30 June she died of peritonitis, with her crucifix at her lips, whilst Bossuet was reciting the *in manus tuas*.

Louis' grief was sincere, but short-lived; and he soon forgot her in his schemes for remarrying his brother into a family which would assist his expansionist policy.

The King's prestige was still apparently low, and unfairly so in the opinion of a foreigner, who was astonished that Louis did not punish his subjects for their grumbling. Their good luck, he said, had blinded them to the fact that they had never had a King who treated them better, nor a braver one; for he himself had seen Louis facing danger with the same calmness with which he attended a ball. But the same observer soon discovered that French discontent was not groundless. For Louis was spending from ten to twenty times as much as any of his predecessors on the Household Troops, stables, music, theatricals, table, clothes, furniture, and buildings.

The rumour that Louis disliked war still persisted. 'Le Roi des Ballets' was his nickname in the army, and this disagreeable piece of news may have reached the King himself; for it was in this year that he gave up dancing in public. And in September he gave his officers a crumb of comfort by invading Lorraine; an affair not worth mentioning except for a letter from Louis to his kinsman d'Enghien which disproves the assertion that the King never unbent:

> Your letter arrived very apropos, for I could not have maintained my proud attitude much longer, and if you had put off writing to me, I should have had to write to you. Seriously, I am eager to re-open our correspondence . . .

A year had now passed since Mme Scarron had undertaken the care of Louis' bastards, and during that time the King's opinion of her had altered considerably. He had begun with such a prejudice against her that in talking to Mme de Montespan he always referred to her as 'your *bel esprit*', but now that he had grown accustomed to the governess, he had learnt to relish her conversation.

The thirty-five year old Mme Scarron was in fact a new experience for Louis; he found in her company a sensation of restfulness, and an enjoyment of the easy unguarded talk which he could never allow himself elsewhere. And perhaps as early as 1670 her coldness, reserve, and wariness had given him a vague idea that the conquest of such a woman would be thrilling; the very qualities which had prevented her from ever having a lover were a challenge to Louis the irresistible.

Mme Scarron had every reason to be wary of men. She had entered society as the penniless daughter of a *declassé* noble, beautiful, unprotected, and fair game for every debauchee; and always, as she tells us rather too often, she had preserved her virtue. The early life of Françoise d' Aubigné, now the widow Scarron, shows what shipwreck could befall a family in one generation. The d'Aubignés were an XIth century House, and Mme Scarron's grandfather had been a comrade of Henri IV's. But her father was an irreclaimable criminal who ended his worthless existence in 1647 as a beachcomber in the West Indies. Half his life was spent in prison, and it was in Niort gaol that Françoise was born in 1635. In 1647 her mother, who disliked her, got her sister-in-law, a Mme de Villette, to take charge of the child, and as Mme de Villette was a Huguenot, Françoise was received into the Reformed Church; whereupon another aunt, Mme de Neuillant, petitioned Queen Anne for custody of Françoise, and placed her in a Paris covent where she was reconverted to Roman Catholicism. When she made her debut her charm, modesty, and beauty secured her the entrée to the Hôtels de Rambouillet and d'Albert where she acquired that 'precious' tone which was then the mark of the best society. In 1652 she made an unconsummated marriage with the helpless cripple Paul Scarron, to whom she was a devoted nurse until his death in 1660; and for the next nine years she eked out a precarious existence on doles begged for her by influential friends. It was a curious background for the woman destined to marry the proudest King in Christendom.

Reticent Louis is an open book when compared with Mme Scarron, the most baffling figure at Court. She was charming, said contemporaries, and much of her correspondence survives; but in it we find none of the charm we were led to expect; and when we have read all that she has left, we are little nearer to understanding her. Mme Scarron's prose is clear, always sensible, sometimes witty, but we never get under her guard; and after a time her perpetual reserve fatigues and exasperates us. When we have finished the letters and the St Cyr papers, all we have learnt is that she was a devout Christian with a cool, matter of fact love for children, and a genius for the role of school-mistress. Did she set herself to attract Louis? No doubt she angled for his 'admiration and respect', for to obtain these tributes was, she said, 'her idol'. But I can find no evidence that she was ever in love with him; on the contrary indeed, much to suggest that she regarded Louis merely as the most difficult and wayward of her pupils. One thing does however become clear as we examine the evidence; the scheming woman who trapped Louis and then spent the rest of her life in plastering over the debauchery of her youth with a hypocritical devo-tion, exists only in the minds of her fanatical enemies, St Simon and 'Madame-Palatine', 'Monsieur's' second wife—both unfortunately much more amusing writers than Mme Scarron. And the portraits which they have drawn have had their colours skilfully heightened by La Beaumelle's forgeries. The old witch who made Louis dance to her tune for forty years is a myth; and in fact we shall see that her political influence was small.

1670 closed with the comedy of 'Mademoiselle's' marriage. All her life she had been as chaste as Diana, and all her life she had been searching Europe for a husband worthy of her; and now at forty-three this woman who had always denounced love as an emotion unworthy of a lady, had contracted a violent passion for Lauzun. He, as might be expected, played his cards beautifully, and 'Mademoiselle' was left to make all the running even to the point of asking Louis' permission to marry him; for he himself had no intention of risking his position by asking Louis for the hand of the richest Princess in Europe. Even 'Mademoiselle' seems to have felt a certain diffidence over the matter, for she begged Louis' permission in writing; and Louis, though astonished, replied courteously that he would leave her to act as she pleased.

We get some idea of the huge sensation the news produced by seeing how Mme de Sévigné passed it on to her daughter:

I am going to tell you the most astonishing, the most marvellous, the most miraculous, the most bewildering, the most extraordinary .. thing ... Well, I suppose I must put you out of suspense at last; Lauzun, on Sunday at the Louvre, is to marry Mademoiselle ... Mademoiselle ...? Why faith, Mlle d'Eu, Mlle de Dombes, Mlle de Montpensier, Mlle d'Orléans, *Mademoiselle*, first cousin of the King ...

But many still doubted the possibility of such an unequal match, and the Duc de Montausier, charged to convey Louis' formal assent to 'Mademoiselle', added on his own account that he advised her to to marry that very day.

Lauzun's vanity wrecked the match; 'Mademoiselle' was for taking Montausier's advice, but Lauzun would have none of it; he would not marry until he could figure in the contract as Duc de Montpensier and Prince de Dombes. Meanwhile heavy pressure was brought to bear on Louis; the Condés were indignant; 'Monsieur', who had hoped to marry his cousin's fortune himself, was clamorous; even the Queen protested. And ministers were quick to point out that the connection would injure Louis' prestige abroad.

So the King sent for 'Mademoiselle'.

LOUIS: Cousin, I am in despair at what I have to say to you, but everyone is saying that I am sacrificing you to make the fortune of Lauzun, and that is doing me a lot of harm abroad. I cannot let the wedding take place. You have every reason to complain of me. Beat me if you like. There is no degree of anger which you can show that I do not deserve and will not suffer. Ah! Cousin, why did you give me time for second thoughts, why did you not make haste?

MADEMOISELLE: Alas, Sire, who could have thought that Your Majesty was going to break his word?

LOUIS: Kings must satisfy the public.

The interview ended in the cousins kneeling to each other—'we were three quarters of an hour in each other's arms, cheek to cheek, he crying as hard as I did'. An absurd, yet pathetic scene.

Then on 11 February 1671 the fashionable world enjoyed another thrill. La Vallière again slipped out at dawn and took refuge in the convent at Chaillot. But this time there was no pursuit by a despairing lover; nor was there peace for the penitent. Louis, who was having further trouble with M. de Montespan, decided that his relations with Athénaïs still needed a cover, and that La Vallière must continue to provide it. Colbert was sent to Chaillot to make Louise see reason, and with a weakness which she herself was the first to condemn, La Vallière returned to Court. And Louis, that enigma of a man, embraced her with tears of joy and talked to her alone for an hour. Even more astonishing, Mme de Montespan wept over the returned prodigal, and soon afterwards all three set out to visit Flanders; ostensibly a pleasure trip, actually a final inspection of the troops prepared for the invasion of Holland, timed for the spring of 1672.

Louis' strenuous activities in 1671 were mainly diplomatic, and we need not enter into them. But it is noteworthy that his preoccupations did not cause him to neglect those courtesies which helped to keep the machine of State running smoothly. Here for instance is a letter to Maréchal d'Albret in June:

> Cousin, I understand better than you do the secret of the magnificent reception at Bordeaux which you describe so pleasantly; it is that the whole province is no less persuaded than I am that I have made a worthy choice in giving you the Government of Guyenne. And whatever honours it may pay to your character, I await the even greater benedictions which it will shower on your conduct.

In September he wrote to Pomponne, French Ambassador to Sweden, recalling him on promotion to a Secretaryship of State:

> Lyonne being dead, I want you to take his place; but we must give some compensation to the son, who holds the *survivance*[1], the value of which is £65,000. I will put up £25,000 and you must find the rest. But so that you will have no difficulty in doing so, I am giving you a *brevet de retenue*[2] for £40,000.

---

1 The right of succeding to his father's office, or, if the King preferred, as in this case, the right of being reimbursed the sum his father had paid for the post.

2 A legal instrument entitling the holder of a bought office to dispose of it at will for a price not exceeding that specified in the *brevet*. Pomponne would have had no trouble in borrowing £40,000 on the security of the document.

Moreover, in spite of his hatred of Jansenism, he invited Pomponne's father, d'Andilly, to Court to hear the news from his own lips. And with his usual forethought in small things, 'the old man (he was eighty-one) was by order of His Majesty served with a bowl of soup on his arrival, on account of his great age'. After which refreshment he was taken to the King, who talked to him very pleasantly for an hour; telling him that he was satisfied with Pomponne, awaited his arrival impatiently, and adding that, as he knew Pomponne was not well-off, he would look after him. Then he gave Andilly dinner and took him for a drive in his coach.

There is indeed a suggestion that in 1671 Louis may have been experiencing a short-lived tolerance towards Jansenism, for in addition to his graciousness to Andilly we find that he bought, and perhaps even looked through, Pascal's *Pensées*. At any rate he made it the book of the year—'all ye Court, Madam Montespan, Vallière, Marshal Turenne, all buy it'.

The winter of 1671 saw the fall of Lauzun, who was arrested on 25 November and sent to Pignerol. His crime is still unknown, but the most likely cause of his disgrace was that he had secretly married 'Mademoiselle' in defiance of the King's express orders, and that Louis had discovered this. There was the usual scramble for the disgraced man's offices, a somewhat undignified proceeding from which only Marsillac, who became third Duc de La Rochefoucauld in this year, emerged with honour. When Louis offered him Lauzun's Government of Berri, Marsillac replied, 'Your Majesty will be pleased to remember that I am an enemy of M. de Lauzun'. A pleasant contrast to Louis' interview on the same day with Villarceaux, an elderly debauchee who came with an offer to procure his fifteen-year-old niece for the King's pleasure. His reception made even Villarceaux 'a little shame-faced', especially when he found that Louis had told the story to the Court.

On 27 November Louis met his new sister-in-law, 'Madame-Palatine', who had married 'Monsieur' on the 16th; and took an instant liking to her. By no means the sort of liking he had felt for Henriette, for 'Madame-Palatine' was not a girl to inspire love. She was perhaps the oddest figure at the French Court, whose inhabitants looked upon her almost as a visitor from another planet. What were they to make of this honest, ugly, out-spoken German girl, who loathed coquetry and would not allow a risky story in her presence, but herself told scatological jokes with enormous gusto? Whose idea of pleasure was to rise at dawn, tramp six or seven miles, and then breakfast on dry bread and cherries; who kept her body clean and her windows open at night; and when her confessor tried to talk to her of the Saints, told him 'not to come bothering her with his nonsense'. For if she had any religion at all, she was a Protestant, and was openly contemptuous of the Romanism which she had embraced in order to marry 'Monsieur'. Her complete indifference to clothes was the despair both of her maids and of her husband, with whom she lived on better terms than might have been expected; for so long as he left her alone, she had not the slightest objection to his peculiar morals.

To Louis, Liselotte was a delightful novelty; he had never met anyone like her before and they had tastes in common. Louis too was a walker—the only one in France, said 'Madame'—and like her he loved fresh air both indoors and out; also they were both extremely fond of hunting. And Louis extracted considerable amusement from her blunt comments on French cookery, courtiers, doctors, and indeed all things French—except the King of France. For stumpy, plain-faced Liselotte fell in love with Louis, and she alone at Court naively failed to realize what had happened to her; all she knew was that she was happy in the King's company, restless and dissatisfied when deprived of it. But there was no doubt of her feelings; we do not need the assurance of her contemporaries, we have only to read her own letters.

Everything was going well for Louis, and his own pleasure was reflected in that which he tried to give to others. In January 1672 Maréchal de Bellefonds asked permission to retire:

LOUIS: Marshal, I want to know why you intend to leave me; is it for religious reasons? Or just a wish to retire? Or is it debt? If it is the latter, I will put things in order and go into the details of your embarrassments.

BELLEFONDS: Sire, it is my debts; I am ruined; I can no longer bear to look those who have helped me in the face, for I cannot pay them.

LOUIS: Well, well, we must settle this; I will give you £5,000 for your house at Versailles, and a *brevet de retenue* on your posts for £20,000, which will be surety if you die; and you will remain in my service.

Next it was the turn of his valet, who solicited a vacant post of Gentleman-in-Ordinary for a friend. 'Hey! Bontemps,' said Louis, 'you are always asking favours for others, I am giving that post to your son'. His friendliness and common-sense were equally apparent in his dealings with another servant, who begged him to speak to the First President about a suit he was bringing against his father-in-law.

SERVANT: Alas, Sire, you have only to say a word.

LOUIS: Yes, and if you were in your father-in-law's shoes, how pleased you would be with me for saying that word.

And he tolerated a good deal of plain speaking in his presence. Stoppa, Colonel of the Swiss Guards, was badgering him for increased pay for his men when Louvois interrupted:

LOUVOIS: If Your Majesty had all the money which he and his predecessor have paid the Swiss, it would pave a road with silver from Paris to Basle.

STOPPA: Very possibly; and if Your Majesty had all the blood the Swiss have expended in the service of France, it would make a canal to float the money from Paris to Basle.

LOUIS (smiling): Pay him what he wants.

In January Louis refused Montausier's request for an Abbey for one of his friends—'It is only ministers and mistresses', said Montausier sulkily, 'who have any influence in this country'. Louis reproached him gently for so addressing his sovereign, reminded him how little cause he had to complain, and next day appointed his daughter a Lady of the Palace. And in the following month, just after the exile of the Marquis de Villeroi, he conferred happiness on his discontented brother:

LOUIS: Well brother, what are they saying in Paris?

MONSIEUR: A good deal about the poor Marquis de Villeroi.

LOUIS: What?

MONSIEUR: Everyone is saying that he has got into trouble for speaking in favour of another unfortunate.

LOUIS: What unfortunate?

MONSIEUR: The Chevalier de Lorraine.

LOUIS: You don't mean to tell me that you are still thinking of

93

that man? Would you be pleased to have him back with you?
MONSIEUR: It would be the greatest pleasure of my life.
LOUIS: Oh very well, I'll make you a present of him; and what
is more, I'll promote him Major-General.

An incident at the close of the 1672 campaign showed in how real
a sense a French King was regarded as 'the father of his people', and
with what confidence his subjects took their troubles to him. Officers
were returning to Paris on winter leave; which was embarrassing for
a certain officer's wife who was about to become a mother, though
she had not seen her husband for eighteen months. She appealed to
Louis as the most honourable man in France to help her in her difficulty;
and Louis, having scolded her for her naughtiness, appointed her
husband Governor of a Dutch town, with orders that he was to
remain in Holland throughout the winter. Which made both happy,
for the husband thought that he had been marked down by the King
as a coming man. On 17 March 1672 England declared war on Holland,
and on 6 April Louis followed suit.

Historians condemn his declaration as an abuse of absolute power,
but had Louis taken a plebiscite he would have had an overwhelming
majority for war; not even when he revoked the Edict of Nantes
was he more truly "democratic" than he was in 1672, and his action
restored his waning popularity almost overnight.

On 23 April the King took command of the Army of France,
eighty thousand strong; and at Sedan was Condé with the Army of
the Ardennes, another forty thousand men; one hundred and twenty
thousand in all, the finest troops which Europe had yet seen. And
to oppose them? twenty-five thousand ill-organized, ill-equipped,
ill-trained Dutchmen led by second-rate soldiers of fortune. Louis'
only anxiety was lest the enemy should rob him of his glory by the
feebleness of their resistance; but it turned out to be by no means the
walk-over which he had anticipated.

At first all went well. Within a week the Dutch were east of the
Rhine, and four days later the French crossed that river at Tolhuis.
The Rhine was low, the resistance pitiable; but Louis' France, in an
orgy of hysterical jingoism, insisted that the corps d'élite, headed by
Louis in person, had swum a navigable arm of the sea and then stormed
a position held by the whole Dutch army.

So far as Louis personally was concerned, this war was 1667 over again on a larger scale; the same energy, the same attention to detail, the same failure to see as a whole the situation confronting him. He slept in his coach, was generally up by three, always before five, and slaved incessantly at tasks which he might have delegated to a junior staff officer; and when he was not writing orders, he was under fire with his troops. Even in the middle of the night he got up to answer a despatch—but one so unimportant that it might perfectly well have remained unanswered until the morning. In short, he never learnt to distinguish between those strategic and tactical concepts which are the art of war, and the mere machinery needed to execute them. He was supposed to be Commander-in-Chief, and here are typical specimens of the orders which he drafted with his own hand:

The Guards will sound the Assembly first, and after them the other regiments as far as the left of the line; the regiment on the right flank of the second line will sound the call immediately after the Guards do so, and then the other second line regiments in the same manner as the first line.

Sergeants will mark the battalion front in order that the line may be straight.

The Commander of each battalion will carry out musketry drill when he thinks fit. All officers will be present. Care will be taken that the exercise is held in a locality where there is no risk of wounding passers by.

Care will be taken that the camp is laid out in a straight line, that the tents are well guyed, Colours properly dressed, and a regular guard maintained.

And even when he attempted to get a little perspective into the picture his plans got no further than the drawing up of a table giving the names of those to be appointed Governors of still uncaptured places, many of which he was never to take.

On 20 June the Dutch halted the French advance by letting in the sea and flooding their country; nine days later they offered abject peace terms which Louis rejected contemptuously; and on 10 July he returned to Court, leaving Luxembourg to command in Holland. He had conquered three Dutch provinces in as many months, and he fully shared his subjects' admiration of his own prowess.

But the effect on his character was disastrous, for he was confirmed in his belief that he was a man equally expert in strategy and in the skilful solution of minor administrative problems. Had he not, in the intervals between taking thirty cities, found time to alter the set of a cross-belt and to site a latrine? So there arose in Louis' mind the picture of an army in which there would be no Turennes or Condés, but only lieutenants to execute the King's commands; indeed, thought Louis, except for considerations of personal glory, there was no reason why he should not conduct a campaign from his desk at Versailles. And thus was strengthened that fatal tendency to over-centralization, which robbed commanders in the field of all initiative and nearly brought the whole French military structure tottering to its fall.

In 1673 Louis was confronted with the problem of accelerating the tempo of a *blitzkrieg* which had already lost its initial momentum, and under conditions which had from his point of view deteriorated. Dutch resistance was hardening under William of Orange, who had murdered the de Witts and made himself Stadhoulder; Vienna and Madrid were awake to the danger of allowing France to annex the Dutch Republic; and even Louis' German vassals seemed to be wavering in their loyalty. Louis, whatever his limitations as a soldier, understood the political situation well enough to realize that if he could not conquer the Dutch speedily, he must fight the whole of Europe; and as a first step towards forcing a decision he laid siege to Maestricht, the best fortress in Holland. It fell at the end of the month, but given Louis' overwhelming superiority, he had no reason for self-congratulation on his conquest. Maestricht was not Holland, and even at Maestricht he could not see the wood for the trees; there was a certain 'demi-lune' in the defence works to which the King devoted his personal attention, and its assault and capture bulk larger in his Memoirs than does the 'help' given him throughout the campaign by Condé, Turenne, and Vauban. Indeed there is in the military portion of the Memoirs for 1673 a puerility which contrasts oddly with the shrewdness of his political observations; 'my cavalry' marched 'proudly'; 'my' infantry advanced 'with drums beating and Colours flying'; 'I myself' sent to Paris for an historical painter to immortalize the scene. But let us do him the justice to observe that he himself was in the trenches when on 25 June d'Artagnan—Dumas' d'Artagnan—'Captain of my First Company of Musketeers', was shot through the head.

Louis XIV as a young man

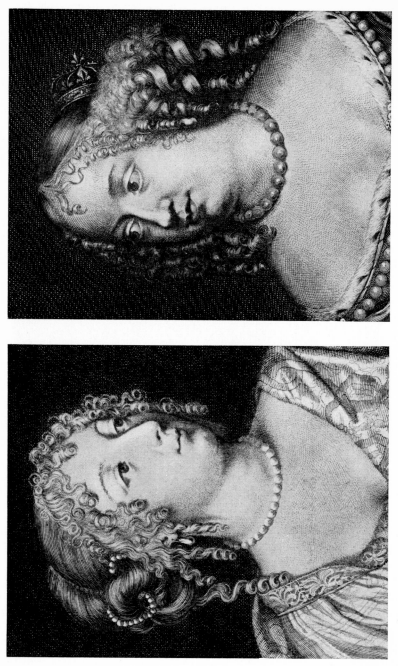

Left: Françoise-Athénaïs de Rochechouart-Mortemart, Marquise de Montespan, *Right*: Queen Marie-Thérèse

In Paris the news of the fall of Maestricht was received with frantic adulation, and even the Generals swelled the chorus; naturally enough, for they had their careers to consider. But that Colbert should have joined in this servile flattery is inexcusable:

> All your Majesty's campaigns produce that astonishment which leaves no room for any emotion but admiration ... one must admit that such extraordinary means to acquire glory as by the capture of Maestricht have never been thought of by anyone but Your Majesty ...

But Colbert could at times write to his master in a very different strain. In August he invited Louis' attention to the fact that the estimated expenditure for 1675 was £7,250,000 whilst total revenue would be approximately £5,436,000; and what did His Majesty propose to do about it? 'The expenses frighten me', replied Louis, 'but you must find the money somehow'.

The versatility which Louis expected of Colbert was amazing; hard on the heels of the financial correspondence he wrote him the following letter:

> In all your letters you have told me nothing about the progress of the work on the terraces of Mme de Montespan's apartments at St Germain. You must finish those which have been started and adapt the others; one into an aviary, and for that all you need to do is to paint the vaulting and walls, put small mesh wire to close the terrace on the courtyard side, and provide a fountain for the birds to drink at; the other needs nothing but a fountain, for Mme de Montespan intends to turf it and make it into a little garden.

On his return from the front Louis did not give Paris the chance of welcoming its hero. It was over twenty years since the Parisians had imprisoned Louis in his own palace, but as time passed the King's resentment at this bygone humiliation grew stronger, not weaker; and it was noticed that on his travels he would make long detours to avoid the necessity of going through his capital. One visit he did make to Paris this year, but that was to wipe out old scores; he insulted his people by driving through the city in the midst of an escort with drawn swords, and on arrival at the Law Courts deprived the Parlement of the title of Sovereign Court; adding that he himself would in future register his own edicts.

The last bar to absolutism was now down.

VI

FROM 1673 onwards Louis' grip on France tightened steadily, he insisted on understanding everything himself, and very little which happened at home or abroad escaped his notice. In the opinion of a clever onlooker Louis was now the best minister France had, and on Lyonne's testimony he had become, by dint of hard work and constant chairmanship of the Council of State, the ablest man in that body. By the private admission of his ministers, his opinion on problems of policy was more often right than was that of his advisers; and so far from leading him by the nose, it was observed that his secretaries always went trembling to a Council meeting. "No Prince was ever less governed," we are told, "and idleness never had a more formidable enemy".

He had by now thoroughly mastered his role of the 'Grand Monarque', and favourite courtiers noticed how consciously he played it. One of them, who had the entrée to Louis' private rooms, tells us that when the door opened, or when the King went out, he would rearrange his face and his bearing, exactly as if he were an actor about to make his entry on the stage.

By 1673 his day was minutely regulated. At eight he held his *lever*, from ten to half past twelve he was with his ministers, whom he then left to accompany the Queen to Mass; from one until two he visited 'the ladies', that is to say Mmes de Montespan and La Vallière, then dined with his wife. In the afternoon he either worked with a minister, walked, hunted, or inspected his buildings. In the evening he played host to his Court until ten o'clock. Then came supper, followed by another visit to 'the ladies', and so to bed.

The nobility had been throughly tamed, and now a courtier's only object in life was to attract Louis' notice by an extravagant devotion and a slavish imitation of his habits. For example, in August Louis discovered that he was going bald, and began to wear a wig; every courtier discovered that he too was going bald, had his head shaved, and bought a wig; and within a matter of weeks the wig had become *de rigueur* at Court. When Louis made the most trivial remark, there was a stampede of courtiers to form a ring around him and stand with their heads thrust forward in breathless silence to hear what he had to say; if at dinner the King let his eyes rest on anyone for a moment, that lucky man was an object of envy to all; Louis was an enormous eater, and so naturally was every courtier; and when Louis had indigestion, every courtier suffered from the same complaint.

Louis would have been more than human if his character had not deteriorated under such treatment, and the more we read about his daily life, the more we realize that the surprising thing about him was not that he was self-opinionated and egotistical, but that he retained his sanity; a state of affairs for which he had to thank first that basic common-sense which never quite deserted him, and secondly, the fact that even now there were a few courtiers who were undazzled by his splendour. The notorious Chevalier de Gramont for instance, who had managed to put himself on a footing of saying anything he chose to the King, even about his ministers. He, entering the billiard room at Versailles one evening, found Louis and his opponent arguing about a stroke, in the middle of a ring of silent courtiers:

LOUIS: Here, Gramont, settle this point for us; I maintain that I am in the right because.—

GRAMONT: Your Majesty is in the wrong.

LOUIS: How the devil can you say so when you haven't heard what the dispute is?

GRAMONT: Because if there was the faintest possibility that your Majesty was in the right, all these gentlemen would be clamorously supporting you.

And meanwhile what of the Queen? Louis continued to treat her with the deference due to her rank; ate, slept, and chatted with her as if there were no such people as mistresses, and for the rest, left her pretty much to her own devices. Half her free time was given to her devotions, the other half she spent with her dwarves and her dogs; the dogs being better treated than the dwarves, who were kept uncommonly short of cash, whereas the dogs, who shared her meals, had their own valets and carriages, which cost the King £1,000 a year. From eight in the evening until ten, when Louis arrived to escort her to supper, the Queen gambled with those who enjoyed that valuable privilege; valuable because she was so stupid that she invariably lost, and to play with the Queen gave a gambler one of the safest incomes at Court. And apparently a large one. Even the magnificent Louis was startled into a protest on the day when he discovered that his wife had lost £5,000 at the card table before noon. For some time past Louis had found the secrecy which enveloped his family by Montespan frustrating; always in the limelight, it was difficult for him to slip off unobserved to the secret nursery in the Rue Vaugirard; and only occasionally could Scarron and the children come to St Germain. Louis did not easily endure constraint, and his self-will was hardening with the years; after many hesitations he decided to brazen things out and admit the existence of his new race of bastards; and on 18 December he caused the future Duc du Maine, aged three, and the infant girl who became 'Mme La Duchesse' to be legitimated.

One result of Louis' act was that Mme Scarron became a familiar figure at Court, and that in their common love for the children she and the King drew closer together. A less observant man could not have failed to contrast Mme Scarron's devotion to her charges with the intermittent and perfunctory notice taken of them by their mother, and Louis was hurt by Montespan's neglect; aand even more so by her contemptuous amusement at his love for the brats. He took to spending more and more time with the governess, whose pleasure in giving him the gossip of the nursery was heightened by Louis' unaffected interest in all she told him. He thought better of Scarron every day; in March he increased her salary from £270 to £500 a year; and by the close of 1673 he found her so amiable and such good company that he could hardly put up with her absence. So in January 1674 she and her pupils were openly installed at Court and the Vaugirard establishment was closed.

The children once recognized, La Vallière's melancholy role became superfluous, and in April her martyrdom ended; still in love with the King, she obtained his permission to enter the Carmelites, and then paid a round of farewell visits, 'with perfect dignity, like a Princess taking leave of an hospitable Court'. But to Marie Thérèse she knelt and publicly begged her forgiveness for the wrong she had done her; saying to those who attempted to dissuade her from so humiliating herself, 'My crimes were public, my repentance must be public also'. And the Queen, who when she forgot she was a Hapsburg was a generous little soul, raised her up and kissed her. Louis shed easy tears in saying farewell, but Louise emerged from the interview dry-eyed; and on 19 April, magnificently dressed, and with the Court thronging about her, she entered her coach and drove to the Carmelite convent in the Rue d'Enfer where as Sister Louise de la Miséricorde she was to spend the remaining twenty-six years of her life.

On the following day Louis left Versailles to reconquer Franche-Comté, and six weeks later, more convinced than ever that Victory and Royalty marched hand in hand, he returned to receive the congratulations of his Court. Many expensive wars were to pass before Louis began to suspect that a King who is not a General is a liability in the field; for when he commanded, tactical considerations had to give way to the necessity of finding an operation for him in which success was certain. It is only a real soldier-king who can afford the luxury of a defeat.

So long as Scarron lived obscurely in the Rue Vaugirard and Montespan queened it at Court, Athénaïs had regarded the governess with patronizing approval; apparently unaware of Louis' visits to the nursery, and of his growing admiration for Scarron. But when this 'excellent upper servant', as she called her, was installed at St Germain, Montespan awoke to her own danger. But she awoke a year too late; Scarron's position was already secure, and knowing this, she made it clear, with a cool, unassailable politeness which maddened Athénaïs, that she was not her servant but the King's; and Montespan lost round after round in the battle between them. For two reasons; firstly she made the fatal mistake of storming at Louis until she repelled him almost as much as she attracted him; and secondly she completely misjudged the governess, seeing in her only an ungrateful adventuress who was scheming to rob her of the King. Whereas in fact Scarron's ambition at this time was to get a sufficient gratuity for her services to form a dowry with which she could enter a convent; an ambition thwarted by a syndicate consisting of Bossuet, Montausier, and her own *directeur*, which insisted that under God she was destined to reform Louis.

It was a task which she undertook with great reluctance, for she rightly foresaw that she would be brought into immediate collision with Mme de Montespan. There were almost daily scenes between the two women, and Mme Scarron more than once complained to her *directeur* that she could not understand how it could be God's will that she, who desired only to serve Him as a nun, should have to suffer as she did at the hands of Mme de Montespan.

Having failed in her frontal assault on the governess, Athenaïs changed her tactics; she unearthed an obscure, impoverished Duke with a bad reputation, and put him forward as a husband for her rival. But this too was unsuccessful, Mme Scarron merely replying that she already had enough worries without seeking an additional one by entering into that state which made the unhappiness of three-quarters of the human race.

In September Louis gave Scarron a gratuity of £10,000, to her infinite relief and joy; as she wrote to her *directeur*, she was now independent, with all her wants satisfied, and to have wished for more would have been mere cupidity. After some consideration she decided to invest the money in land, and on 27 December she bought the Marquisate of Maintenon for £12,500, thus acquiring the title by which she is best known to posterity; a sound bargain, for Maintenon brought her in £750 a year.

The transformation of the widow Scarron into a Marquise with landed property awakened even the dullest to her growing importance; and this added to Mme de Maintenon's troubles; a swarm of new friends, anxious to assure her of their devotion, besieged her door. But the task of these ingenuous ladies who had suddenly discovered Mme de Maintenon's charm proved unexpectedly difficult. She had served a hard apprenticeship, and repelled gushing flattery with a cold politeness; it was not easy to 'sprinkle her with Court holy water' as the slang of the day called it.

But the Court sycophants were to Maintenon a mere flea-bite compared with the nerve-racking strain of her continual and unavoidable collisions with Montespan; for Athénaïs was now attacking with teeth and claws. And by February Louis could no longer ignore the facts; 'terrible things', wrote Maintenon, 'happen daily between Mme de Montespan and myself; and the King witnessed one of our quarrels. A quarrel which was a turning point in Mme de Maintenon's career. What happened was that Louis surprised the two women at the height of their fury, and not unnaturally asked what was going on. Before Montespan could speak, Maintenon had invited Louis to enter the next room and there hear her explanation; which the King did, leaving the raging Montespan to the enjoyment of her own reflections.

One can well believe that Maintenon, having secured the King's ear, 'painted Mme de Montespan's conduct in lively colours'. But her hour was not yet come, and Louis made some attempt to defend his mistress —asking Maintenon if she had never observed how Montespan's lovely eyes filled with tears when some touching or generous act was related in her presence.

It sounded well, but in fact Louis' heart was not really in the task of defending his mistress; he had reached that stage in an ill-assorted union when a man realizes that, except as a bed-fellow, the woman of his choice has become intolerable. Lust for Athénaïs still enslaved him, but he was beginning to be ashamed of his bondage and was wondering whether it was not in his power to escape from a liaison which in his cooler moments now disgusted him. Though satiety had not yet been reached, boredom was setting in; as we learn from Montespan's confidential maid, who left it on record, that often when the King was supposed to be with Montespan, he was actually sitting alone in her anteroom over the fire, 'pensive for hours, sighing heavily from time to time'.

But the greatest danger to Montespan's position lay not in her tantrums and her insolence but in the revolution which was being worked in Louis by his own conscience, aroused by the syndicate vowed to his reformation. He had promised the Queen that at thirty he would settle down to being a good husband, and now, when nearing forty, his life was a bigger scandal than when the promise was made. And by this time Mme de Maintenon was rebuking him openly:

MAINTENON: Sire, your Musketeers are the apple of your eye; what would you do if you learnt that one of them was living with the wife of another man?

LOUIS: You are very right, Madame.

And Bossuet, who never got credit for his courage in the matter, told Louis that he would refuse him Communion at Easter if he was then living in mortal sin. To us, Bossuet's warning seems merely a case of a priest performing his bare duty. But we forget Bossuet's background, and the bad example set him by the many who were courtiers first and Bishops afterwards; also that Bossuet remained all his life the provincial bourgeois, trained to adore his King, and thirty years, contact with him did nothing to modify his rather childish amazement and joy at finding himself on a familiar footing with his hero. It must have called for great resolution on Bossuet's part to tell Louis that his feet were of clay.

He had his reward. Louis was won over by his fearlessness, and shortly before Easter he sent a message to Montespan saying that he could no longer commit the sin of living with her. And King and ex-mistress both made their Communions on Easter Sunday.

On 10 May Louis set out for the army.

It is significant that this year it was to Maintenon that he wrote first from the front, and not to Montespan; the governess, on her way to Barèges with the crippled Duc du Maine, wrote to her *directeur* on the 20th, telling him that there was only one man from whom she now received letters; but that it was a man whose friendship for her was perhaps warmer than a confessor would wish.

Bossuet and Maintenon both thought that the discreditable Montespan incident was now a closed chapter in the King's life; Bossuet because he had been fooled by Montespan's sham penitence, and Maintenon because being herself both frigid and unimaginative, she was quite unable to realize the physical strain of continence on such a man as Louis. Both would have been shocked and astonished had they seen Louis' letters from the front to Colbert:

The cost is excessive, from which I can see that to please me you find nothing impossible. Mme de Montespan writes that you acquit yourself splendidly in carrying out my orders . . .

And a week later:

I am very pleased to hear of your purchase of orange trees for Mme de Montespan; if Mme de Montespan wishes it, continue to buy her the best you can.

The fact was that Louis' passion for Athénaïs was still hot after five years of intercourse, and he was now regretting his precipitancy in discarding her. And she, so far from thinking of repentance and oblivion, was fighting desperately with the aid of powerful allies—human and diabolic—to recover her position. Helped too by a stroke of luck, for Bossuet, going from boldness to audacity, had just written Louis a severe letter on his extravagance and the miserable state of his over-taxed people. He should have known Louis better; memories of the Fronde instantly awoke in the King, engendering suspicions that Bossuet planned to become a second Cardinal de Retz; and the Bishop's stock fell disastrously. In July Louis sent orders to Versailles that Montespan was to be there to meet him on his return, and when he arrived, his welcome to Athénaïs was such as to arouse dismal forebodings among the devout. But even now Louis struggled against the inevitable; Montespan, he said, returned to Court merely as his old friend, and he would never see her again except in a roomful of people. In due course the first of these much advertised public meetings took place; Louis drew Athénaïs into the window, where they talked in whispers, with tears running down their cheeks; then they turned, bowed to the company, and left the room; and the result was that Louis' third family was increased by Mlle de Blois in 1677 and the Comte de Toulouse in 1678.

To the unobservant, it was the old liaison renewed, and Montespan triumphant. But not quite; for neither could forget Bossuet's rebukes, and each now saw in the other the cause of sin persisted in with full knowledge and consent. Their quarrels were more frequent and more bitter, the reconciliations shorter-lived and more perfunctory; and as Louis fought against his conscience he grew colder, whilst his mistress became more shrewish.

In 1676 Louis dug the grave of such military reputation as he had acquired. At first all went well; on 21 April he commanded at the siege of Condé, and the fortress surrendered on the 26th—a paltry triumph, regarded by Louis with a modesty which was as pleasant as it was unexpected. On 3 May he wrote to 'M. le Prince' thanking him for his congratulations 'to a mere apprentice', and a few days later the First Equerry received a letter from him in which he said that 'if it was not Antwerp which he had taken, at least he had not taken Condé for Antwerp'.

On the morning of 10 May 'Monsieur' was besieging Bouchain, whilst Louis at Heurtebise, covering the siege, found himself face to face with the allies under William of Orange who was advancing to the relief of Bouchain. By eleven o'clock both armies had deployed into line of battle, Louis with forty-eight thousand men to William's thirty-five thousand, and having also the advantage that French morale was higher than that of the enemy. It was as certain as anything could be in war that if Louis had ordered a general advance, victory would have been his.

And Louis funked it.

Having assembled his Marshals, he asked their advice as to whether he should attack; and the very fact of his asking the question showed them all what answer he hoped to get. Louvois was the first to come to his master's assistance; the King's task, he said, was to cover the siege of Bouchain, and it was for the enemy to attack him if he pleased; therefore tactical considerations imposed a defensive, not an offensive role on the King. After this, the verdict of the Council of War was a foregone conclusion—four votes to one against an attack. 'As you have more experience than I have,' said Louis, 'I yield to you, but I do so with regret'.

He had lost his chance and he knew it; and he never forgave Louvois for his advice, nor himself for having accepted it; and for the first time, his courtiers' flattery of his tactical genius rang false in his newly sensitized ears. He was to pay for his blunder with a remorse which no subsequent successes could obliterate; in 1680 he said that the faults which he had committed, and which had caused him infinite sorrow, had been through complaisance, and through following the advice of others too uncritically. And the wound to his pride was still hurting after another nineteen years had elapsed; whilst he was walking in the gardens at Marly on an April afternoon in 1699, some tactless person mentioned Heurtebise. And the King said in a low voice that it was the day of his life on which he had made his greatest mistake; that he never thought of it without extreme grief; and that sometimes he still dreamt of it, and awoke in anger.

He has been accused of showing at Heurtebise an ineptitude which was dictated by nothing less than personal cowardice. But to accept this is totally to misunderstand his character; no one who has studied it with any care will reject the frequent evidence of Louis' courage, moral and physical; whatever may have actuated him on that 10th May it was certainly not fear for his own skin.

Surely the fact was that he was too proud to risk a defeat? True, defeat seemed impossible, but suppose he had been beaten, what sort of figure would the ever victorious *Roi-Soleil* cut as he slunk back to France amidst the laughter of all Europe at the hero who had been thrashed by a pack of cheese-mongers? He decided to play for safety.

On 4 July Louis reliquished command and returned to Versailles, where he endeavoured to restore his morale with a liberal dose of self-praise; but though he could write, 'I have shown that my mere presence is enough to embarrass the enemy', he was evidently still kicking himself for his folly in commanding the covering army, with all its incalculable risks, instead of besieging Bouchain. 'Large sieges please me best,' he wrote to Louvois, 'but in the present state of affairs we must postpone them to a more favourable time'.

Sentiment at Court was more favourable to Louis than had been that of the camp, but even at Versailles Heurtebise produced an occasional discord in the hymn of praise:

LOUIS: I am afraid we shall lose Philipsburg; but after all if we do, I shall be none the less King of France.

MONTAUSIER: And Sire, you will still be King of France when your enemies have retaken Metz, Toul, Verdun, Franche-Comté and several other provinces which your ancestors did without.

LOUIS: I understand you; what you mean is that my affairs are in a bad way; and I am pleased that you should tell me so, for I know you do it only out of affection for me.

Louis could be gracious to the outspoken Montausier, but not to Louvois, who was a victim of one of the King's rare sarcasms this autumn. An old woman of the people accosted Louis in a corridor at Versailles, begging him to get her an interview with Louvois—a request which could hardly have been improved upon had the object been to flick the King on the raw. But he replied politely, pointing to Louvois' brother, the fat, greasy, brutal Archbishop of Rheims, 'Look, Madame, here is M de Rheims. Try him. He has much more influence with M. de Louvois than I have'.

Throughout the year the war between Montespan and Maintenon continued to rage with a ferocity normally hidden behind smiles and compliments; and keen eyes watched the duel with breathless anxiety, for the courtiers, in the slang of the day, did not know which foot to dance upon. In May Maintenon appeared to be winning; Montespan's women were at her service, one holding her rouge pot, another offering her her gloves, and a third putting her to bed. But when Louis came home in July, he greeted Montespan so warmly that Maintenon went back in the betting; but by the middle of the month Maintenon was in higher favour than ever, though Louis' attentions to her rival were still marked. It would have been an anxious enough year for the courtiers if it had been a straight fight between the two, but in fact there was a growing doubt if Louis' final choice would be either. For the King, in that spirit of *carpe diem* which is the reaction of the man of pleasure to the disagreeable knowledge that he is nearing forty, was throwing all restraint to the winds. Mme de Louvigny, whom the Duc de Gramont's second son had been forced to marry at sword's point eight years earlier; Mme de Soubise, a lovely red-haired Rohan, whose son, the Cardinal de Rohan, was generally supposed to have been fathered by Louis XIV; Mme de Ludres, Canoness of Pussay, and Mlle de Théobon—all enjoyed Louis' favours in that hectic summer. The battle swayed to and fro until September, when Mme de Sévigné decided that if Maintenon had not won, at least Montespan had lost; her star was paling, she wrote, and there had been tears, chagrin, sulks, unnatural gaiety. Some trembled, others rejoiced, but the majority of the court was looking forward to a change.

As for Maintenon herself, she longed for retirement; she had stayed at Court solely to reform the King, and the only result was that the sinner's last state was worse than his first. Louis' sexual promiscuity was now being reprobated in secret, even by his courtiers; and the most servile were taken aback by his liaison with Mme de Ludres, a Canoness; not quite the same thing, said everyone, as debauching a nun, but perilously near it. If Louis was aware of these murmurs he gave no sign, but continued on his way, serene, impenetrable, the master of his world; no one, said a courtier, ever saw him lose his temper, and only once had he been heard to swear; and always he was anxious to avoid hurting the feelings of others. And he still managed to keep his head, though every day the flattery offered to him became more extravagant; here for instance we have a harangue to the French Academy:

> Admiration (of the King) becomes stupour, and the Academy, after having cultivated the art of good speaking, is at a loss for words, and can now honour the King only with silence and confusion. I often think that Homer must have been inspired to foretell our King when he describes a hero . . . Louis is Your work, Oh God, and You well know how to uphold him; command Your angels to camp round and watch over him.

And though Louis was now overburdened with work and women, he still kept the machine of Court gaiety running at full speed. 'Madame-Palatine', writing to a friend in Germany, has given us a typical day in the life of a Court lady at this period. From early morning until three o'clock she hunted, then came home, changed into full Court dress, and sat down to gamble until seven. Then she went to the theatre until half past ten, after which came supper, followed by a ball which did not end until three in the morning—an eighteen hour day in fact, assuming that the hunt lasted for the average six hours.

But for those who were merely occasional guests at Court and did not have to live there, it was still an enchanted land; as witness Mme de Sévigné, whose account of a day at Versailles is so vivid, so lively, that it must be quoted:

> I spent Saturday at Versailles . . . and this is what happened . . . You know all about the Queen's toilet, Mass, and dinner . . . Then at three the King, the Queen, 'Monsieur', 'Madame', 'Mademoiselle', all the Princes and Princesses, Mme de Montespan and her suite, all the ladies of the Court assembled in that beautiful room of the King's . . . wonderfully furnished, everything magnificent . . . One wanders from place to place without the least crowding. A gaming table is the pivot on which the party turns . . . Dangeau offered me to go partners in his game, so I was comfortably seated. I made the bow you taught me to the King, and he returned it as if I was still young and pretty. The Queen talked to me for a long time . . . 'M. le Duc' paid me a thousand compliments . . . M. de . . . well you know the sort of thing, a word from everyone one meets in walking round the room. Mme de Montespan tells me that the waters of Bourbon, so far from curing her knee have made the other one sore as well. Her beauty is astonishing . . . this delightful confusion without confusion lasted from three until six . . . the band plays all the time, which has a very good effect. The King chats with the ladies . . . At six the King, Mme de Montespan, 'Monsieur' . . . get into the King's coach, the Queen into another with the Princesses, then everbody else into the others . . . One embarks in gondolas on the canal, where again there is music. At ten we return to the palace, when a comedy is acted. The clock strikes twelve and supper is served.

Pleasant enough for Mme de Sévigné, the bird of passage, flattered by the King's politeness. But what must it have been for Louis, who had to go through it twice a week for fifty years? It is understandable, if reprehensible, that he should have snatched eagerly at any distraction within his reach.

In 1677 it seemed as if Louis had chosen Mme de Ludres to succeed Montespan. Sharp eyes detected the King at St Germain, travelling in a private sedan chair from his lodgings in the Old Château to those of Mme de Ludres in the New; and this was enough to prostrate the Court before the rising star. On the mere suspicion that Mme de Ludres had become Louis' mistress, Princesses and Duchesses sprang to their feet at her entry as they did for Montespan, and remained standing until Ludres made them a sign to sit down; and this in the presence of the poor Queen, who thus learnt of her husband's latest infidelity.

But Mme de Ludres' triumph was short-lived; Chamarande, Louis' valet-de-chambre, was the *entremetteur* in this affair, and him the stupid woman tried to replace by her rakehelly friend Montataire. Louis was so surprised and shocked to find such a fellow in his presence on such business, that he immediately 'advised' Mme de Ludres to retire to a convent; offering her £10,000, which she refused. She returned to her Canonry where the rest of her life was said to have been extremely edifying.

On 4 March Louis arrived before Valenciennes and assumed command of the investing army, fifty-thousand strong. It was the usual Louis victory, a foregone conclusion, and the town fell on the 17th. We will skip Louis' praise of his own doings, but let us note that Valenciennes was saved from sack by the King's exertions. He himself hurried through the streets and personally saw to it that his orders to spare the townspeople and their property were obeyed; so successfully that at two o'clock in the afternoon the shops were all open and the streets full of passers-by, as if nothing out of the ordinary had happened.

We notice without surprise that the usual hymn of King-worship went up all over France, but it is startling to find that it was now obligatory to insert a eulogy of Louis in official correspondence. Here is an extract from a despatch sent to the Foreign Office by Louis' plenipotentiaries at Nimeguen:

Neither the Forces of so many Enemies, nor the Rigour of the Season are capable to hinder His Majesty from making great conquests; but at what a dear rate does France purchase them! Since it is at the Peril of so precious a life, and it were to be wish'd that we could shortly preserve it by a good and speedy Peace which would give him occasion to enjoy in Tranquillity so inexhaustible a Stock of Glory etc., etc.

On 21 March Louis detailed 'Monsieur' with twenty-thousand men to besiege St Omer; a manoeuvre intended to distract the enemy's attention from Louis' own siege of Cambrai, which was to be the high light of the campaign. But things did not work out as Louis had intended. On 4 May 'Monsieur' learnt that William of Orange was advancing from Ypres to raise the siege of St Omer by attacking him in the rear. 'Monsieur' acted speedily and intelligently; he called no Heurtebise-style Council of War, but, leaving a detachment to mask St Omer, he marched to Cassel, where on the 11th he fell upon William's army, which had arrived the previous evening. Fortune offered 'Monsieur' a chance to show his metal, and he did not fail to take it; bravery was expected of him, but not the leadership and tactical skill which were praised by those whose approbation was worth having. And his leadership was not such as Louis XIV was accustomed to exercise; 'Monsieur' fought, said an eyewitness, like a grenadier, had a horse killed under him, his cuirass pock-marked with bullets, and twenty of his staff killed at his side in the final charge. It was a decisive French victory, and the trophies were fifty-four Colours, two thousand five hundred prisoners, all the enemy artillery, and William's baggage, with his private papers.

On hearing the news Louis exclaimed, 'On my honour, I am better pleased for my brother's sake than for my own'; and he has been branded as a hypocrite in consequence. But were not his immediate and subsequent reactions perfectly natural? First joy at a well-loved brother's success, followed by a stab of self-reproach at the glaring contrast between Heurtebise and Cassel. It is true that he never gave 'Monsieur' a command again, and at first sight Louis' conduct in retiring him seems ungenerous; but to label it jealousy is to ignore the fact that the King's carefully guarded prestige was an integral factor in the maintenance of the social structure; the King must have no rival, least of all a rival who stood so near to him as did Philippe. Louis' real fault was not that he excluded 'Monsieur' from his armies, but that he included himself in them.

Left: Françoise d'Aubigné, Marquise de Maintenon. *Right:* Louise de la Vallière

Louis XIV in old age: from a wax mask by Benoist at Versailles

On 18 April Cambrai surrendered to Louis, but for the first time on record a Royal victory passed almost unnoticed; for Paris, where 'Monsieur' was extravagantly popular, was too busy toasting the victor of Cassel to have any time to waste over the annual routine victory of its King. On 31 May Louis returned to Versailles, where no doubt the delicate flattery of Racine and Boileau afforded him some comfort:

> LOUIS: I am vexed that you did not witness my last campaign. That would have shown you what war really is.
>
> RACINE: Sire, we are two quiet cockneys, and we had no country clothes. We ordered them; but Your Majesty had taken two cities before the tailor could finish our coats.

Louis' return momentarily settled the question of who was to be queen of the harem. During his absence, Montespan had plied him with amusing letters in the *dégagé* tone of a woman who had not a care in the world, and Louis, piqued at her seeming indifference to himself, had determined on her reconquest. Needless to say he was successful, and there was positively a second honeymoon for the King of forty and his mistress of ten years standing. Their affection was now stronger than ever, reported Mme de Sévigné. Maintenon despaired, and we gather that by the autumn she had given up all idea of reforming the King; it was impossible, she said, that she should sacrifice her whole life, her liberty, her health, and her salvation in such a hopeless cause.

But whatever his morals, Louis was growing in impressiveness as the years went on. He spoke Italian as if it was his native language, said an admiring foreigner in 1677; Spanish too, and a little Latin. His natural judgement was good, and he had a smattering of all sorts of subjects, war, architecture, painting, and music; on music alone he spent £2,500 a year. But the very sight of a book bored him, though he was always pleased to get one as a present; on the other hand he wrote much and often, kept his own accounts, and his lack of book knowledge was to some extent made good by his prodigious memory, which retained almost any information which he had ever collected. 'All fear him', concluded the foreign visitor. But this was not quite the case; for in this year we learn with astonishment that the Great King, when confronted with a strike, was as powerless as a trades union leader. In November Mansart, builder of Versailles, who had begun life as a working stone mason, reported to Colbert that all his stone-cutters were out on strike, claiming—perhaps truly—that their pay was four weeks in arrear, and positively refusing to resume work until their claim was settled. And it was the strikers, not Louis, who won.

On 7 February 1678 the King, accompanied by the Queen and her ladies, left for Flanders, arriving before Ghent on 4 March. The town surrendered to Louis on the 13th, and on the 27th Ypres followed suit; and the King, having had his annual victory, resigned the command and returned to St Germain where he arrived on 7 April. Much to the satisfaction of the women, for they had had the customary and abominable Flanders weather, to say nothing of bad quarters, bad food, and intense boredom. And of the men none were better pleased to be home than Racine and Boileau who had been dragged along to immortalize the 1678 conquests. They had followed Headquarters, sometimes on horseback, sometimes on foot, but always 'in mud up to their ears'; and when Louis asked them jovially what they thought of a soldier's life, it was Boileau who replied with Johnsonian vigour that he no longer marvelled at a soldier's courage. Anyone, he said, would wish to be killed to be quit of such an intolerable existence.

Louis' ministers never led him by the nose, because he understood the work of their various departments as well or better than they did themselves. But it was different with his Marshals, who often took skilful advantage of his unwarranted belief that he was a strategist. This year for example Créqui, commanding the Rhine Army, submitted his plan of operations to the King and was permitted to carry it out; but leave would probably not have been forthcoming had he not represented his scheme as a mere filling out of the project 'which Your Majesty had the goodness to sketch for me'.

And Louis really believed that he had done this.

The war ended on 17 September with the Peace of Nimeguen, whereby Louis obtained a fortress barrier stretching from the Meuse to Dunkirk; but it has been argued that this gain counterbalanced neither the outlay, nor the undying hatred engendered in Holland. La Fare, retired Guardsman and minor poet, admittedly a captious critic of the whole reign, said that all Louis had really accomplished was to turn a pacifist Republic into a formidable enemy, and that if in the 'seventies he had sung Europe to sleep, he would have been irresistible when the real trial of strength took place at the turn of the century. It is a plausible argument, but such are easy to produce after the event, and La Fare, we must remember, lived to see the débâcle of the Spanish Succession War, dying in 1712; and even so, was Louis at fault in using his continental superiority in the 'seventies to ensure that if and when he had to fight for the Spanish succession, it would be with a north-eastern fortress barrier as far removed from Paris as possible? To me it seems that where Louis made his fatal mistake was in not drawing in his horns *after* the Peace of Nimeguen, quietly strengthening his army, restoring his finances, and waiting patiently for the death of Charles II of Spain. Had he done so, there is a chance, perhaps a probability, that he would have got the Spanish inheritance in 1700 without having had to fight for it. But had he so acted he would not have been Louis XIV; adoration and easy victory had satisfied him that he was invincible, and his foreign policy for the next ten years united all Europe against him. And unfortunately during the same period his conviction that he could govern France single-handed grew stronger. His ministers, said the same hostile critic, no longer thought of telling him the truth, but only of flattering and pleasing him. His son was educated in a servile dependence, and not trained for his future tasks. Louis did not confide in his generals, whom he wanted submissive rather than talented, and as his able men died off he replaced them by their young and badly educated sons. It is an overcharged picture by a man who hated the King, but he certainly hit the nail on the head when he spoke of 'Monseigneur's' 'servile dependence'; to give only one illustration, the heir to the Crown was now seventeen, an age at which his contemporaries were many of them married men, and commanding regiments; but this unfortunate Prince had still to apply through his tutor to his father for permission to attend a performance at the Opera. Though in passing let us note that there was no truth in the assertion that Louis disliked 'Monseigneur' and kept him at arm's length; as we shall see later on, he was, according to his lights, an affectionate father, even to his legitimate son.

Amongst much which is conjectural about Louis the soldier, one thing is at least obvious, and that is that in 1678 he was as satisfied with his own military exploits—always barring Heurtebise—as he had been ten years earlier. Hear him on the subject:

I must admit that having in previous years succeeded in the

possible, I felt pleasure in being forced (in 1678) to besiege places which the greatest captains of our age had not dared to attempt, or before which they had been unfortunate.

And in addition to self-injected flattery, he continued to receive a heavy dosage of it from his courtiers. Maréchal de La Feuillade for instance, 'a man whose only god was the King', established his position with Louis completely at a party where, pretending to be drunk, he was cunning enough to say that he loved the King, not as King, but by the personal fascination which he exercised over him as a gallant man.

Louis, in 1677 completely occupied with the reconquest of Montespan, turned again to Mme de Soubise in 1678; and a remarkably astute woman took the opportunity to contrast the two rivals. In her view neither of them loved the King; both were ambitious, the first for herself, the second for her family. Mme de Soubise wished to raise and enrich the House of Rohan—for she was a Rohan both by birth and by marriage—whilst Mme de Montespan wanted to govern, and make her power felt. Mme de Soubise, who had the beauty and the warmth of a marble statue, had nothing with which to fight Mme de Montespan in Louis' favour; and moreover, as she was interested in nothing but money, her conversation was dull, whilst Mme de Montespan could make the dreariest topic amusing.

Mme de Soubise was not an attractive woman, but one cannot help admiring her for becoming Louis' mistress in more senses of the word than one. When she came down in the evening wearing a certain pair of earrings, it was a signal that she would welcome a visit from Louis that night; but if she was not wearing them, the King soon learnt that her door remained closed, even to him; she steadfastly declined to play odalisque to Louis' Grand Turk.

But the day of both women was nearly over, for in September a new star, Mlle de Fontanges, destined to be Louis' last mistress, appeared on the Versailles stage.

VII

MARIE Angélique Scoraille de Roussilles, Demoiselle de Fontanges, 'beautiful as an angel and stupid as a basket', was a provincial girl who had been equipped and sent to Court by family subscription in the hope that her remarkable likeness to La Vallière would catch the King's eye; and this worthy project succeeded. Her assets were an excellent figure, lovely eyes, a 'delicious little mouth', an admirable complexion, and 'a certain soft and modest air'; which latter was misleading, for so far from being modest, this seventeen-year-old was as eager to become the King's mistress as was her family to see her installed in that coveted position. She had been groomed for the post, and as soon as Marsillac sounded her on Louis' behalf, she said that she received this declaration with joy; that the King was a glorious Prince, but that she could have no great faith in him so long as Montespan enjoyed his favours; that she herself was intensely jealous. And perhaps this was only a passing flame which might soon be extinguished; but if this great Prince really loved her, he could prove it by loving her only; as she for her part was ready to love him.

Fontanges was a Maid-of-Honour to 'Madame', so lived not at the Louvre but in the Palais-Royal, 'Monsieur's' town house; and it was under his sister-in-law's roof that Louis, who was not remarkable for his delicacy, seduced her. He went to Paris by night, with no escort except a few lifeguards, and came to the Palais-Royal. A Mlle des Andrets opened the door of the Maids' quarters to him, and this was where he enjoyed Fontanges for the first time. But unfortunately not without arousing suspicions which he would fain have avoided; early risers detected him returning to St Germain. And when his brother and 'Madame' came to stay at St Germain, he was again unlucky in that inquisitive eyes saw him crossing the park at night on his way to Fontanges' lodgings. Later on, the girl was given a room next door to the King's cabinet, but in public Louis always pretended not to know her. In fact the secrecy which had so titillated his passion for La Vallière was again brought into play in the hope that it would add the same piquancy to his final liaison. The whole intrigue is at once pathetic and disgusting—the King at forty vainly trying to recapture in the arms of a succubus the delights which he had shared with Louise when he was twenty-three.

The first result of Louis' new adventure was a monumental quarrel with Montespan, provoked by her; she reproached him for his ingratitude; Louis retorted that for her he had lost his reputation; from generalities they proceeded to personalities; and the last word rested with Montespan—'Well, I may have faults in my person, but at any rate I do not *smell* as nasty as you do'.

This is the closing scene in Louis' long intimacy with Montespan, who thenceforward found herself playing the role which she had formerly imposed on La Vallière; her only usefulness to the King now was that she distracted attention from the fact that Fontanges was his mistress. The Court had a curious appearance in this, the last of Louis' debauched years. The King lived with his wife, his mistresses, and his children, legitimate and bastard, as if they all made one united family; and Marie Thérèse received the visits of the left-hand queens and their offspring as if this was one of the routine duties of a Queen of France. And they all attended Mass together. At St Germain, Montespan, her children, and Fontanges sat side by side opposite the King, but at Versailles the former was on the Gospel side of the Altar, the latter on that of the Epistle. And Louis? He looked restless, we are told, and gazed with more devotion at Fontanges than at the Altar; and when he was tired of so doing, he 'lowered his nose, opened his mouth, and shut his eyes'. Alongside him sat the Queen, with the sweat running down her face; for she always dressed in a brocade heavier than that used for horse trappings. And throughout Mass courtiers chuckled at the spectacle of the rival mistresses, 'rosary or missal in hand, lifting their eyes to heaven in ecstasy like the Saints'. And yet the same courtier to whom we are indebted for this picture can go on to say that it would be impossible to find a man of more regular and exemplary life than the King. It is a striking proof of the fascination which Louis exercised over all who were brought into contact with him.

If Louis' conduct at Mass was unedifying, he was still showing himself zealous for orthodoxy and a good hater of Jansenists; though his objection to Port-Royal was obviously political rather than religious:

His Majesty dislikes too great an intimacy between persons of the same way of thinking, such as is frequent in the Faubourg St Jacques . . . the King particularly desires that no union, sect, or coterie should excite remark.

The pen is Pomponne's, but the diction is Louis at his most characteristic. By 1679 we notice a lifelessness, a hushed, scented, oppressive atmosphere at a Court which had become a mere setting for the over-whelming figure of Louis. And this atmosphere was the King's own fault; he was reaping the harvest of servility which he himself had sown. The great nobles of 1679, said one of them, lived in as much fear of their King as did schoolboys of their master, or novices of their Father-Superior.

But Louis' own family had not yet been steam-rollered down to the general level, and in 1679 we find the little 'Mademoiselle', 'Monsieur's' elder daughter by his first wife, making a desperate attempt to avoid marriage with the King of Spain. For the poor girl was passionately in love with 'Monseigneur' and pleaded with Louis to marry her to him:

> LOUIS: I am making you Queen of Spain; could I do more for my own daughter?
>
> MADEMOISELLE: You could do more for your own niece.

And even after her betrothal, the girl still fought with despairing courage, throwing herself under Louis' feet as he was on his way to Mass. But for all answer to her prayers, she received only the characteristic negative, 'Madame, it would be a nice thing indeed to have it said that the Most Catholic Queen had prevented the Most Christian King from attending Mass'.

Next to war, building was Louis' favourite hobby, and this year he completed Marly. It was the fulfilment of his long cherished dream of a country house where Louis, the private gentleman, could entertain his intimate friends. But Louis, like Scott, had no self-control where building was concerned, and the little box in the country ultimately cost his subjects some £600,000; but the place was always a favourite with the courtiers, and Louis' personal care was evident in the service and appointments. It was probably the only house in France to which ladies did not have to bring their own toilet sets, and certainly the only

Royal residence in which a courtier could have meals from the King's table served in his own room.

In January 1680 the great Poisoning Scandal, on which the police had been at work since 1673, broke on a terrified France and ruined Montespan. A grim story of professional murderers, renegade priests, Black Masses, and ritual slaughterings; but these horrors are outside the scope of this book, and the subject is mentioned only for the effects which the denouement had on Louis and his ex-mistress.

The King had at first taken a creditable attitude when informed of these abominations, directing that suspects should be dealt with regardless of rank or sex; but when he gave these orders he did not foresee that Montespan was going to be one of the suspects most deeply implicated. Now it emerged that as early as 1667 she had endeavoured to bind Louis to her with 'conjurations' performed by a renegade priest; that in 1668 she had used the same method to compass the death of La Vallière; and that on at least six occasions between 1673 and 1680 she herself had taken part in the horrid ceremony of the Black Mass to ensure Louis' death if he should abandon her. Can we blame Louis if he refused to face the huge scandal which he would have provoked by allowing the mother of his children to be tried on a charge of attempting to bring about the death of their father? All the evidence against Montespan was suppressed, and that Louvois and Colbert approved of its destruction seems to furnish conclusive evidence that they too were convinced of her guilt. And perhaps her punishment was not so light as it seems to us; she remained at Court, nominally the King's mistress, actually deprived of all position and influence. Louis visited her daily and exchanged a formal word or two with her; but he took no trouble to conceal either his determination never to see her again except in the presence of witnesses, or the shuddering disgust with which he now regarded her.

Fear of poisoning, never absent from the XVIIth Century French mind, attained panic proportions in 1680, and even Louis shared his subjects' anxiety. But to him poison was an occupational risk; and when warned that his life might be in danger, he said, 'I have already had many warnings about this; but I should die under the burden of perpetual anxiety if I took constant precautions. Let it be as God pleases. I have no intention of making any change in my usual way of life'.

The scare had the odd result of bringing Louis a monetary windfall; glass, according to the then current theory, could not be 'impregnated' with poison whereas metals could, and consequently there was a run on glassware from Colbert's State factories. The replacement of the silver goblet by the wine glass had its origin in the poisoning scare of 1680.

On 17 March marriage at last released 'Monseigneur' from the school-room. The bride, Marie Anne Christine Victoire, was the twenty year old sister of the Electors of Bavaria and of Cologne, and the match, which was of course purely political, was designed to enlarge the French army's eastern combat zone in the next war. Marie was an ugly girl apparently, for every man knows what it means when one woman praises the beauty of another's 'arms, hands, teeth, and hair'. And yet such was the magic of rank that it was *de rigueur* for courtiers to pretend to be in love with her.

In 1680 Mme de Maintenon was climbing rapidly to the summit of her fantastic career; by March we hear of endless conversations between her and Louis, and in April it had become part of his routine to spend two hours with her after dinner, chatting in an easy, friendly, natural manner. In June 'the conversations were of a length which set everybody speculating', and by midsummer the King was spending from six to ten o'clock every evening with Maintenon, 'each in an arm-chair', whilst Fontanges wept openly at Louis' neglect; a neglect which a less stupid girl would have seen to be imminent as early as 6 April, when Louis had made her a Duchess with an allowance of £5,000 a year—'A separation which', as Mme de Sévigné observes, 'did much credit to the severity of their respective confessors'.

Maintenon's position was now secure; she was Lady-of-the-Ward-robe to the Dauphine, confidante of the King, and 'Mme de Mainte-nant' to the courtiers; and she could afford to be magnanimous to Montespan. The two women were no longer on visiting terms, but whenever they met they chatted with such liveliness and apparent cordiality that an outsider would have thought them the best friends in the world. Nor was this behaviour entirely humbug on the part of either; habit, and a genuine enjoyment of each other's wit, made it a pleasure to each of them to have a talk when opportunity arose.

Nothing showed more clearly the mastery which Maintenon had already gained over Louis than her achievement in bringing about a

rapprochement between him and the Queen this autumn; and incidentally nothing better demonstrates the falsity of the suggestion that in
1680 Maintenon replaced Fontanges as the Royal mistress. It was
noticed that Louis began to show Marie Thérèse an attention and
tenderness to which she had long been unaccustomed, and which
made her happier than she had ever been since 1661. She was moved
to tears, saying repeatedly, 'God has raised up Mme de Maintenon
to give me back the heart of the King'. Louis had in fact surrendered
to Mme de Maintenon, whose influence over him was so different to
that which any other woman had exercised. Charm, coupled with an
uncompromising forthrightness, was the secret of a triumph in which
sex as yet played no part; she opened Louis' eyes to the horror and
degradation of his state, talked sternly of David and Bathsheba, and
frightened him with thoughts of his destiny in the life eternal. Louis
was converted, and the first result of his change of heart was an immediate and striking revolution in the manners of his Court. An officer,
coming back to France in 1680 after twenty years absence, discovered
with astonishment that he was a stranger in his own country. In 1660
Court life had been a perpetual round of balls, concerts, banquets,
and love-making; but now everyone lived as silently as if in retreat,
spending little, and circumspect in their behaviour; whilst debauchery,
drunkenness, immodest dress, and even obscene language, ruined men
and women with the King. But, concludes our informant with a
certain grim satisfaction, in spite of all, he felt that Louis was not a happy
man.

Probably not. But a more contented man, with his feet firmly
planted on the ground. To this year belongs his own pamphlet, *Le
Métier du Roi*, which did credit to his common-sense; and though in
September he tacitly allowed his subjects to christen him 'Louis Le
Grand', his innate sense of the fitting still prompted him to reject
flattery which made him look ridiculous. Whilst inspecting Versailles
he noticed two of Lebrun's paintings, one called 'The Unbelievable
Passage of the Rhine' and the other 'The Marvellous Capture of
Valenciennes'; and he at once ordered that the adjectives be
obliterated.

On 28 June 1681 the Duchesse de Fontanges died, 'to the sensible
displeasure of His Majesty, who still had a tenderness for her'; and
nothing remained of the King's last adventure but the financial hang-

over. In three years she was said to have cost the State something over £120,000, though it is only fair to point out that this scandalous figure included much lavish generosity to the Roussilles family after her death.

Louis' reformation came as an unpleasant surprise to many who had not the slightest inclination to be reformed themselves; and it is doubtful if the new regime did much but add hypocrisy to the other vices of the recalcitrant section. The Court became more splendid from now on, but duller than heretofore, a whispering gallery honeycombed with spies. All letters, said 'Madame', were opened in the post, though she admitted that in her own case the officials did her the honour of resealing them very cleverly. But those of the Dauphine generally reached her in 'an unbelievable mess'. All that glitters is not gold, she continued, and in spite of the much vaunted French liberty, all amusements were pursued under an indescribable constraint. The walls and ears of Versailles, she went on to say, had tongues, and it was very dangerous to whisper anything which would be displeasing to the King. As for the Princesses, except as regards their conversation they were more in slavery than the women of the seraglio; their glances were watched, and every man in their entourage was a spy of the King's; for Louis' position was such that either through fear or ambition there was not a man who did not think it an honour to serve him in any fashion. And boredom, she said, weighed heavier on all every day; it would be difficult to say whether the performers in a Court ballet or the spectators longed more earnestly for its conclusion, for 'when one cannot choose one's own pleasures, those in which one is compelled to join, are more often pains'.

In the autumn Louis inspected Strasbourg, the Imperial key to the Rhine, which he had just annexed, together with Casale, the gateway into the Italian plain; and returned to complete a transaction as discreditable to the man as was his latest display of *realpolitik* to the King. He released Lauzun, allowed him to return to Court, and gave him a kind reception; but the price paid for his liberty by 'Mademoiselle' was the settlement of her Principality of Dombes on Louis' favourite bastard the Duc du Maine. Not of course that the matter had been thus nakedly represented by either party to the bargain; but each well understood the terms. It was a transaction which, if it showed Louis' love for his children, demonstrated no less clearly his abuse of the Royal power to provide for their future at the expense of a legitimate member of his own family.

On 16 May 1682 the Court, led by its King, made a formal entrance into Versailles. At last Louis felt that he had a setting worthy of himself, one which he could stamp with his own personality in a way which was impossible in the palaces which he had inherited from his predecessors. And he must have enjoyed the symbolism of the act, for Versailles was the crowning stroke of his revenge for the Fronde; by making his new home the seat of government he reduced the capital to the status of a provincial city, and published an edict in stone and marble that the Louvre was now merely an historical monument.

But there were common-sense reasons for abandoning the Louvre. The King loved big rooms, full of fresh air and sunlight, and the Louvre was a warren of dark little closets, filled with the dreadful stench of the open moat which was the only drainage system of the palace; reeking too with the scarcely less offensive odour from the neighbouring butcher's market. To have remodelled it would have been difficult, and to enlarge it impossible.

We cannot look at Versailles without asking ourselves what it cost; or remembering the fable that Louis, horrified at his own extravagance, burnt the accounts. Revolutionary propaganda appears wildly to have exaggerated the cost of Versailles, some writers putting it as high as £60,000,000; whilst according to Peignot, Louis' total expenditure on building, public works included, was under £24,000,000. And when we recollect that in addition to public works this figure would include the capital outlay on Marly, Trianon, and probably Clangy, it is not easy to see how Versailles could have cost more than £10,000,000 at the outside.

A formidable sum, but we must not accuse Louis of reckless extravagance in devoting it to housing himself and his Court; first because the bulk of the money was spent inside the Kingdom, and secondly because it was what he intended it to be, a European advertisement of the French genius and a magnet to the polite of all the world. And to scholars as well; for though Louis himself was no reader, his library, open to the public, increased between 1643 and 1715 from five to seventy thousand volumes. In fact the only building extravagances with which he can be reproached belong to the period before he found his feet; he might for instance have spared the £7,000 which he paid for the visit of the Italian architect Bernini in 1665. These accounts make interesting reading, and one wonders if Louis himself had a hand in their compilation; certainly the meticulous recording of trifles, side by side with the expenditure of millions, is very characteristic of him. As for instance the entry showing that the daily subsistence allowance for swans and carp at Fontainebleau was 3½d. and 1d. respectively; and the stray grant of £21 to the mole-catchers at Versailles.

Louis now had the house of his dreams; not comfortable to be sure, but then he was indifferent to comfort so long as he had magnificence, and this he certainly achieved. Achieved, too, certain things always longed for by Louis the man—far horizons, light and air indoors, and flowers everywhere, arranged both indoors and out so as to afford striking contrasts and brilliant effects. For like all sensualists, Louis delighted in colour; a fact so well known that a cynical courtier accused him of inviting Cardinals to Fontainebleau in summer, purely in order to enjoy the effect of their scarlet against the deep green of the foliage.

He now had his vast gardens where he could find comparative solitude, and into which he could slip to tranquillize himself amidst his statuary, labyrinths, 'green carpets', and fountains; for he had inherited from Spanish Anne a passion for the sight and sound of sparkling water falling into a marble basin. Le Nôtre, creator of the gardens, had had a similar career to that of Mansart, builder of the château. Beginning as a gardeners' labourer, he had become the Capability Brown of his century, but never lost his common-sense peasant outlook, even when ennobled and given the Order of St Michel in 1693. As his arms he selected a potato and a cabbage, supported by a spade and a rake, 'because he did not choose that his descendants should forget what he had been'. Louis loved him, and towards the end of their lives the two old men used to be pulled round Le Nôtre's masterpiece in bath chairs; Le Nôtre exclaiming at intervals, 'If only my mother could see me now!' In the 'seventies Louis had lent him to the Pope, whom Le Nôtre was said to have embraced heartily at his first audience:

A COURTIER: I bet that story about his throwing his arms around the Pope's neck and kissing him is untrue.

LOUIS: I should not bet on that if I were you; it is what he does to me whenever I have been away from home; very probably he did kiss the Pope.

The gardens did not exhaust Louis' out-door amenities, for when he was tired of them he could walk to Trianon, where he kept a zoo containing a rhinoceros, an elephant, ostriches, gazelles, seals, and a large aviary. When he was in the house he could amuse himself with his cabinet of medals and curios, which he was always ready to show to visitors; for he was something of a connoisseur and collector, having picked up these tastes from Mazarin in his youth. But his chief indoor relaxation was music, which he loved passionately, and at last he had the space which he needed for its performance; from 1682 onwards he maintained a full orchestra, a chamber orchestra, and a choir; and did too a little music-making himself, for he was a competent performer on the clavecin, the lute, and the guitar. The acres of lofty rooms were on an ascending scale of magnificence which culminated in the Throne Room with its silver throne, the walls flanked with orange trees in silver tubs, and hung with Titians and Vandykes; and the Great Gallery, where the chairs were of silver, and whose seventeen windows had white damask curtains bearing the arms of France in gold thread which had cost £90 each; then the *sanctum sanctorum*, Louis' private office, full of flowers, the walls panelled with mirrors, and in the middle of the room the great writing table with its crimson, bullion-fringed cloth; small wonder that Versailles dazzled the world. But let us come down to earth and remember that the huge château had drawbacks which we would not tolerate today; all the chimneys smoked, and in hard weather wine froze on the King's own buffet; food was served in congealed gravy, owing to the distance which separated the kitchens from the dining room; the courtiers were housed in little cubicles in which we should hesitate to keep a dog; and, impressive as the £90 curtains no doubt were, what would have struck us on pulling them aside was that the inhabitants of the château were not house-trained. But none of this would worry Louis, who looked upon his creation and saw that it was good.

Louis, at forty-four, was no longer the Prince Charming of twenty years earlier, but a pock-marked man with full, almost purple cheeks, who was putting on weight; 'certainly not handsome, but giving a vivid impression of grace and majesty'. And he, formerly something of a fop, now dressed 'in brown cloth without decoration except for the vest; he wore no rings; his only diamonds were the buckles of his shoes, his garters, and his hat,—that hat which looks so well in the portraits, but with which we wish no closer acquaintance; for as he wore it at meals, ate with his fingers, and always pulled it off when he spoke to a lady, the brim was permanently coated in stale grease'.

In the new palace on 6 August was born 'Monseigneur's' first child, the Duke of Burgundy, and the reception of the news gives a curious picture of a France still largely feudal in sentiment. The King was the first to come into the anteroom with the news, 'Mme La Dauphine has just given birth to a Prince'. Instantly, everyone went almost off their heads, and all—servants included—rushed to embrace the King, who was carried by the crowd from the Surintendance to his own rooms. He let anyone who wished kiss him. The *canaille* lit bonfires, and the chairporters burnt the Dauphine's gilded chair. There was a big fire ablaze in the Court below the Gallery of the Princes, which was being stoked with the wainscotting and parquetry intended for the Grand Gallery. Bontemps, Louis' confidential valet, came in a rage to report this to the King, who only laughed and said, 'Let them enjoy themselves, we can get fresh materials'.

Perhaps the only discontented face was that of 'Madame-Palatine', already imbued with her long-cherished hatred of Mme de Maintenon. And it is easy to see why she hated her; many women had fought each other for Louis' love, but only these two were to fight for his friendship; and until Maintenon's rise, 'Madame' had been his most intimate female friend. It had been an alliance in which even the most spiteful courtier could smell no hint of scandal, in fact much the sort of intimacy which was now recognized as existing between Louis and Maintenon. 'Madame' lost the battle for a variety of reasons, but mainly because she was fourteen years younger than the King, whilst Maintenon was three years older; 'Madame' wanted Louis to be always as light-hearted as herself, whilst Maintenon 'dared to speak to the King seriously on serious matters'. Given the new Louis, the issue of the struggle was never in doubt, and gradually the bond between 'Madame' and the King slackened. And Liselotte never really forgave Maintenon; for years she believed any lie about the ex-governess, for whom her mildest names were 'the old slut', or 'the old ordure'.

On 27 July 1683 the Queen complained of a swelling under her arm, took to her bed, and died on the 30th in the presence of her husband and the Court—'In the twenty years I have lived with her', said Louis tearfully, 'she has never given me cause for annoyance, nor has she ever opposed my will'. And the great egoist's obituary notice said all that there was to say about poor stupid little Marie Thérèse. The King, according to Mme de Maintenon's niece, was more touched than afflicted by the Queen's death, and his Court was touched with him. But the grief of Mme de Maintenon appeared to be sincere. As soon as the Queen was dead, she wanted to retire to her own rooms, but M. de La Rochefoucauld took her by the arm and pushed her towards the King, saying, 'This is not the time to leave him; he has need of you'.

This was on a Friday. On the following Monday the King left Versailles for Fontainebleau, and during this trip the favour of Mme de Maintenon increased by leaps and bounds. The King could not do without her, lodged her in the Queen's apartments, held his Council in her room, did most of his work there, and consulted her frequently. And it would seem that it was during this visit to Fontainebleau that Louis proposed to Mme de Maintenon and was accepted, for, said her niece Mme de Caylus, at Fontainebleau 'her spirits were so agitated that I have since thought that this was due to her uncertainty as to her future, to her thoughts, hopes, and fears. Then her vapours passed off, and before the end of the visit calm had replaced agitation'. And on 7 August Mme de Maintenon wrote herself to her importunate wastrel of a brother, the Comte d'Aubigné, to say that the reason she was unable to see him was so useful and glorious that he should have nothing but joy. And shortly afterwards she begged her *directeur* not to forget her in his prayers, for she had much need of strengthening to make a worthy use of her good fortune. There is too a significant ring of assurance in a letter to her sister-in-law, Mme de Villette, in which she said that Villette's last news was false, and that she might spread it throughout her province in complete certainty of its accuracy that the King was indulging in no gallantries.

But Louis' preoccupation with Mme de Maintenon did not interfere with his plunge into the Spanish Netherlands in September, on the pretext that the Spaniards were evading their obligations under the Treaty of 1678. The operation hardly deserves mentioning except that it affords an example of Louis' intervention in favour of the common soldier. He learnt that the officers were making illegal deductions from their men's pay, and that in a certain regiment a man had been court-martialled and shot for organizing a protest against this fraud:

His Majesty regards what has been done to the soldier as murder . . There was nothing which justified such an example being made of him . . . I am sending orders to M. de La Chétardie to suspend the officers who sat on the court-martial, and to imprison the command-ing officer who permitted the retention of the men's pay . . . and to teach Commissary St Germain to permit such disorders, the King commands his imprisonment in the château of Landscroon, and has forbidden me (Louvois) ever to employ him again.

It is pleasant to read of this sympathy with the under-dog, and it would be even more pleasant if his dealings with the weak states on his perimeter had been tinged with something of the same sentiment. But there is no trace of it; on the contrary, his arrogance and brutality to his neighbours were intolerable. Which was a grave blunder on Louis' part; for the time was coming when he would need every ally he could get in a Europe in which he was no longer paramount—'Each day the pupils were catching up on their master'. But Louis despised the small powers too much to conciliate them, and ignored the fear and hatred aroused by his incursion into the Netherlands; a hatred considerably quickened when in August the French Navy bombarded Genoa for the 'crime' of having built galleys for Spain. And when in the same month Europe was compelled to guarantee Louis undisturbed posses-sion of his thefts for the next twenty years, it was obvious that the time was approaching when France would be confronted by a world in arms.

At Versailles on 12 June 1684 at midnight, Louis was married to Mme de Maintenon; Father La Chaise officiated, the Archbishop of Paris gave the nuptial benediction, Louvois and Montchevreuil were the witnesses, Bontemps prepared the Altar and served the Mass.

It was an intimate little party which assembled in the Chapel that night and every member of it was to preserve Louis' secret inviolably. La Chaise was not only the King's confessor for over thirty years, but was also a valued friend; a friendship which had originally sprung from their common enthusiasm for the collection of rare medals. On account of his official position, Harlay de Champvallon, the Archbishop of Paris, could not be excluded from the wedding, though doubtless both bride and groom would have wished him elsewhere. For he was a disgrace to the priesthood, a man whose least offence was that all the world knew that the Duchesse de Lesdiguières was his mistress; and for whom no funeral eulogy was delivered when he died in 1695—'two little bagatelles made such a composition impossible, his life and his death'. Henri de Mornay, Marquis de Montchevreuil, 'honourable, brave, and as poor as a Church mouse', had been a friend of Mme de Maintenon's as far back as 1658, and was also in high favour with the King, who appointed him Governor to his bastard by La Vallière, and afterwards to the Duc du Maine, his favourite of the Montespan brood.

No record of the marriage exists, and some have doubted whether Mme de Maintenon did in fact become Louis' wife. Certainly there is no irrefragable proof, but there is a mass of detail which when examined carries conviction that the ceremony was performed. To go into the evidence supporting the marriage theory would need a chapter in itself, and here only some of the more suggestive facts can be touched upon. In the middle of July d'Aubigné, who had hoped great things from 'the brother-in-law' as he called Louis, wrote bitterly to his sister—'So then, yours is a personal distinction which is not to benefit me?' and Mme de Maintenon replied bluntly that that was the exact position. Then there are passages in her own letters which cannot be explained unless we accept the fact that she was married. To her brother for instance—'Our lots are different; mine brilliant, yours tranquil. God has put me where I am, and He knows that I have not sought for this position'. And again to the same—'I could not make you Constable when I would have wished to do so, and now that I can, I do not wish; being incapable of making unreasonable requests to one to whom I owe everything'. To another correspondent we find her writing, 'My favour is embarrassing, even in the confessional'.

Godet Desmarets, Bishop of Chârtres, was an austere priest, incapable of conniving at a royal liaison, and this is how he wrote to Louis of Mme de Maintenon:

You have an excellent companion, filled with God's spirit, whose tenderness for you is unequalled . . . no one loves you more tenderly or respectfully than she does . . . It is plain that God has wished to support you . . . by giving you a woman who, like the good wife of Scripture, occupies herself with the salvation of her husband.

Then in 1692 came a Papal Bull giving Mme de Maintenon permission to lodge in any convent in France for so long as she pleased; a compliment paid by the Vatican to no one in France except the Queen. And dozens of small details strengthen our conviction that she was Louis' wife; for example the King's insistence that she should be seated in an arm-chair whilst Royal Princesses sat on *tabourets*, a distinction belonging only to the Queen of France; a letter of her own deprecating the 'respect' with which the Royal family treated her; the tone and diction of her letters. Small points all, but combining to produce certainty in our minds. But perhaps the negative evidence clinches the matter. St Simon, most spiteful and most credulous of contemporary memoirists, and a fanatical hater of Mme de Maintenon, had no doubt at all that she was Louis' second wife; and this means that even he was unable to find any shred of evidence on which to base an argument that she was the King's mistress. And the same is true of 'Madame', in whose frenetic ravings against the 'old ordure' there is not only no hint that Louis did not marry Maintenon, but on the contrary much indignation with him for having made such a ridiculous and degrading match.

So here at last was Cinderella married to Prince Charming. And they lived happily ever afterwards? Many years later Mme de Maintenon said that it was true that the King loved her, and more than he did anyone else; but all the same, only as much as he was capable of loving; for men in general, she added, except when driven by passion, knew little of love's tenderness. About the same time, in a letter to an old friend, she said that she looked back on her life as a miracle when she reflected that she was by nature impatient, and that the King never knew how often she was at the end of her tether. She had been born open in manner, but with Louis she had always to dissimulate. She had planned, first to withdraw him from women, and then to give him to God, and in this she could never have succeeded if she had not been so compliant. Only God, she said, knew what she had suffered, but she had been placed where she was in order to sanctify the King.

It is not the letter of an ex-mistress in a reminiscent mood.

Maintenon's secretary, Mlle d'Aumale, has left a depressing sketch of her employer's married life. She had often seen her, she wrote, tired, ill, chagrined, and restless, and yet when Louis came in she would assume a laughing air and a contented voice, and them amuse the King with a thousand fancies, entertaining him for four hours on end without repetitions, without a hiatus, and without a slander. But when he left at ten o'clock, and the maid drew the curtains of her bed, she would whisper to Mlle d'Aumale that she had only strength left to say that she could talk no more.

But marriage brought Maintenon one great happiness; she was able to create for herself the post for which nature had intended her, that of Headmistress of a large girls' school. She had always dreamt of doing something to ease the burden of her own class, the poor nobles, and had long since decided that no help would be of more value to them than the free education of their daughters. And by adroitly timing her suggestions to Louis in the first flush of his honeymoon, she secured his assent, and subsequently his enthusiastic co-operation. The King, whose love for children was perhaps his finest quality, took fire at the plan; and with his infallible knack of choosing the wrong site for a building, selected the marshy plain of St Cyr for the establishment which was to become one of the chief interests of his life. But only in his choice of a locality did he blunder; we have his own notes outlining the constitution of the new school, its revenue, furnishing, estimated expenses and so forth, all stamped with his usual dry common-sense. And on one point husband and wife were in complete agreement; St Cyr was to have nothing of the convent about it, for both had a contempt for the education given in such places. France, said Louis, had enough good nuns and too few good mothers; and it was the latter class that Mme de Maintenon's school was designed to produce.

But St Cyr by no means absorbed Louis in 1684 to the exclusion of other interests; Versailles, though formally taken over, was far from finished, and the King, with his usual love of detail, scrutinized even the most trivial accounts—the locksmith's for one, and that for nails, bolts, and screws for another. And as usual, he was on the alert to gratify those whom he thought had a claim upon him; the grand-daughter of his old nurse for instance, to whom he remembered to send a hundred guineas when she married a policeman; and at the same time he was busily engaged in soliciting his friends' votes for Boileau in the forthcoming election to the Academy; into which Louis did in fact lobby him in this year.

Maintenon and the reformed King speedily imposed their own tone upon the Court, and there was an outburst of austerity at Versailles which horrified the worldly. Comedies were forbidden in Lent; courtiers were reproved for not fasting rigorously, and even for whispering at Mass; the King spent nearly the whole of Christmas Day in the Chapel, and ordered Brissac, Major of the Bodyguard, to give him the names of any courtiers whom he saw talking during service; even 'Monsieur', always a prime favourite, was reprimanded for his disorderly household; and 'Madame' was reproved for her gross language. Edifying reforms no doubt, but unfortunately the worst features of an imposed code of morals soon appeared; hypocrisy was rampant, the informer flourished in every religious house, tavern, street, and home, and nowhere was the surveillance of the secret police more ubiquitous than at Versailles itself. Yet the lure of the Court remained irresistible, and the country nobility came in swarms to install themselves in a palace which was rapidly becoming a miniature police state. The figures are striking; when Louis XIV was born in 1638 the noblesse resident at Court had numbered about six hundred; by 1684 this figure had risen to seven thousand.

We are often told that after 1684 Louis was driven in blinkers by his confessor, but this is to forget that he had one of those strictly compartmented minds which enabled him to define unerringly where religion ended and politics began. Louis never pretended to be a theologian, and to him his confessor was the expert responsible for the King's salvation, whose orders were therefore to be obeyed in religious matters; but let him beware of attempting to infiltrate into politics. Only in Louis' France among the Catholic powers were Bishops forbidden to correspond with the Vatican, except through the Foreign Secretary, who read the correspondence on the rare occasions when permission was given for an interchange of letters; and so jealous was Louis of priestly power that even routine correspondence with the Pope on such matters as Bulls and Dispensations was conducted, not by the Church but by the Paris banks.

In his forty-seventh year the pace was beginning to tell on the King; he was losing his teeth, not sleeping as he used to do, and suffering from indigestion and nightmares. But his grip on Court and State was as firm as always. And to the surprise of his entourage he was still, after six months of marriage, as attentive to Maintenon as ever; when in January 1685 she had rheumatism, 'he was much grieved, and visited her two or three times a day'.

1685 is the high water mark of Louis' Kingship, and perhaps too of the stream of flattery which would long ago have poisoned a less well-balanced mind; and he could still acknowledge a compliment with a graceful if assumed modesty. Meeting Racine one day soon after the poet had eulogized him before the Academy, he said, 'I could have praised you more for your speech, M. Racine, if you had praised me less'. And if he loved to be praised, he could still reject the coarsest of the flatteries offered to him. In this year a religious Order, the Minimes, dedicated a thesis to him in which they compared him to God, but in a way which let it be clearly seen that God was the copy. It was shown to Bossuet, who drew Louis' attention to it, and he immediately sent the document to the Sorbonne for censure, and to the hangman for burning.

We lately saw Louis' indignation at abuses in the army; and in 1685 we find him angrier still at a gross injustice done to the work-people at Versailles. The men who dug the trenches for the pipes had to work in water up to their knees, and Louis, noticing this, gave orders that they were to be given thigh boots and extra pay. A fortnight later he returned, and saw that some were still labouring bare-legged; among them a man of over sixty, who said that M. Berthelot, the Intendant, had not given him any boots nor increase of pay. Investigation showed that six hundred of his fellows were in the same plight. It was nine in the morning; Berthelot was immediately arrested; by mid-day he had been tried, convicted of peculation, and condemned to death; and at half past one he was hanged.

1685 was enlivened by a scandal in the Royal family, the culprits being Louis de Bourbon, Prince de Conti, and his wife, the King's favourite child, that daughter who had been described a few years earlier as 'all love'. The two had fallen in love with each other when they were children, and had had a rare stroke of luck; it happened to suit the King's plans that they should marry, and since they had become man and wife in 1680, 'they had loved as lovers do in a romance'. In March, Conti had committed the crime of leaving France without permission to enjoy a campaign with the Austrians in Hungary; and from Mons had written an apology to Louis, enclosed in a letter to the Princess. 'Madame', said Louis when she presented it, 'I can refuse nothing from your hand; but you will see the use I shall make of it'; and with these words he threw the letter into the fire unopened. Which was ominous enough for Conti, but worse was to follow; the young couple apparently did not know that letters were opened in the post, and exchanged a number which were, to put it mildly, indiscreet; several ladies' reputations were compromised; a good deal of nastiness came to light; and worst of all, Louis was spoken of in a tone which horrified him. He was tolerant of abuse, and indeed in this year when he saw a particularly stinging libel on himself, all he had said was, 'I am consoled by the fact that no one ever wrote like this about a *roi fainéant*'. But that anyone could think him *comic* enlarged his concept of the possible; with incredulous eyes he saw his sacred self and his Maintenon described as 'the old boy from the country and his old woman'; and there were other flippant references in the same vein. Conti, luckily for himself, was out of Louis' clutches, and it was on the Princess that the King's anger fell; and perhaps he was angrier with her than he was with her husband, for she had written telling Conti how she had been obliged to take a new Lady-of-Honour at random in a great hurry, 'lest she should be saddled with one of those horrors from old Maintenon's academy'. Louis' treatment of the Princess was characteristic. When next she had to encounter her father she was, to translate literally, 'thunder-bolted with a look'; but also characteristically Louis, angry though he was, promised his daughter that he would save the good names of all the women compromised in her letters; and to this day we do not know the identity of one of them.

But it was not in the King's nature to hold out long against a pretty woman, and the Princess was soon restored to favour. She got off with the fright, and the shame of having to appear before a justly offended father; and with the humiliation of having to beg Mme de Maintenon to intercede for her pardon. The latter spoke to her strongly, not deigning to refer to the insults to herself; and whilst telling the Princess many home truths, she did all in her power to soften the King.

On 18 October 1685 Louis signed the revocation of the perpetual Edict of Nantes.

It is often alleged that the revocation was the fruit of Louis' conversion, an offering up of the heretics as an expiation for his own sins; a theory which would be tenable only if Louis' attitude towards his Huguenot subjects had changed suddenly between 1680 and 1685, whereas all the evidence shows the contrary. Petty persecution of the Huguenots was active as far back as 1666; in 1668 the King began to offer bribes to Huguenots who abjured their faith; in 1670 he considered their extermination; in 1674 the underground persecution was intensified; in 1676 the King was pondering an ingenious plan for bribing Huguenot pastors to be 'converted' after defeat in a pre-arranged debate with Catholic priests; and in 1678 began the persecution which preluded the tragedy of 1685. Whatever else Louis' action may have been, it certainly was not impulsive. And the theory of the vicarious sacrifice was quite alien to a man of the King's literal cast of mind. Indeed the revocation was precisely the opposite of a sacrifice for past sin, it was evidence of a determination to cease from sinning henceforward.

Let us try to see the matter as Louis did. He had indulged in a spiritual stock-taking since 1680 and had realized that there were other sins than those of the flesh. He was God's lieutenant on earth, entrusted with the care of twenty million souls, and for nearly two decades he had looked on idly whilst no inconsiderable number of them had marched down into Hell. And what, his confessor may well have asked him, could Louis plead at the Day of Judgement when asked for an account of those souls whom he had allowed to go to perdition? Persuasion had failed to bring back the lost sheep; temporal suffering was as nothing when compared with eternal damnation; let Louis ponder the dominical *compelle intrare*. And this we know Louis did; getting essays on those two difficult words from every Bishop, and wading through them all himself. There is no reason to attribute base or selfish motives to Louis; granted the premiss of his Church, the truest kindness he could show his heretical subjects was to 'compel them to enter in'. And that once admitted, brutality became charity —'the surgeon's knife', 'cruel only to be kind', and so on.

We cannot blame Louis for not being in advance of the thought of his day; but we can and do blame him for insufficient examination into the authenticity of the mass of 'conversions' which preceded and produced the revocation. Nor can he be forgiven the resultant atrocities on the ground that he did not know what was being done by his evangelising dragoons in his name. Louis cannot have it both ways; either he was an autocrat or he was a tool in the hands of others. We believe him to have been an autocrat; to have decided hastily on insufficient data; and to have failed to control his subordinates after the plunge had been taken. That he rushed into the revocation without considering its military, economic, and political repercussions does not seem to have been the case. Hébert, the parish priest of Versailles, who knew him well, tells us that the King had foreseen all the consequences of his act; he knew that a great number of his subjects of all classes would flee to Protestant countries and would enter the armies of his foes. He knew also that in abandoning their own land they would carry with them an implacable hatred against their King, whom they would denounce as a tyrant, a cruel persecutor, and a bad Prince, and that everywhere they would become firebrands urging their adopted countries to declare war against France. And, said Hébert, he was not deceived in his forecast; his revocation of the Edict showed the grandeur of his soul, for he put the honour of his faith before his temporal interests.

As for Mme de Maintenon, generally represented as spurring Louis on, the fact is that he reproached her for her tepidity. She herself told the nuns of St Cyr that the King, burning with zeal and wishing to see more of that quality in her, said more than once that he feared that the consideration she wished him to show to the Huguenots came from a lingering tenderness towards her old religion. And if any further evidence is needed to disprove her bigotry, we find it in her treatment of her Huguenot maidservants. The King in his new-found fervour pressed her to get rid of the girls, or else force them to enter the Church, but Maintenon bluntly refused to comply with his wishes, saying, 'Let me go my own way; I know what the outcome is going to be; I must beg you to leave me mistress in my own house'.

Whatever the rights and wrongs of the revocation, its immediate result was to increase Louis' popularity with all classes, and France applauded him as it had not done since he declared war on Holland in 1672. Abroad, the reactions of both Protestant and Roman states were much what Louis had anticipated. With one disquieting exception; the Pope alone amongst Catholic sovereigns sent no message of congratulation to the Eldest Son of the Church—'He could never be brought to express the slightest approval of the onslaught against the Huguenots'. Which from Louis' point of view was all the more unfortunate because Innocent XI was the only Pope of the century whose uprightness and integrity were unquestioned by all Europe, Protestant as well as Catholic.

VIII

On 23 February 1686 Louis had to put himself into the hands of his surgeon Felix, an enterprising practitioner who was to die sixteen years later as the result of attempting to operate on himself. Felix diagnosed the King's complaint as an anal fistula, and this not yielding to treatment, Louis decided to undergo what was then called The Grand Operation. On 18 November it was performed in the presence of Mme de Maintenon, Louis prefacing the ordeal with one of his infrequent sarcasms—'Do not treat me like a King,' he said, 'I want to get well like a peasant'. Not a groan escaped him whilst the surgeon was at work, and only one untoward incident disturbed the calm; Montespan attempted to enter the room "with that imperious manner which a long domination gives". But the usher on duty refused her admittance, and she returned to her own apartments, in a fury which she was foolish enough to let everyone perceive.

That same afternoon Louis presided in bed at the Council of State, and on the 20th, still in bed, spent the day, 'singing with surprising gaiety'; though as late as 11 December, 'he suffered for seven hours as if he was being broken on the wheel'. But by Christmas day he was completely cured.

Though he had been more or less ill throughout the year, there had been no diminution in Louis' normal and incessant activity. The military reviews this summer, designed as a warning to the formidable anti-French League of Augsburg, were even more elaborate than usual; and the untried younger generation jeered at the King behind his back, making songs whose burden was that Louis was fonder of reviews than of active service.

But the flattery offered him in public was as extravagant as ever, and perhaps reached its peak with La Feuillade's extraordinary performance before the King's statue in the Place des Victoires. He marched round it three times at the head of the French Guards, prostrating himself before it at each circuit, 'as the pagans used to do before the statues of their Emperors'. And not content with this, he broadcast the news that he had bought a vault in the nearest Church, from which he was having a tunnel constructed to the middle of the Place so that he could be buried under the statue of the King. He was also, he said, leaving a trust fund to pay for lamps which were to burn day and night before the statue in perpetuity. But it was all in vain, for Louis, who disliked him, merely laughed. The King's illness had been kept so secret that as late as August 'Madame' thought that he was contracting tertian ague; and her survey of the position is illuminating. 'God guard us from his fever', she said, fearing that it would make the King a hundred times more morose than he was already. Adding sourly that Louis fancied himself devout because he was now sleeping with an old woman instead of a young one; and that his devoutness in fact consisted in having spies everywhere, and in tormenting everyone.

'Madame's' furious jealousy of Maintenon makes her a tainted witness, but Hébert, who was appointed parish priest of Versailles in November, has left an unattractive picture of the Court at its zenith. The first thing that struck him was its amazing luxury, and he was particularly shocked to find Bishops living 'with a profusion which would have been blameworthy in the women'. They degraded their office by their greed, he said, and many of them rarely visited their Dioceses because their energies were concentrated on obtaining translation to richer ones; and to win preferment they paid servile court to the King's confessor, to those in favour, and to women who, if these Bishops had done their duty, they would have rebuked sternly for their disorderly lives. The next aspect of Court life which offended him was not only the unbelievable rage for gambling, but the fact that people of any rank could play with the highest in the land, provided that they had enough money; and he added that he himself had actually seen a butcher playing with Knights of the St Esprit. Lastly, and perhaps worst of all, was the depth of corruption evinced by the fact that a noble who was faithful to his wife was laughed at as a man who lived à la bourgeoise.

But Hébert, I feel, generalizes from isolated examples after the manner of Macaulay; if we imagine a bigoted, uncouth Elder of the Scottish Kirk transplanted to the Whitehall of Charles II and there recording his impressions, we get an idea of the spirit in which Hébert wrote.

Of the King alone has he any good to say, and here we need not follow him, for it is the now familiar verdict—gracious, kindly, courteous, and of an incomparable majesty.

Louis was indeed seen at his best in 1686 and 1687. Even in the realm of international politics a prudent moderation replaced his former arrogance; though to be sure he knew that France was overstrained, and he was trying to husband his resources. And he relented towards that official Paris which he hated so implacably; on 30 January 1687 he accepted an invitation to dine with the city magnates at the Hôtel de Ville, and did the thing handsomely; refusing to have his route from Nôtre Dame, where he had heard Mass, lined with troops, in order that his people might be better able to see him.

And in the matter of taxation his conscience now prompted him to attempt to relieve his people of some of the burdensome weight of 'the glory of France'. When in 1687 a new contract was placed with the Tax-Farmers, he refused to accept the highest tender, much less force the bidding higher, as he could easily have done; being persuaded that 'when these gentlemen bid extravagantly, they always recoup themselves by fleecing the people'. And early in the summer he sent officials into the provinces to scrutinize instances of abuse in the collection of taxes, and to invite complaints from individuals and municipalities. Further, he set the Court a good example by paying off his own private debts. Which incidentally give us a startling insight into the fortunes which could be made by picking up the crumbs from Louis' table; in twelve years he had run up a bill for £22,000 with his valet Bontemps, for 'collations and suppers'.

Now as always Louis was at his happiest and his most human at Marly; understandably, for his dream house of Versailles was developing into a small town, and not altogether a pleasant one, harbouring singularly undesirable visitors from Paris. In January 1687 for example, an officer of cavalry had his pocket picked in the King's presence, and the King repaid him the £50 which had been stolen, saying that it was not fair that a poor officer should lose what might be his savings from a year's service in his host's house.

Small wonder that he relished Marly, and when a trip there was impending, courtiers could detect a certain added graciousness in Louis' manner; as for instance in his invitation to a Bishop in December —'Others beg me to take them to Marly, but I beg you to accompany me'. Racine, who was one of Louis' guests on this occasion, wrote from Marly to say that no one who had not been there could imagine how pleasant it was, and how different the Court was at Marly and at

Versailles. For at Marly the party was small, and no one was there who had not been specially invited, consequently everyone felt highly honoured and in the best of humours. The King, he went on to say, was caressing and free in his manner; 'he did me the honour to talk to me several times, and I emerged as usual, that is to say delighted with him, and in despair at myself; for I never have so little wit as at those moments when I need it most.'

And as we are on the subject of Racine, let us here demolish the absurd story that he was disgraced for mentioning Scarron's plays in the presence of the King and Mme de Maintenon; to begin with he was not disgraced, and secondly we observe that on 14 February 1688 Scarron's *Jodelet, maître et valet* was played by command before Louis and his wife.

As usual at Marly, Louis wanted his domestics to consider the trip their holiday as well as the master's; and Racine noticed that on 4 December, when *Le Bourgeois Gentilhomme* was played, the King fixed the performance at six instead of in the later evening, so as not to interfere with the servants' supper hour.

But the most noticeable thing about Louis in these days was his continued attention to Mme de Maintenon after four years of marriage; even 'Madame' had to recognize it. Writing to a friend in Germany in April 1688 from St Cloud, she said it was certain that the King had never entertained such a passion for any of his mistresses as he did for this hag; adding that it was curious to watch them when they were together. If Maintenon went to another part of the room, Louis would follow her almost immediately and begin to whisper in her ear, even after having spent the whole day with her.

1688 was for Louis a year fraught with anxiety and the burden of momentous decisions; the European sky was dark, with storm clouds stationary over England where James II had in three years dissipated the good-will which Charles II had built up over a quarter of a century. Here it would be irrelevant to enquire how that brave and competent sailor, James, Duke of York, had degenerated into that miracle of ineptitude, King James II; it will suffice to say that, having alienated every section of his own people and every European ruler save Louis, he was now trying to snub his French cousin into leaving him to his fate. England had endured James in the confident knowledge that his successor would be his Protestant daughter Mary, wife of William of

Orange; but when on 10 June the Queen bore a son, it resolved to endure no longer, and on the 30th the Whigs invited William to invade their country. In the same month Louis, to whom it was vital that James should remain King of England, invaded the Electorate of Cologne and forcibly installed Cardinal Prince von Furstembourg, 'the French master-key to Germany', as Elector; thus getting control of the back door into Holland as well as a springboard into North Germany, but making war with the Empire a certainty, and with the whole of Europe a strong probability.

Had he possessed the initiative, it was not the moment that Louis would have chosen for a general war; he was straitened financially; he was relatively weaker than he had been since pre-Louvois days; and he was without allies whilst his enemies, actual and potential, included the Empire, Holland, Sweden, Spain, England, and the Pope. But Louis could not stand idly by to watch William become King of England, and he chose what was probably the best course open to him; he rejected Louvois' advice to attack Maestricht, thinking, and no doubt correctly, that even its capture would not deter William from invading England. Instead, Louis struck at Philipsburg on the Upper Rhine, the only available gateway into France for the Imperialists. On 24 September he 'published his just grievances' against the Emperor, and on the 27th his armies attacked all along the Rhine front. It was sound strategy, marred only by one fatal miscalculation; Louis thought that the English revolution, like the English Civil War, would be a long, slow business.

The Duc du Maine, making his military debut at the siege of Philipsburg, acquitted himself creditably, and his father's mingled pride in and anxiety for his favourite child came out clearly in his very human letters to the youth's Governor. He had been impatient, he wrote, to hear himself from him, though grateful that the Governor had written to Mme de Maintenon. He was delighted to learn of 'the bearing and firmness' of the Duc du Maine, but he was in great anxiety for his son, and it was a comfort to him to know that the Governor was at his side; then he added that good and bad news was to be given to him without reservation—'I want the whole picture, and I am confident that you will not deceive me'.

This favourite, now eighteen, proved a disappointment to Louis whose love for him could not warp the King's judgement of character;

a negative disappointment, for there was no vice in the boy. A cripple from childhood, he had been educated by Mme de Maintenon, and was the governess's chef d'œuvre; and had she loved him less, it might have been better for him. He had been an infant prodigy, and when his schooling was complete, there emerged a timid, retiring youth, more at home amongst women than with men, still tied to Maintenon's apron strings, and lacking the ambition, the drive and vitality which alone could win success in the world for which his father destined him. With a privileged place in the shade, either as a Churchman or the husband of an understanding wife, he would have led a blameless and contented existence, dabbling in literature, hunting, and pretending to manage his estates; but for a prominent role he was totally unfitted.

The daily round of duties, trivial and important, continued despite the war. On 29 June Louis visited Conti to inspect his trousseau; and he particularly admired 'the magnificent *déshabillé*', also 'a gold brocade shot with flame colour and green to match the dressing gown'. This by the way is not the same Conti, Louis' son-in-law, whom we recently saw in disgrace, but his younger brother François, the fourth Prince. The third Prince had died in 1685; died as he had lived, passionately devoted to his wife, whom he nursed personally through an attack of small-pox; her he saved, but in doing so he lost his own life.

Next day we find Louis righting a poor widow, whose estate had been annexed by the old legal family of de Mesmes, whose present head, Jean Jacques, had been a Judge since 1671:

As soon as the King sat down, Brissac ushered in the mother and son. M. de Mesmes recognized them, and changed colour, but it was worse for him when the King drew the woman's petition out of his pocket.

Louis: Read this, M. de Mesmes, here is a fine eulogy of your conduct.

Mesmes: Sire, I . . .

Louis: Read it, and then I will speak to you. Is this complaint true?

Mesmes: Yes, Sire.

Louis: (angrily): And you dare to admit it? On what grounds do you retain this property?

Mesmes: Sire, my father and I have been in possession for over thirty years.

LOUIS: Does that make it any the less theirs by right?

MESMES: But, Sire, the lapse of time gives us a prescriptive right, and if Your Majesty is going.—

LOUIS: On what does your prescriptive right rest?

MESMES: On the law, Sire.

LOUIS: Well then Monsieur, learn that between God, me, and Justice, there is no Law; before leaving Versailles you will restore the property which you so unjustly hold. I advise you not to let me hear of this matter again. Your conduct, Monsieur, is odious.

On 5 November William landed at Torbay and advanced towards London, establishing contact with James II's army near Salisbury; from where James, betrayed by Marlborough, retreated on the capital. On the 21st his Queen landed at Calais, smuggled out of England with the little Prince of Wales by Lauzun, who received the Garter and his full restoration to Louis' good graces for his services; and on 6 January 1689 the party reached St Germain. The fall of the Stuarts was the gravest setback which Louis had yet encountered, and a particularly exasperating one, for had James heeded Louis' warnings and accepted his proffered assistance, he might have been shored up on the English Throne. But no hint of Louis' anger showed itself in his reception of the fallen King and Queen, which was both generous and chivalrous; St Germain was hastily prepared for their occupation, and it is pleasant to discover that it was Louis himself who remembered to stock the nursery with toys.

The meeting of Queen Marie and Louis took place at Chatou, five miles short of St Germain. As soon as the King saw the little Prince of Wales, he ran to to kiss him; then turning to the mother who, to mark her gratitude, had got out of her carriage, he said, 'Madame, this is a very sad service which I do you today; but in the future I hope to render you greater and more useful ones'. At St Germain the Queen found all that would have been prepared for a Queen of France; and in addition, on her dressing table was a purse containing £3,000.

The Queen was followed by James II, who reached St Germain on 7 January, where he found Louis waiting to receive him; and let us note that the most arrogant monarch in Europe welcomed his guest, not in the Hall of the Guards, but beyond it, and 'gave him the hand'; honours which according to French etiquette would have been denied to every King except the Emperor. Courtiers hinted their surprise, but Louis said that on such an occasion as this he felt he must go beyond what was customary, in order to emphasize his respect for fallen Royalty, and the tender compassion with which he regarded a King in exile. It was a pattern of behaviour towards the Stuarts to which Louis adhered punctiliously for the rest of his life; even when James, with typical boorish ineptitude, insisted on retaining amongst his titles that of 'King of France', Louis made no protest; and years later, when Louis was an old man, if 'James III' danced at Versailles, the King of France got up and stood bare-headed until the 'King of England' sat down.

But to return to this 7 January. The two Kings were 'locked in a long embrace', and then Louis conducted his brother King to the Queen of England's room and presented him, saying, 'I bring you a man whom you will be very relieved to see'. And when the two Kings separated, Louis said to James, 'I do not want you to show me out; today you are still my guest; tomorrow you will come to see me at Versailles. I will do the honours there and you will do the same when I return your call; and after that we will live together informally'.

Louis was now spending much of his time at St Cyr; 'he had an air', we are told, 'of being at home there'. And on 26 February at a performance of *Esther* we find him acting as door-keeper; he stood outside the door of the theatre and held his cane across it to act as a barrier; and remained there until all who had invitations had entered; then he had the door shut.

This afternoon of February 26 has been immortalized for us by the lucky accident of Louis having Mme de Sévigné among his guests; who preens herself with a naive and joyous snobbery which is irresistible; Maréchal de Bellefonds 'came of his own choice' to sit beside her, and immediately in front of her were two Duchesses and a Princess. And after the final curtain she had a brief conversation with the Sun-King himself:

LOUIS: They tell me, Madame, that you have enjoyed the play.
SÉVIGNÉ ('Without losing my head') Sire, I am charmed with it; I have no words to say what I feel.
LOUIS: Racine is a man of parts.
SÉVIGNÉ: Yes Sire, indeed; but truly these girls have great ability;

they enter into their roles as if they had been acting all their days.

LOUIS: Yes indeed, that is true.

Nothing could be flatter, but it is worth preserving this artless example of the way in which France hung on the lips of her King.

But Louis showed up better than this when James II left to reconquer Ireland—'I hope I never see your face again', was his farewell to the exile.

In this year Louis devastated the Palatinate, a far blacker crime than the revocation of the Edict of Nantes; and his apologists make the same excuse in both instances—he was ignorant of the brutalities which were perpetrated in his name. Possibly he was, but why? And it is of course true that Louvois conceived this strategic operation, which smells rather of our own century than of the XVIIth. The plan, faithfully executed, was that the Austrians were to be denied the Palatinate as a zone of manoeuvre by turning it into a desert; towns and châteaux were blown up, cattle, crops, vines, farms and their utensils were destroyed, bridges demolished, and the inhabitants were forbidden under pain of death to attempt the rebuilding of their burnt-out villages. Only one thing can be said for Louis, namely that in spite of Louvois some compensation was ultimately paid, and those Rhenish peasants who were lucky enough to escape starvation and strong enough to survive the journey, were allowed to settle in Alsace tax-free for ten years. But this was a drop in the ocean, and the appalling misery inflicted left an indelible impression in Germany; up to the first World War, and perhaps still, Palatinate children learnt their alphabet from picture books in which each letter illustrated some aspect of the atrocities of 1689; and the ruins of Heidelberg castle were preserved as a monument to French barbarism.

The devastation widened the breach between Louis and 'Madame-Palatine'; for these outrages were committed ostensibly 'to enforce the claims of my sister-in-law, the Duchesse d'Orléans'. Thus, as 'Madame' lamented, she was made the destroyer of her dear native land, and of her favourite town, Mannheim, which had been converted into a heap of ruins. And when she thought of all that had been blown up, she was so sad that she could not sleep; or if she did doze off, it was only to dream of the tragedy and wake with a start to a fresh realization of her people's sufferings. 'And', she concluded with angry bitterness, 'the King is offended at my grief!'

Nor does 'Madame' exaggerate, for we know from other sources that Louis was much hurt by her failure to rejoice at the success of his arms in the Palatinate. Louis' 'annoyance' at his sister-in-law's 'unpatriotic' attitude was perhaps the most striking example of that insensibility which in his worst moments was the product of his amazing egotism. He was a paradox—cynically corrupt in foreign politics, at home fair and just; brutal, kindly, insensible, considerate, he was all these by turns.

At the very time he was committing these outrages in Germany, at home he sentenced Hervé, doyen of the Paris magistrates, to dismissal and exile for using his official position to evade the payment of his debts; gave a Court lady £500 to compensate her for losses suffered from a fire in her apartment whilst she was his guest at Compiègne; and appeared to his own subjects to be 'truly Christian and truly great . . . spurred on by religious enthusiasm in the unequal struggle which he was maintaining against half Europe . . . defending Justice, Right, and God's cause'.

1690 provides what is easily the most valuable contemporary impression of Louis XIV which we have; for it is taken from a secret document, compiled by the Brandenburg Resident in Paris, who had been instructed by his master to prepare a complete dossier on France. It was of course sent to Berlin, not through the French post but by special courier, and was therefore safe from prying eyes; in other words it is an objective portrait of Louis by an experienced diplomat.

The King of France, he said, was not a man of outstanding ability, and had been badly educated; but he had made himself capable of carrying the whole burden of government on his own shoulders. Without being brilliant, profound, or particularly enlightened, he had in him the stuff which made a great king. He had discernment and penetration, was neither ill-tempered nor violent, judged men and affairs sanely and fairly. He had no forgiveness for those who, even by accident, betrayed his confidence. He talked little, but what he did say was both apropos and dignified. He had a natural leaning towards justice and equity, when he did not allow himself to be led astray by false maxims of La Gloire; and he was moderate in his passions, not easily angered, and of a sober and regular way of life. But, continued the Resident, he also had less praiseworthy qualities; he was extremely jealous of his authority, and absurdly sensitive on the subject, so much so that he became incapable of a fair, or even a reasonable decision when once he had got it into his head that his Royal authority was being disputed. His generosity was by no means disinterested, but was practised from ostentation, and he was always wavering between thrift and profusion; consequently often prodigal when he should have been thrifty, and vice versa. His early victories, coupled with the servile instincts of the French people, and incessant flattery, often tricked him into accepting eulogy as a candid appraisal of his actions. It would be a mistake, continued Spanheim, to imagine that his devoutness was feigned, for it was founded on religious principles so far as he was capable of understanding them; but his religion apparently had not taught him humility, charity, or compassion. Another thing to the King's credit was that he had no favourites, unless 'Monsieur' was counted as one; for he was allowed liberties forbidden even to the rest of the family. At meals his babble dominated and drowned all other conversation, a state of affairs tolerated by the King because he thus kept abreast of the gossip of the day. Underneath the glitter of the Court, said Spanheim, what had struck him most was the method and economy employed in its administration, and the excellence of the police service. And also the fact that gallantry, 'in which from time immemorial the French Court had been the instructress of all Europe', had disappeared as completely as blasphemy and impiety.

Another man who endeavoured to sum up Louis in this year was Fénelon, who was to become Archbishop of Cambrai in 1695, and upon whom Louis' verdict was 'the finest and most visionary thinker in my Kingdom'. This charming but ambitious ecclesiastic had first met Maintenon in 1688, had made a conquest of her, and by 1690 was her chief adviser on the delicate matter of promoting Louis' salvation. In January he wrote to her advising that she should make no rules for handling the King, and should not initiate any religious conversation with him unless she could do it naturally, and by interior guidance. She should behave to the King, he said, with simplicity, complaisance, liberty, and joyfulness, without foresight or reflection, like a little child; and in the long run Louis could not but relish that freedom of God's children which now scandalized him. Above all, she was not to be secret, reserved, or austere with him, and he, Fénelon, would prefer to hear that Louis rebelled against Mme de Maintenon's efforts rather than that he was distrait and indifferent.

From which it appears that Fénelon understood Louis better than he did Mme de Maintenon; who, one would imagine, would have found the role of a playful little child a difficult one to render convincingly.

On 20 April the Dauphine died, and 'the King saw her expire after he had spent an hour in prayer at the foot of her bed'. Her passing caused scarcely a ripple on the surface of Court life, and she is worth an obituary notice simply because she was the only woman who ever got her own way at Versailles in defiance of Louis' wishes. The King had wanted her to fill the place left vacant by Marie Thérèse, and the Dauphine had wanted to lead a retired life. Louis, backed by Maintenon, had made vain efforts to draw her out; he had thought that by dint of good treatment, and the 'noble and gallant turn he gave to his kind-nesses', he would induce her to hold a Court. But she responded so ill that at last he tired of rebuffs and left her to her solitude; and she passed her life in the dark, airless little closets behind her reception rooms, where her only amusement was to cook German messes with her favourite maid, Bessola.

But collectively, the women proved too much for Louis in one respect; they refused to alter their fashions at his bidding. In 1691 he found that to abolish the *fontange* coiffure 'gave him more trouble, and cost him more time than all his conquests'; and as soon as his back was turned, the *fontange* quietly reappeared. As late as 1712 he was still grumbling about female obstinacy, confessing that he was annoyed to find that with all his kingly authority, he had complained in vain about the height of ladies' head-dresses; not one of them would do their hair a fraction lower to please him. Then one day an English woman of no great position had arrived, with her hair dressed low; and immediately all the Princesses had gone from one extreme to the other.

In Louis' present war, that of the League of Augsburg, Maréchal de Luxembourg came into his own as the foremost soldier of his day. To the Parisian mob he was 'The upholsterer of Nôtre Dame', a nickname bestowed upon him in recognition of the number of enemy standards which he hung in the metropolitan Cathedral after each of his victories. But he himself was far prouder of a more esoteric distinction, his European handicap in the game of war; where he commanded for France, his opponent reckoned his presence as the equivalent of an additional 5,000 French troops of the first quality. And had Louis utilized his services to the full, his reputation would have stood even higher than it did. In 1690 the King chose him as his second-in-command for the 1691 campaign, and it was with considerable disgust that Luxembourg heard that his role would be to cover Louis' siege of Mons; and with misgiving, because he knew that France no longer had the safety margin needed to squander resources on a pompous siege, and also because his professional instincts were all opposed to the offensive-defensive to which the King was wedded. But he could only obey orders.

On 16 March Louis handed over Maintenon to the Dames of St Cyr, saying, 'I leave you all that I hold most dear'; and on the same day he finally rid himself of Montespan.

For twelve years Athénaïs had hung on at Court, neglected and despised, and she might have continued to do so indefinitely had not Louis taken the care of their daughter Mlle de Blois, afterwards Duchesse d'Orléans, out of her hands. This was for Montespan the last straw. Losing her temper completely she sent a bitter message to Louis asking his permission to quit the Court, 'and the King joyously gave her leave to do so'; and to make sure that the lady should have no second thoughts, he on the same day gave her rooms at Versailles to the Duc du Maine.

On 17 Louis left for the front, arriving before Mons on the 21st. As usual, the King's success was a certainty, and on 8 April he had the 'triumph' of accepting the surrender of the town. But with the disappearance of his youthful ardour he was less fitted than ever to command his armies. At Mons he had more troops than he knew what to do with, yet he was so nervous that he sent for heavy reinforcements; and had he been attacked, there were so many of them that they could not have been deployed on the ground available. The best that can be said for Louis' generalship in 1691 is that he was still attentive to the comfort of his men; in inspecting the lines, he used to visit the hospital to satisfy himself that proper care was being taken of the sick and wounded, and to the delight of his troops, he made a point of tasting their soup to see that it was of good quality.

Louis' absence from Versailles has given us his only surviving letter to Mme de Maintenon in which he betrays his feelings:

I take advantage of the departure of Montchevreuil to assure you of a truth which is too pleasant to me for me ever to tire of repeating it; it is that I love you always, and to a degree which I cannot express; and whatever affection you have for me, I have more for you, being with all my heart entirely yours.

Louis rarely showed anger, but this year the annual siege was enlivened by a quarrel with Louvois. The King altered the siting of a guard, and Louvois, dissatisfied with his master's judgement, took it upon himself to move the guard back to its old post; and Louis detected the alteration:

LOUIS: Who has posted you in this place again?
CAPTAIN: M. de Louvois, Sire.
LOUIS: But did you not tell him that I myself had selected the site?
CAPTAIN: Yes, Sire.
LOUIS: Well if that isn't Louvois all over. He thinks himself a General apparently.

And Louvois, in the expressive French phrase, had his head well washed by the King, who henceforward regarded his War Minister with a good deal of jealousy and suspicion; so much so that when Louvois died suddenly on 16th July, it was rumoured that he had committed suicide to avoid dismissal. But there appears to have been no truth in this.

With Louvois' death ends the age of the great ministers; Colbert had gone in 1683, and Seignelay, Louis' best Navy Secretary, in 1690; that Seignelay who has survived in Mme de Sévigné's exclamation on hearing of his death—*c'est la splendeur qui est morte!* And now Louvois. On Colbert's death his posts had been divided between several ministers; Seignelay was succeeded by the incompetent Pontchartrain; and Louvois by his young and inexperienced son, Barbézieux, who had inherited all his father's vindictive brutality along with a good deal of his capacity; but he was lazy and dissipated. From now onwards Louis was to be virtually his own War Minister and Navy Secretary; by October his working day had lengthened by four hours, whilst in December he could no longer spare the time to play the host at his evening receptions. Those who saw him, we are told, were astonished at his energy; he was holding more Councils than ever, and from six until ten at night he worked with Barbézieux or some other minister; and frequently he returned to his office for another spell of work after supper.

Everything that Louis did was news, and the change of ministers was no exception, attracting notice so far afield as Holland:

A DUTCH COURTIER: The most curious thing I saw in France was a king provided with a young minister and an old mistress.
WILLIAM (dryly): Which should have made it clear to you that he uses neither.

A *mot* which however contained less truth than William imagined.

Whether Louis realized in 1691 that his military exploits were no longer admired we do not know, but for some reason he was unwontedly modest about them this year. When in January 1692 the Provost of the Merchants was delivering a complimentary harangue on the King's victories, Louis turned to Luxembourg and said, 'You were mainly responsible for them'; and in August he wrote almost apologetically to Luxembourg, who had relieved him in command of the Army of Flanders:

I am satisfied that if I do not give you all my ideas, you will do as well without them; but *amour propre* makes me think that what I say may not be entirely useless, and that, capable though you are, I may be able to give you some hints.

Even the flattery of the Dames of St Cyr was not received as formerly:

A DAME: Sire, you should not have exposed your life as you did at Mons.
LOUIS: I did no more than my duty.
DAME: But the good of the State demands the preservation of your life.
LOUIS: A King's job is never vacant for lack of candidates; another would do better than I can.

1692 found Louis busily engaged in consolidating the position of his bastards; in February he married Mlle de Blois to his nephew, the Duc de Chartres, in spite of the frenzied opposition of the Duc's mother, 'Madame-Palatine'; and in March his favourite, the Duc du Maine, married Mlle de Charolais, daughter of the Prince de Condé; with the enthusiastic approval of her greedy and servile father. It was thus far Louis' most striking move in that elevation of his bastards for which he has been so much blamed; but what is generally ignored is that here as elsewhere, he was careful not to move in advance of what public opinion would tolerate. If the greatest Houses in France had not made their eagerness to intermarry with Royal bastards so shamefully obvious, it is unlikely that Louis would ever have withdrawn them from a luxurious obscurity.

In May the King assumed the Flanders command, taking with him a very reluctant Racine, who was fortunate in not having his letters to Boileau opened in the post. In the first of them he reported that on the previous day Louis had reviewed his army, with Racine in his entourage. The cortège set out at eleven, and, moving always at the trot, was on horseback until eight in the evening. The mere passage down the line took two hours, and, said Racine, he himself was so tired and dazzled by the glitter of swords and muskets, so deafened by drums and trumpets, that he let his horse go as it pleased and paid no attention to the spectacle—'I wished with all my heart that these people were in their own cottages with their wives and children, and I in the Rue des Maçons with mine'. And he concluded by saying that however tiresome reviews might be in an epic poem, they were infinitely more so in real life.

Whilst Louis besieged Namur the news arrived that his fleet had been decisively beaten at La Hogue, and was unfit to keep the sea. But the tidings affected him very little, for he was incapable of appreciating the significance of the disaster; to him a fleet was rather an appanage of Royal state than a vital instrument of policy. And he was too pleased at taking Namur 'under the moustache of William' to have any thought to spare for a setback on an alien and treacherous element.

His self-satisfaction over Namur is only too evident in his own Memoirs:

> The King left camp on 3 July to return by short stages to Versailles, the more satisfied with his conquest in that this great expedition had been entirely his own work; that he had undertaken it with his own lights, and executed it so to speak with his own hands, in full view of the enemy's army; that by the breadth of his foresight he had . . .

And so on for another page and a half.

But all the same, without him Namur might not have been taken; an admission made by his bitter enemy St Simon, who says that it was certain that without the presence of the King, they would never have carried the siege to a successful conclusion. The fatigue of mind and body which the King underwent, he says, brought on the most painful attack of gout which he ever had; but this did not prevent him from superintending everything from his bed, nor from holding Council meetings as if he had been at Versailles. And boastful though Louis was in his Memoirs, he showed himself a different man at St Cyr; one of the Dames congratulated him on 'his glorious prize, Namur':

LOUIS: (laughing): You should rather offer me your condolences, for all I did was to take a town, whilst M. de Luxembourg won a battle.

THE DAME: Your Generals, Sire, were acting under your orders.

LOUIS: Yes, but they accomplished more than I did.

Even after more than thirty years of continuous adulation, Louis still retained something of his innate common-sense.

By 1693 the King realized that, in the modern phrase, 'he had too much on his plate'. France was beginning to grow uneasy, and he himself 'wished at all costs to see his people happier'—if it could be done without relinquishing his role as arbiter of Europe's destiny. A position which he had in fact lost for ever, and his obstinate struggle to recapture it made it impossible to ease the burdens of his subjects. Twenty years of unbroken success had given him the subconscious conviction that it was part of the settled order of things that he should declare war when he felt like it, and make peace on his own terms when France had had enough; and it is hardly surprising that he was slow to realize that the initiative had passed into enemy hands for good. Indeed it required the shock of having his peace proposals rejected by the Allies in November to awaken him to the change which had come over Europe since 1667.

Among his minor troubles in this year was the conduct of Barbézieux. Louis had always been accustomed to submissive ministers, with whom he could live and work on friendly terms, and here was an ungrateful youngster whom he had raised to a high position, behaving with an *insouciance* which irritated Louis profoundly. But with his usual forbearance, he now tried what a warning might do. In May he wrote to Barbézieux' uncle, the Archbishop of Rheims:

I know what is due to the memory of M de Louvois. But if your nephew does not alter his way of life, I shall be forced to take drastic action. I shall be sorry to do it, but it will be unavoidable. He has ability, but does not make good use of it. He gives too many supper parties to Princes when he ought to be working; he neglects my business for his pleasures; he keeps officers waiting in his anteroom too long, and speaks to them haughtily and sometimes harshly.

Even in youth Louis had not been an easy man to entertain in his leisure hours, and as his anxieties deepened, the task became more difficult, as we learn from Mme de Maintenon herself; every day, she was at St Cyr before dawn, and when she got back she found the King in her room—'and I am badly in need of a rest when he has left me'. It must have been a considerable relief to her when, after a tedious journey with Louis to Flanders, he installed her at Namur on 18 May and proceeded to take command of his army at Gembloux on 7 June.

Much controversy has raged over Louis' actions in the next two days; those eager to defame him say that Gembloux, 1693, was simply Heurtebise, 1676, over again—Louis fumbling and irresolute, at best too fearful to seize victory when it was within his grasp, at worst too frightened for his own skin to risk a battle. The facts are that on 7 June the armies of the King and Luxembourg were within a couple of miles of each other, and together were stronger than that of William, who was entrenched at Park within easy striking distance of the French. The plan was that the combined French armies should cut William's communications by capturing Huy and Liège, and then exploit that favourable situation in a manner yet to be decided. And Louis' acts were to inspect his army on 8 June; announce on the 9th that he was handing over command to Luxembourg; that 'Monseigneur' would proceed to reinforce the Army of the Rhine; and that he himself would return to Versailles. And so far from being dictated by moral or physical timidity, Louis' sudden decision to reduce Flanders to a secondary theatre was the result of a prefectly tenable strategic concept; he had heard at Namur of the unexpected capture of Heidelberg by his Rhine Army, and decided to exploit this success vigorously in the hope of forcing the Emperor out of the war, rather than to employ his full strength in gaining a limited objective in the north which would not materially improve the long-term position of France. And as for the 'certain victory' over William which his detractors say he threw away, an attack on Park could not have had a better than even chance of success; as is clearly shown by the fact that Luxembourg, given a free hand, reconnoitred the Allied position on 18 June, decided that it was unattackable, and had to spend a month in coaxing William into a position where he could be assaulted with a reasonable prospect of success. So the parallel between Heurtebise and Gembloux turns out on investigation to have existed only in the imagination of Louis' enemies; and those of them who call attention to the fact that 'soon after' the King's return to Versailles Luxembourg did defeat William at Neerwinden, fail to point out that Luxembourg's victory was won on 19 July, after a month of manoeuvering had produced a tactical situation entirely different from that which had existed when Louis made his decision of 8th June. Finally, it is worth noting that Louis himself, who to the end of his days was ashamed of Heurtebise, had no misgivings whatever about his conduct at Gembloux; unless we count as a misgiving a certain regrettable jealousy of Luxembourg's brilliant exploits which Racine detected; he wrote to Boileau and asked his advice on how he should speak of Luxembourg in his official account of the campaign—'for you know how touchy the master is about anyone linking praise of others with that of himself'.

It was Louis' last campaign. The search for *la gloire* was finished, and from now on the King was to be found in his proper place, directing his Kingdom from Versailles; to the great relief of his Generals. Though their relief would have been greater still if Louis could have brought himself at the same time to abandon that meticulous control of detail which he still attempted to exercise from his desk.

Once back from the front Louis plunged into his usual many-sided activity, the trivial jostling with the important in the customary manner, and each receiving the same degree of attention. Economies great and small were now the order of the day; he cut off the chocolate and liqueurs which were normally served at his evening entertainments, and which had involved him in considerable expense; and he did not full up vacant abbeys as quickly as he had used to do, but kept them empty to distribute the revenues to the poor of the district in which the abbeys were situated.

Then he turned his attention to hooliganism, in dealing with which he showed sounder views than those held by many magistrates today; the Chevalier de La Vallière, nephew of his first mistress, was arrested about this time for breaking street lamps in Paris, and was by the King's orders sent to the prison of the Châtelet for two days; whilst his companion, the Duc d'Uzès, thought himself lucky to escape to his regiment on the frontier. Having no doubt fled to it to avoid the dread penalty of exile, which under Louis XIV had become the most potent instrument for disciplining the nobility; for what could be more terrible than to be shut off from the radiance of *Le Roi-Soleil?* But it is interesting to note that Louis' sentences of banishment were usually tempered by that paternalism which mitigated the severity of the *ancien régime.* When in August 1694 Mme du Roure was ordered to set out instantly for one of her father's estates 'for making certain remarks in Paris which had not been well received', Louis, knowing the condition of her finances, sent her £200 'to make things easier for her'. The lady's real offence by the way was that 'Monseigneur' was conducting a liaison with her.

'Monseigneur' was now a man in his thirties, the widowed father of three sons; but after the unbending custom of the day, imposed equally in Royal and peasant households, he was still primarily the obedient son of his father; seeking Louis' advice on all points, even the most trivial. As for instance, on what people he should, and should not ask to dinner:

> I shall give you no orders as to what guests you have to eat with you; you can pay that honour to whom you choose; but remember that it *is* an honour, and do not make it too common.

And here we may contradict the popular story that Louis regarded 'Monseigneur' as his 'official' son, and a man to be kept at arm's length. Louis' own letters tell a different tale:

> Trianon, 6 August 1694... I was at Marly today to see the accommodation; I hope that when you come home you will be pleased with yours.
> Versailles, 19 August 1694 ... I have not yet decided about a trip to Fontainebleau. I could not bear to pass Choisy (his son's country house) while you are not there; but after your return I will stop there with the greatest of pleasure for as long as you wish. I shall find myself very lonely at Fontainebleau without you.

And these letters were written at a time when Louis had good reason to be annoyed with his son; for 'Monseigneur' had, as the courtiers put it, 'set up his own Maintenon' by secretly marrying Mlle Chouin, a Maid-of-Honour to the Princesse de Conti. But Louis' soreness at 'Monseigneur's' furtive conduct was neither deep nor lasting, and he ended by accepting the situation. When the news leaked out, Mlle Chouin was expelled from Court, but 'Monseigneur' and she continued to meet, first at Choisy and afterwards at Meudun. These interviews were kept secret for a long time, but first one person, then another, and finally everybody, was told about them; and at last the King and Mme de Maintenon consented to meet Chouin. They dined at Meudun, at which meal Mlle Chouin did not appear, but afterwards the King and his wife had a long talk with her.

Though Louis was not on active service in 1694, he continued to keep a sharp eye on the army which was nominally under the command of 'Monseigneur'; in June he wrote to him asking for news of desertions, which he feared were rather heavy, in spite of all 'Monseigneur's' efforts to catch the culprits; and with his usual sense of fair play, he advised his son to make careful enquiries as to whether it was not the Captains who were encouraging desertion by not looking after their men properly. And the King apparently exercised some disciplinary control over 'Monseigneur's' command from his office at Versailles; for a few weeks later he wrote to inform his son that he had sent the Colonel of the Regiment d'Angoumois in arrest to the château of Namur, because his regiment was worthless; adding that he would be kept there for a good long time 'so that other officers may see the necessity of applying themselves to carrying out my wishes'.

IX

In May 1694 Louis felt himself strong enough to take another step in aggrandizing his bastard sons, the Duc du Maine and the Comte de Toulouse; he created an intermediate rank for them between the Princes of the Blood and the Dukes. It was the most daring move which he had yet made, and he must have been conscious that he was sailing very close to the wind; but though there was a certain amount of grumbling, the necessary business was steered through the Parlement without any open protest from either the Princes or the Dukes. It was not Louis but his two bastards who were to reap the whirlwind of this audacious sowing.

The two boys were in their father's good books this summer, but it was otherwise with the girls, who seem to have been in constant hot water. The trouble began in August when Louis decreed that the youngest of them, the Duchesse de Chartres, should on the strength of her rank be addressed as 'Madame' by the other two, whilst she would address them as 'Sister'. La Vallière's daughter, the Princesse de Conti, though eleven years older than the Duchesse de Chartres, submitted with a good grace; but 'Mme La Duchesse' reacted characteristically. She did not positively refuse to obey, but she began to address the Duchesse de Chartres in public as 'my little pet'; and as St Simon remarked, nobody could be less like a little pet than the Duchesse de Chartres was in face, figure, and general appearance. The Duchesse, who saw that she was being laughed at, was furious, and Louis had some trouble in quelling the storm. One which would probably have had serious consequences for 'Mme La Duchesse' had not the King, like every other man at Court, found her irresistible. Now twenty-one, 'her whole appearance showing that she was the offspring of the tenderest love', she had been the wife of 'M. Le Duc', Condé's eldest son, for seven adventurous years; and handled that brutal and ferocious degenerate with such skill that he believed her to be in love with him whilst in fact she was the mistress of the Prince de Conti; for she was as clever as she was pretty. Selfish, but like so many clever and selfish people, quite charming; gay, witty, lively, the best of good company—'It was impossible to refrain from trying to please her'. No one ever saw her out of temper, and she had a free and gracious manner which put all at their ease; for the rest, she had a talent for composing witty and indecent verses, some of which have survived on their merits; could drink most men under the table; and hid a good brain behind a mask of frivolity. Unlike the Duchesse de Chartres, she was not in the least afraid of the King, knowing that his irritation at her pranks would always be short-lived. Though at times Louis would talk to her very severely, as for instance in 1696. She and her sister had just been reprimanded by him for letting off fireworks under 'Monsieur's' windows in the middle of the night, when they were detected in a further outrage; 'Monseigneur' found them one evening in the room they shared at Marly, smoking pipes which they had borrowed from the Guardroom. Knowing what the consequences would be if their conduct came to light, he made them leave off; but unfortunately the smell of burning tobacco had already penetrated into the King's room. And on the next morning the two culprits had a dressing down from Louis, of which the peroration was a reminder that they both owned country houses to which they were in danger of paying long visits. 'And the threat', we are told, 'had a good effect'.

On 4 January 1695 Louis' only remaining first class General, Maréchal de Luxembourg, died at Paris, and for the King this was almost as damaging a blow as had been the Stuart *débâcle* in 1688; France was in the middle of a critical war, and there was no one to fill Luxembourg's place. 'Monseigneur', with unprecedented courage, urged his father to give the Army of Flanders to Conti, a real soldier and one of the most popular men in France, but was well snubbed for his pains. Louis does not even seem to have considered Conti's qualifications for the post; recollections of what he had suffered at the hands of the Great Condé in the Fronde excluded all other aspects of the matter from his mind, and he could only see in Conti another pretender to a share in his Kingly authority—'I am surprised that you dare to ask a Command of this importance for a Prince of that House', he said to 'Monseigneur'; 'interests of State demand that the Condés should never be allowed to be more powerful than they are now'. The incompetent Villeroi replaced Luxembourg, and of his campaign all that we need say is that on his return, the Paris mob hung a wooden sword in a straw belt on his front door, whilst his Maître d'Hôtel, visiting the Paris market, was pelted with rotten apples and turnips.

But unpromising as the military situation was, the financial was even more serious, and taxation increased by leaps and bounds. In January came the notorious Poll-Tax, often represented as the last straw that broke the French camel's back; but was it as bitterly resented as some of Louis' contemporaries would have us believe? As soon as its terms were published, the officers of the Swiss Guards petitioned the King to cancel their exemption from the new tax, assuring him that the whole regiment was as well-intentioned towards him as were his born subjects. And in the following month the liveried servants in Paris sent a deputation asking that they too should be permitted to pay, on the ground that domestics were as well able to do so as were soldiers and peasants.

No doubt these incidents had a tonic effect upon Louis, but it was a momentary one, and his increasing depression was evident throughout the year. He was more than usually resentful of minor illnesses, and in his religious life Maintenon found 'a tepidity which drives me to despair'. Writing to Cardinal de Noailles, the Archbishop of Paris, on 27 December she said that to call what had passed between the King and herself before his Christmas devotions a conversation, was a misnomer. She had been unable to get anything out of him, though she had told him a little about St Augustine; and as this had been well received, she had suggested that it might be both amusing and instructive if they made a habit of reading some pious book together, 'and that I thought it must be Father La Chaise who opposed the idea'. Whereupon the King had said that on the contrary, La Chaise had made the same suggestion. That she had then gone on to remind him how he had formerly pressed her to read Fénelon and St François de Sales to him, and spoke of her grief at his subsequent loss of interest in these matters; and that for all reply, the King had said that he was not a man to follow anything through to a logical conclusion.

As Louis' religious zeal cooled, he seems to have fallen back on his old idea that piety consisted in living disagreeably, in refraining from amusement, and in cultivating boredom; and of his entourage only 'Monsieur' was outspoken in his annoyance at the formal devoutness which had fallen like a wet blanket over Versailles and Paris. Telling

161

the King indignantly at supper one night that he was just back from the St Germain's Fair, where he had found that gambling had been forbidden, and that 'M. Le Duc', when he called for dice, had been refused them; that even eating and drinking were discouraged, and that the porters and water-sellers no longer dared to ply their trades on a Sunday. To which tirade Louis returned no answer.

As regards amusements at Court, let us hear 'Madame', who about the same time was pouring out her complaints to a friend in Germany. An *appartement* she said, was an intolerable business. One went to the billiard room, where one lay on one's belly almost, and remained doubled up in absolute silence until the King had finished his game. Then came a concert where was sung an act from some old opera which everybody had heard a hundred times before. After this, a ball, where those who did not dance sat for two hours watching an interminable minuet. Then at quarter to ten there was country dancing, 'one performing after another like children saying their catechism'; and so at last the 'entertainment' came to a close.

Even in Louis' effortless compliments, the note of sadness and disillusionment was becoming apparent; 'Here everything grows old except your eloquence, Monseigneur', he said to Mascaron after hearing him preach in this year.

There is no more surprising trait in Louis' character at this time than the tolerance which he, with so exalted an opinion of his own status, exhibited towards his critics; against the Paris pamphleteers he disdained to act, and he was more than magnanimous to Fénelon when in December the Abbé attacked him savagely and personally in a letter which was really a fair sized pamphlet. It is much too long to quote, but a few sentences taken at random, will give its general tone:

You are praised to the skies for having outdistanced the grandeur of your predecessors, that is to say for having beggared France to introduce a monstrous luxury at Court ... Your extended frontiers have been unjustly acquired ... those who have signed treaties with you have done so in the spirit of a man who gives his purse to an armed robber ... You have always wished to give peace as the master, and impose conditions instead of negotiating fairly and with moderation ... and meanwhile your people die of hunger ... France is nothing more than a desolate and impoverished hospital

... You do not love God, and your fear of Him is that of a slave; your religion is superficial and formal ...

And what was Louis' revenge? To promote Fénelon to the Archbishopric of Cambrai, the richest See in the gift of the Crown.

In fact throughout his life we notice that, except when bigotry blinded him, Louis' anger was seldom aroused by boldness, even effrontery, provided that it was not merely factious; he kept his wrath for conduct that was mean and unworthy of a man of quality. When in 1696 the plot to murder William of Orange was uncovered, Louis was genuinely indignant that he should be suspected of having had any hand in the matter. The Prince of Orange, he told his Court, would do him the justice to believe that he had no intention of procuring an assassination, for he knew very well that he, Louis, had kept certain people in prison for the last two years merely for having suggested such a thing.

In this summer Louis at last succeeded in breaking the formidable ring of enemies by which he was surrounded; the Duke of Savoy made a separate peace with France on 25 August 1696, and his defection paved the way for the general peace which was to come next year. From Louis' personal angle the important clause proved to be that whereby the Duke's daughter, Marie Adelaide, was to marry Louis' eldest grandson, the Duke of Burgundy; for this wholly delightful little person was to be the last of the King's child-friends, and was to win him more completely than anyone had ever done before; was too to conquer Maintenon, who as early as 5 August was preparing for the arrival of the Savoy Princess. A conversation which she had with the King on the subject shows by the way that she was not so chary of intervening in matters of business as she would have had posterity believe:

LOUIS: I am going to see a man (Father La Chaise) whom you think a good sort of fellow, but of no ability.

MAINTENON: You must think the same, or more so; for you see him oftener than I do.

LOUIS: True; and my opinion of his talents gets lower every day.

MAINTENON: Well, do not let him give me some stupid as confessor for the Princess (of Savoy); tell him to consult the Archbishop, who has the highest opinion of some of the Jesuits.

LOUIS: Do you make some enquiries for a suitable man, and I will ask for him.

In September it was big news that Louis had a carbuncle on the back of his neck; which at first strikes us as yet another instance of that exaggerated interest in the Sun-King with which we are now familiar. But in fact the anxiety was not unwarranted; with the insanitary surgery of the day, any incision was more likely to produce blood-poisoning than not, and all Europe was quite justifiably agitated as to what would happen if Louis died in the middle of the war; but he was fortunate, and by the end of the month he was entirely cured.

On 16 October the eleven year old Marie Adelaide of Savoy arrived on French soil, where Dangeau, her Chevalier d'Honneur, met her on behalf of the King; and almost from that moment the unfortunate man was deluged with advice and admonitions from governess Maintenon, all agog to take possession of her last and most important pupil. If the Princess did not give the lie to first impressions, she wrote they would be only too happy to have such good material to work upon. Dangeau should encourage her to play 'Madame', a game which would accustom her to conversation; blind man's buff would fortify her health; and there was nothing like spillikins for promoting dexterity.

On 4 November Louis met the child at Montargis, and at half past six he sat down to give Maintenon his first impressions:

> I arrived here before five, and the Princess just on six. I went to greet her at the carriage. She let me speak first, and then answered very nicely, with a touch of shyness which would have pleased you. I led her to her room through the crowd, showing her from time to time by bringing the flambeaux close to her, and she played her part with grace and modesty . . . She has the best grace and figure I have ever seen; though thin, as befits her age . . . I find her just what I wish, and would be sorry if she were more beautiful . . . I hope I shall be able to maintain the easy, familiar air I have adopted until I get to Fontainebleau.

> Ten o'clock.

> The more I see of the Princess the better pleased I am . . . We leave tomorrow at half past ten, and will be home at five by the

latest. I am entirely contented; nothing in her which is not apropos in answering questions ... her politeness is remarkable ... her air noble, her manners polite and polished. I am pleased to be able to tell you all this good of her, for I can do so without flattery.

On the 8th the new Princess was formally welcomed by the Court, and from 'Madame' we get a more dispassionate opinion of her than that given by Louis. She was, said 'Madame', not exactly big for her age, but she had the figure of a pretty doll, nice blonde hair, and plenty of it, black eyes, long eye-lashes, a fine skin, a little nose, and the Hapsburg lips and chin. She was very serious for a child of her age, took little notice of 'Monseigneur', and barely looked at 'Madame' or the Duc de Chartres. But as soon as she caught sight of Mme de Maintenon she smiled and threw herself into her arms; 'from which', says 'Madame', 'you can see what a little courtier she is already'. Everyone at Court, she continued, had turned childish, and 'Madame' herself had led a party of ladies to play blind man's buff with the Princess on the previous day.

Marie Adelaide's conquest of Louis was immediate and complete, and their undisturbed affection for each other was to be the King's chief solace for the next sixteen years. His own children, even the Duc du Maine, never quite succeeded in forgetting that their father was the King of France, nor could they throw off a certain constraint in his presence which Louis himself was powerless to dispel; they never for instance dreamt of entering his presence unsummoned. But to Louis' delight Marie saw in him only Grandpa Louis, an agreeable old gentleman who was more amusing than most of the men about his vast and bewildering Court. And she gave him a good deal of her company; bursting into his private room unannounced, even when he was working, perching on his knee or the arm of his chair, pulling his wig, shuffling his papers, and flitting restlessly about the office; then, after an impetuous kiss, flashing off elsewhere. That she should have won the heart of Louis, who spoilt her outrageously, is not very surprising, but we should hardly have expected her to make an instant conquest of Mme de Maintenon. But she did; behaving to 'Aunt' as she called her, with a blend of affection, obedience, and familiarity which Maintenon found irresistible. But all the same, 'Aunt' had no intention of letting Marie develop into the spoilt darling of the Court;

and soon after her arrival the child found herself transformed—with her own enthusiastic consent—into 'Mlle de Lastic', a day-girl at St Cyr. There she occupied herself with the Dames in charge of the various departments, and with the other pupils in their work and lessons, submitting to the rules of the house, even to that of silence; running about at recreation with the Red Class in the garden, going with them to Chapel, confession, and catechism; several times appearing in the chorus of *Esther;* and often shut up in Mme de Maintenon's private room, where she acted as her secretary.

It would have been better for other precocious great ladies, and for France, if they had had the same upbringing; how childish, we say as we read of their fits of rage, their extravagance, their complete lack of self-control. Forgetting that these Duchesses, Countesses, and Marquises were literally children; on 3 September 1698 Louis, being then at Compiègne, took five married ladies of title for a drive in his coach; and noted with amusement that their combined ages fell short of seventy.

One of the five was Marie Adelaide who on 7 September 1696 had been married to the Duke of Burgundy, though so far the marriage was mere ceremonial, Louis having decreed that the couple would not live together until the bride was fourteen. The fifteen-year-old groom, Louis de France, Duke of Burgundy, was a very different character to his wife. Fénelon's masterpiece he has been called, but there were few contemporaries who approved of the education which had been given him. The general opinion was that 'Monseigneur's' three sons had been 'horribly ill brought up'. They ate by themselves, went for walks by themselves, and attended practically no Court functions. At nine in the morning they visited the King, who did not see them again for the rest of the day; and though they showed themselves at an *appartement*, they came in just as the concert began, and fled the moment it ended; and they never visited or received visits.

From this disparaging account we see that Burgundy was the son of that mother whose love of solitude had been strong enough to enable her to defy the wishes of Louis XIV; and he had started life with the further handicap of being a neurotic valetudinarian, a condition due to his surgeon's clumsy and painful treatment of a misshapen bone. Consequently when Fénelon took him over at the age of seven, he found a child who would have been the despair of most tutors—'he was born terrible, and in youth made all men tremble'. Greedy, insatiable in his demands for pleasure, given to insane fits of rage, and with an arrogance which prompted him to regard his brothers as a species intermediate between himself and mankind. But on the credit side, a boy with good brains, who was both open and truthful.

It was on this unpromising material that Fénelon worked a miracle. Out of the depths there emerged a Prince gentle in all his ways, penitent, modest, kindly, affable, and austere towards himself so far as the duties of his station would allow. Conscious of his responsibilities, he thought only of combining his duties as a son and a subject with those which he would be called upon to perform hereafter. One great piece of good fortune the youth had; he fell so passionately in love with his little wife that from 1699 onwards his existence may be described as one long honeymoon; and if she, as we are told, 'was touched by his passion rather than passionately in love with him', she at any rate made him very happy; and their married life was regarded as a model by the whole Court.

The Duke had need of all the marital comforts with which he could surround himself, for in the family at large he was never persona grata. His father disliked him as much as 'Monseigneur' was capable of disliking anyone; and his grandfather regarded Fénelon's masterpiece with a dubious eye. 'A St Louis strayed into the age of Voltaire', was to be the verdict on the Duke in years to come, and had Louis heard it, his doubts would have been confirmed. That His Most Christian Majesty should be represented at the Heavenly Court by St Louis was all very well and proper, but a second St Louis on the throne of France might spell disaster. However, the situation never arose, and we are left to speculate on what would have been the fate of the Monarchy had Burgundy come to the Crown in 1715.

To a considerable extent it was Louis' dissatisfaction with Fénelon which was reflected in his dissatisfaction with the shy and awkward dévot with whom Fénelon had saddled him; for the brief days of that ecclesiastic's favour were over. Always a mystic, Fénelon had been steadily deviating from orthodoxy for some time past, and in this year Louis found it necessary to banish him to Cambrai for his sympathy with Quietism. And the King reflected with increasing bitterness that it was Maintenon's fault that Fénelon had been promoted; for she could almost be said to share Church patronage with Louis, as is evident from this letter of hers to the Archbishop of Paris:

> Would it not be a good idea, Monseigneur, to make a list of good Bishops when you have time, and send it to me so that on those occasions which are always cropping up, I could uphold their interests ... I am always asked for my opinion on these matters, and I could take a bolder line if I were better informed.

On 20 September 1697 peace between France, Holland, and England was signed at Ryswick, and on 30 October between France and the Empire. Among the clauses of the first treaty was one whereby Louis recognized William of Orange as King of England, and in connection with it we notice one of his scrupulous attentions to the feelings of the exiled Stuarts; he gave orders to his choirmaster that nothing was to be sung at Mass which referred to the peace, lest it should hurt the feelings of James II and his Consort.

Almost at once Louis turned his attention to the problems raised by the peace which his country so badly needed; and on 30 September his opening words to the Council of Finance were, 'We must now seek means to reduce taxation with as much diligence as we sought to increase it during the war'. And in the field of international diplomacy he bent all his energies to negotiating such a partition of the Spanish Empire after the death of Charles II of Spain as would obviate the risk of another European conflict.

But nothing could conceal from the King the fact that the Peace of Ryswick was a heavy blow to French prestige; after nine years of fighting, Louis had emerged from the war almost in the position which he had occupied after Nimeguen in 1678; with however the fatal difference that he was now much further on the road to bankruptcy. He was at best a King who was standing still, and that by his own definition was a King who was going backwards. Even his subjects were aware of how greatly Louis' prestige had declined, and were proportionately indignant. In November the Venetian Ambassador reported to his masters that the Paris fishwives were protesting that they would have consented to go on paying the Poll-Tax for many years more rather than have such a peace as this. And he added that the blame for such an ignominious treaty was generally imputed to Mme de Maintenon, who had become odious in all eyes.

Maintenon had never been popular with the public, but so far her stock had not sunk so low as it did in 1697; in this year the King had to dismiss the Italian Players for putting on *The Mock Prude*, a piece in which Mme de Maintenon was openly satirized; an impertinence which would have been unthinkable ten years earlier. Louis was not the man to under-rate the significance of such an incident, and his gloom threw a deeper shadow over the Court than usual; 'except by piety', sighed Mme de Lafayette, 'there is no salvation at Court'; and her view is strikingly corroborated by Prior, who accompanied Portland to Versailles after the signature of peace. The whole Court, said Prior, was sad and sombre; and bigotry reigned to such a degree that one saw girls kneeling at prayer in the galleries as if they were in a convent. Whilst the Lifeguards would lay down their arms and knot fringes, as girls did in England.

In 1698 Louis was a tired and anxious man, and it is small wonder that he could not always hide his irritation; when in this year 'Monsieur' saw fit to harangue him on the misery of the people, the King burst out:

Well, when four or five hundred thousand of this *canaille*, so useless upon the earth, have died, will France be any less France? Be so good as not to meddle with matters which do not concern you.

And he had of course been reproached for a remark 'worthy of a tiger rather than a Christian'. Just as if he were in fact the passionless demigod his idolaters claimed him to be. It was a deplorable remark no doubt, but surely to anyone with insight, nothing more than the exasperated outbreak of a very human man, tormented beyond endurance by the gadfly persistence of 'Monsieur'?

For he had at this moment several causes for exasperation, notably the mud stirred up by Fénelon in the Quietist dispute, which showed no signs of subsiding; rather the contrary. Louis' worldly commonsense was outraged at the thought that mysticism, a cult so entirely alien to his temperament, and which he was incapable of understanding, should have set his Kingdom by the ears. To him it was a 'novelty' like the Jansenism with which he confounded it, and once Louis had got it into his head that anything was an innovation, the novelty and its sponsor were irretrievably damned in the Royal eyes. And in his anger Louis cut blindly and injustly at the theological

169

spider's web in which he was entangled. In June he banished four gentlemen of the Duke of Burgundy's household on the mere suspicion of their being 'warmly attached' to the new opinions, and worse still, cashiered Fénelon of the Guards, apparently for no better reason than that he was the Archbishop's brother.

But it was upon Mme de Maintenon that the brunt of Louis' anger fell, and in this same month they had the only serious quarrel of their married life. He reproached her sharply for having persuaded him to appoint to Cambrai a man who was little better than a heretic, and so bitter was his wrath against her that she herself afterwards confessed that she had never been so near disgrace as she was in 1698.

So deeply wounded was Mme de Maintenon at Louis' treatment of her that she was unable to hide her grief from the Court; the *Pantocrate*, wrote 'Madame' gleefully, had great power; but at the same time she was not the happiest woman in the world, for she was often seen to shed hot tears, and she was constantly speaking of her own death. But Maintenon was rather given to saying that she wished she was dead, though only once did she so express herself to her brother, whose retort ran round a delighted Court—'Why? Has God the Father promised to marry you then?'

Her lot however was much less enviable than brother d'Aubigné thought it. Writing to the Archbishop of Paris from Compiègne in September, she told him to correct his impression that she was having a holiday. The King, she said, was in her room three times a day, which prevented her from doing anything which she wanted to do. Her desire, she continued, was to occupy herself with good works—'It seems to me that I would be more fittingly employed on a charitable committee than in running about an army camp with a child of twelve' (the Duchess of Burgundy).

It was not until the end of June that Maintenon was restored to Louis' good graces; but by 2 July all had been forgiven, and the King resumed his visits to St Cyr:

> 2 July 1698. I think I shall be able to go to Compline at St Cyr, if you approve, and we will walk back together afterwards ... Should you agree, find some ladies to walk with us, and let me know your wishes that I may comply with them.

To be able to revisit St Cyr must have gratified Louis almost as much as did the reconciliation with his wife, for there he not only found the deepest content left to him, but also experienced a religious quickening which died amidst the formal pomp of Versailles Chapel. The taste for pleasures, said Mme de Maintenon, was now dead in him; age and religion had brought serious reflections on the vanity of what he used to enjoy. He now patronized fêtes and theatricals with reluctance, and grumbled to her about the constraint of rank which forced him to take part in pleasures which were no longer such to him. And he admitted that nowhere could he pray as he did at St Cyr, where the order, silence, and calm refreshed and delighted him. He had by now accustomed the Dames of St Louis to treat him familiarly and to chat freely with him. And better still, had habituated the children to regard him as an old friend; often in summer he could be found sitting under a tree in the garden with a little girl on his knees, who chattered to him with a freedom which she would never have attempted with her own parents. And whenever one of the girls married, Louis would have a talk with her before signing her marriage contract; for such was still the glamour of his prestige that his signature was as good as a dowry. More than one noble went to St Cyr for a wife, only in order to have that magic 'Louis' sprawled at the foot of the contract of marriage.

Before July was out, Maintenon had, with female resilience, recovered from the fright which Louis had given her over the Fénelon affair, and had resumed her role of guardian angel; not always with success. In a note written to her *directeur* in July she confessed that she had 'failed to please' in a conversation with the King on his building extravagances, and that she was grieved to have vexed him to no good purpose. That he was again building at Marly, and the new work was to cost £9,000. Marly, she said, would soon be a second Versailles, but there was nothing to be done but pray and be patient.

But husband-like, Louis, though feeling it due to his dignity to administer a snub, apparently took his wife's expostulations to heart. For a few days later we hear that when Pontchartrain proposed to him that he should pull down the buildings on the Place Vendôme and reconstruct the Square after a design of Mansart's, Louis' dry response was that all ministerial gentlemen were anxious to do something that would ensure that their names were remembered by posterity; that they were skilful enough to persuade the public that it was the King who was wedded to these vanities; and that he had no intention of falling into that trap again.

On 15 April died one of the greatest figures of a great century, Jean Racine; and Louis' behaviour during his last illness and after his death completely destroys the romantic story of Racine's 'disgrace'. From 15 March, when the poet was reported to be at his last gasp, until the end, Louis, who so hated to be reminded of death and shrank from all contact with it, not only sent daily to enquire for his Historiographer, but granted the dying man's last request, that he should be buried at Port-Royal. Soon after his death Louis spent an hour with Boileau, Racine's oldest friend, and opened the conversation by saying, 'We have each lost a good friend'. And on 7 May he bestowed a pension of £175 on Racine's widow.

We may remember that back in 1690 Spanheim had praised the admirable police of Versailles. Either he was mistaken in its efficiency or else it had deteriorated considerably since Spanheim's time, if we are to judge from two curious incidents this summer; on 3 June over £12,000 worth of harness was stolen from the Royal stables, and neither the thieves nor any of the missing articles were ever traced. And at about the same time the bullion tassels and fringes of the velvet curtains in the *Grande Suite* were cut off and removed, without any arrest ever being made. But this time there was a sequel; five or six days later, whilst the King was at supper, a large parcel, thrown by no one could discover whom, fell on the table, and on being opened was found to contain the missing fringes, with a note—'Take back your fringes, Bontemps, they are more trouble than they are worth. My respects to the King'. But if the thief was present at the denouement it must have been a disappointment to him. 'That', said Louis quietly, 'is a great piece of insolence'. And he continued his supper as if nothing had happened.

In August occurred an odd event which remains one of the lesser mysteries of the reign. The blacksmith of the little Provençal town of Salon arrived at Versailles, demanding a private audience of the King, to speak to him on a matter of the highest importance; and by his persistence he at last got access to Louis himself. He had, he said, seen and spoken to the late Queen Marie Thérèse, who had appeared to him in a glow of light in a dark lane and given him a message for the King; and as proof of its genuineness had entrusted him with a secret which could be known to no one but the King himself. Louis saw the man alone on two occasions, and talked to him each time for more than an hour; after which he gave him a present of money, paid his travelling expenses back to Salon, and ordered the Intendant of Provence to see that he lacked nothing for the rest of his days. All that ever came to light about the affair we have from Louis himself; Maréchal de Duras, a man who was on a footing of being able to say whatever he liked to the King, tried the day after the first interview to draw Louis when they were out shooting together. Duras approached the subject by quoting the vulgar proverb that if the man was not mad the King was not noble. At which Louis stopped, a thing which he seldom did whilst walking, and turning to the Maréchal, said, 'If that is the case, I am not noble, for I have talked to that blacksmith for a long time. He spoke most sensibly, and I can assure you that he is very far from being mad'. And the words were uttered with 'an emphatic gravity which surprised the bystanders'.

Louis is frequently berated for his extravagance, but too often his effort, at economy are ignored by the same critics; take the Budget for 1700 for instance, in which we note that, as against that for 1699, the army vote had dropped by £500,000, the Navy vote by £200,000, and that for the Galleys by £150,000. And at Versailles he refused any longer to pay for alterations which courtiers had made in their rooms. At first one assumes the latter to have been one of those window-dressing economies so popular in democratic budgets, but on investigation it appears that in ten weeks of 1699 the expense under this head had been £5,000.

By 1699 Louis was definitely tiring of his white elephant, Versailles, which became less of a château and more of a town every day, swarming with an unauthorized population. In the spring of 1700, for example, we find that fifty Swiss had to be turned on to the task of expelling beggars from the passages. Even the King had reached the stage of admitting in public that Versailles had its faults; and when an impudent nonentity called Villiers loudly disparaged the King's taste, as exemplified by his paintings, architecture, and gardens, Louis merely remarked, 'It is strange that Villiers should visit me solely in order to find fault with my house'. Ten years earlier Colonel Villiers would have been 'advised' to air his opinions with his regiment.

It is indeed probable that to Louis the only attraction Versailles now had was its proximity to St Cyr. And when for any reason St Cyr was out of bounds to him, it was to Marly that he turned for recreation; there we find him on a November evening in this year, singing with Maintenon and the ladies whilst his daughter, the Princesse de Conti, accompanied them on the clavecin; a favourite instrument with Louis, who on another Marly evening was 'greatly amused' by the playing of a nine-year-old girl, whose touch he found 'delicious'. And he was always on the alert to see how he could make Marly more attractive to his guests. On this same visit, while strolling in the gardens, he ordered the men to put on their hats; much to the surprise of some visiting Spanish nobles. 'Gentlemen', said Louis to them, 'one is never supposed to wear a hat in my presence, but I don't want anyone to catch cold'. And indoors too, further efforts were made to emphasise the difference between Marly and all the other royal residences; drinks were served in the salon to anyone who called for them, so that they would not be put to the trouble of procuring them from outside; and low screens were placed around all the chairs, behind which courtiers were deemed to be invisible, and consequently did not have to get up when Princes of the Blood, or even 'Monseigneur' himself, entered the room.

But in spite of his multifarious activities and his restless journeyings from palace to palace, Louis could not shake off his depression; he saw in the public a new climate of opinion, increasingly critical of his regime, and the significance of Fénelon's *Télémaque* did not escape him; for its huge vogue was due to the fact that it was everywhere being interpreted as a satire on Louis' government. For the King's state of mind Maintenon is always the best barometer, and her reports to Noailles at this time were pessimistic. The King, she said, wished to accommodate religion to himself, not himself to religion; he desired its external practices, but not its spirit. He would never miss a Station or a Fast, but he did not understand the need of mortification and true penitence. And she concluded by saying that though she made every effort to cheer him up, she was not always successful.

Ever since the end of the war Louis had been working with his usual patient skill to frame a treaty for the imminent partition of the Spanish Empire which would appear satisfactory to all Europe; and in March one was at last ratified. By its terms a Hapsburg of the Austrian branch was to become King of Spain, whilst France was to be compensated with sundry territories, the most important of which were to be a large part of Northern Italy, and Sicily. The Spaniards were of course not consulted on this carving up of their possessions, but it was known both at Versailles and at Vienna that they were violently opposed to any partition whatsoever.

That Louis should have agreed to his old enemy the Emperor having the bigger slice of the cake showed his astonishing moderation; or rather it would have done so if we could be sure that he was acting in good faith. But according to Villars, the most brilliant of Louis' long succession of soldier-diplomats, the French King did not really believe that the Emperor would stand by the treaty; and as the Emperor entertained exactly the same misgiving about Louis, each began to put his house in order for a struggle which both regarded as inevitable. The Emperor had in fact signed only because he thought it would draw his former allies more warmly into his interests when war came, and Louis signed because he thought that his apparent moderation would go a long way to break up an incipient coalition hostile to France.

Such was the situation when at three on the afternoon of 1st November 1700 Charles II of Spain died at Madrid, leaving no children. It was an event which had been expected at any time since his birth in 1661, and indeed his survival until 1700 was nothing short of a miracle; son of a middle-aged, diseased father by that father's fifteen-year-old niece, he had inherited Philip IV's complaint; at four years of age he was as helpless as an infant, and at thirty-five he was senile. He could neither eat nor speak properly, and in addition to his inherited disease he suffered from dropsy and epilepsy; the Planet King he was called by his flatterers, but his grim unofficial title was Charles the Sufferer.

What was to occur when the Spanish Hapsburgs became extinct had been the major preoccupation of every cabinet in Europe for forty years; and the situation had grown more tense after 1679, when Charles's marriage had proved that he was incapable of begetting children. After 1680 hardly a move was made on the European chessboard which was not influenced by the momentous question of the Spanish inheritance, always in the background; and it is one of the chief indictments of Louis XIV's foreign policy that though he was as conscious as were his rivals of the supreme importance of the Spanish question, he frittered away in the Augsburg war, entered upon to escape an illusory encirclement, resources which it was his obvious duty to husband for the greatest struggle of the reign. An argument which begs the question as to whether the encirclement of France in 1688 was in fact a myth.

On 9 November a courier reached Versailles from Madrid with news of the Spanish King's death, and bringing with him a copy of Charles's will, whereby he bequeathed his vast Empire to the Duc d'Anjou, Louis' second grandson; but with the reservation that if Anjou refused to accept the donation in its entirety, the whole Spanish Empire was to be offered to the Austrian claimant; in other words, in no circumstances was there to be any partitioning.

In his will Charles explained away the renunciation made by his half-sister, Louis XIV's Queen, of any share in the Spanish inheritance by asserting that such renunciation was intended to be valid only on behalf of whatever Prince issuing from her, was in the direct line to become King of France. That Prince was the Duke of Burgundy, the eldest grandson; and therefore the indisputable heir at law was the late Queen's second grandson, the Duc d'Anjou. The courier bearing this weighty document seems to have reached Versailles about mid-day; and Louis, on hearing the news, cancelled the hunt he had ordered for that afternoon, and at three called a Council meeting in Mme de Maintenon's room, at which she was present. And the situation was debated until seven, when the Council broke up.

X

THE WEEK which elapsed between the famous Council Meeting on
9 November and Louis' decision on the 16th was the most momentous
in his long reign. During the whole time the King kept his thoughts to
himself, and no one could hazard a guess as to how he would decide;
not even his daughters, who on the 13th could get nothing from him
except the non-committal remark that he was certain that whatever
course he adopted would be condemned by many people. We now
know however that his decision had then already been made, for on
the 14th he wrote to his Ambassador at the Hague saying that he had
examined the pros and cons of standing by the Partition Treaty or of
accepting the Will. That if he stood by the Treaty, he quite understood
that he would enlarge his kingdom and weaken the power of the
House of Austria; but he also foresaw that he would have great
difficulty in getting peaceful possession of what had been allotted to him
by the Treaty; in fact so far as he could see, to give effect to the Treaty
would entail the conquest of the whole Spanish Empire as a preliminary
to carving it up—a move which would start a war to which he could
see no end. And that in brief, he had decided to accept the Will;
thinking that as he would almost certainly have to fight whatever he
did, he might just as well fight for the whole cake instead of a slice of it.

On 16 November there took place at Versailles what is perhaps the
most theatrical scene of a theatrical reign; so stagey that we miss the
limelight on the two Kings, and the crashing chord from the orchestra
as the doors open. The King's *lever* was just over, and the courtiers were
outside his private room, when to their surprise both leaves of the door
were flung open and Louis invited all who could, to enter. There they
found the Duc d'Anjou; and Louis, taking him by the hand, said,
'Gentlemen, I present you to the King of Spain; his birth called him to
that Crown. It is God's decree'. Then addressing his grandson, he said,
'Be a good Spaniard, that is now your first duty; but remember that
you are also a Frenchman, so that you may preserve the union between
our two nations'.

The youth of nineteen thus dramatically transformed into the Most

Catholic King, Philippe V, 'already had the manner of a King of Spain'; which is 'Madame's' indulgent way of saying that he had inherited the flaccid torpidity of 'Monseigneur', his father. He hardly ever laughed, very rarely spoke, and his mouth always hung open except when someone told him to shut it; and he was the least intelligent of the brothers, though a truthful, clean-living youngster whose only vice was sloth. But even had he been a clever man abounding in energy, and backed by capable advisers, his position for the next few years would have been an impossible one. For he was not a free agent; Louis might talk soothingly to Europe about the complete divorce between the French and Spanish Crowns which the renunciations guaranteed, but his frequent letters to his grandson show that this was flagrant windowdressing; and in these letters Louis appears as the business man who has bought up a semi-bankrupt concern, installed his grandson as manager, and is increasingly disappointed at the sloth and inefficiency with which the lad handles the orders and advice given him by Head Office at Versailles. And as for Philippe's advisers on the spot, Louis supplied them from Paris after consideration of a brief and pungent despatch from the French Embassy in Madrid; he had asked what were the occupations and possessions of the leading Spanish nobles, and had received the answer, 'Occupations, idleness. Possessions, pride, misery, and the pox'.

Louis wasted no time in hustling Philippe off to take over his inheritance, and on 4 December the new King left Sceaux, the Duc du Maine's country seat, for Madrid. After a highly emotional scene; even 'Monseigneur' was touched, and 'Madame' says that she thought both he and the King of Spain would die of grief, so deeply were they moved. After repeated farewells Louis escorted his fellow King to his coach, and Philippe set out for the frontier, surrounded until the last moment by a dense crowd, in which 'one heard nothing but sobs, and saw nothing but handkerchiefs held to streaming eyes'.

Before leaving Sceaux Philippe had had a private interview with Louis, and we know the gist of the orders which he then received; hold in esteem, said Louis, those who for good reasons risk your displeasure. Never neglect business for pleasure. Never make snap decisions, always listen to your Council before making up your mind. Never say anything that will wound anyone. Do not receive presents from your subjects, or if you must, give the donor a much richer present. And above all, never have a favourite or a Prime Minister.

The ease with which he installed Philippe at Madrid in January 1701 seems to have gone to Louis' head, and to have convinced him that the good old days when he had dictated to all Europe were come again; for on no other assumption can we explain his rash and provocative conduct in a situation of such delicacy as now existed. Hardly six weeks had passed since he had assured the world that the divorce between the French and Spanish Bourbons was absolute; then on 1st February he signed Letters Patent reserving to Philippe V and his heirs their places in the line of succession to the Crown of France. On the 5th, taking advantage of the fact that England and Holland were, as usual, wholly unprepared for war, he loosed his magnificent army into the Low Countries. And by the end of the month he had occupied Luxembourg, Namur, Mons, Charleroi, Ath, Oudenarde, Nieuport, and Ostende, in fact all the vital places from which it had taken nine years to dislodge him in the previous war. Not content with which, he must needs further exasperate Europe by refurbishing the old sophistry of 1667; he was, he said, merely acting as caretaker for his grandson until the new King of Spain could make his own arrangements for garrisoning the Spanish Netherlands, and when Philippe had done so, every French soldier would be withdrawn from Spanish soil. And on 17th April Louis was further encouraged in his high-handed policy by England's recognition of Philippe V, in the teeth of William III's efforts to force his country into war with France. In fact Louis was in a most favourable position. True, he was at war with the Empire, but an Empire handicapped by the defection of Bavaria and Cologne, and with its communications to Italy hamstrung by Louis' alliance with the Duke of Savoy; and at its strongest, the Empire had never been a match for Louis' France.

Even now it might have been possible to keep England neutral, or at worst a luke-warm enemy, in spite of the anti-French Grand Alliance signed on 7 September, had not Louis indulged in one of his reckless chivalric gestures which roused unwarlike England to a white heat of indignation. On 13th September he visited the dying James II at St Germain and told him that he could die at rest as regarded the Prince of Wales; for France would recognize him as King of England, Scotland, and Ireland.

Three days later James II died, and Louis formally recognized the

Old Pretender as James III; apparently forgetting, or being indifferent to the fact that he himself had recognized William III by the Treaty of Ryswick, and that not three months had passed since the English Parliament had by the Act of Settlement excluded the Stuarts for ever from the Throne. It was a piece of French insolence which England was unlikely to overlook.

Domestically as well as in the political field, it was a tragic year for Louis, who in it lost his well-loved brother, vicious, chattering, affectionate, ridiculous 'Monsieur'; who died of apoplexy at St Cloud on 9 June. And something of Louis himself died with him, for in losing 'Monsieur' he lost the only person with whom he could share his memories of Anne of Austria and of that old Court which, even to the brothers, now seemed so incredibly remote. And he lost too the one man with whom he could live in private on terms of complete familiarity. The King, said St Simon, had always allowed 'Monsieur' to use the freedom of a brother in private; and in public he had treated him as a brother, with all kinds of favour and consideration, taking care however that he should not become too important a personage. But if 'Monsieur' had an ache in his little finger the King used to go at once to see him, and repeated his visits until he was well again.

One pleasant result of Philippe's death was to bring about a reconciliation between Louis and the widow. 'Madame' tells us that on 12 June the King came to see her, and though in great sorrow himself, did all he could to comfort her; and that on the same day Mme de Maintenon advised her that this was the opportunity to become reconciled with the King. Whereupon 'Madame' sought an interview with Maintenon and confessed that she had long hated her for having deprived her of the King's good graces; but that she would forget the past in return for Maintenon's friendship—'She advised me to speak to the King with complete frankness. I followed her advice. The King embraced me, begged me to let bygones be bygones, and promised to restore me to his favour. In fact everything went off splendidly'.

'Madame' was as naive in her pleasure at Louis' graciousness as could be any provincial girl newly arrived at Versailles; on 19 June, 'the King is so kind'; on 14 July, 'I receive great consolation from the King'; and on the 28th Dangeau notes that 'The King desires "Madame" to take part in everything that is going on; he says that here she is *en famille*, and therefore there is no need for her to live in retirement'. The hunting parties were resumed, Louis and 'Madame' tête-à-tête in the King's four horse curricle, and a special performance of *Absalom* was staged at St Cyr for her benefit. In fact Louis, having determined to make up the quarrel, did the thing handsomely.

The King was now in his sixty-third year, but for him there could be no slackening of the pace; on the contrary, the burden was becoming heavier. Forty-seven years earlier he had plumed himself on the fact that he worked six or seven hours a day, now he not only maintained the old routine, but had sacrificed to his additional tasks the pleasant hours between five and ten in the evening. Nor did he make war an excuse for sparing himself the more ornamental duties of Kingship; on 14 July for instance, we find him going to the Invalides to watch his old soldiers dine.

A pleasant little trait in Louis' character, this care for the crippled, but as he began to grow old, he showed others which were less agreeable; notably his hatred of Jansenists, which was rapidly developing into a phobia. In this year a letter written by Mme de Maintenon to Cardinal de Noailles gives us an ugly impression of the witch-hunting atmosphere of the Court in 1701. The King, she said, was aware that Noailles had dealings, direct and indirect, with persons at Rome who were rabid supporters of the Jansenists. Everything, she warned the Cardinal, came to the King's ears, and it was not without reason that he suspected Noailles. Nor must Noailles imagine that it was Father La Chaise who had denounced him, for 'the old chap no longer has any credit'. But other people had written and spoken to the King, she said, and she reiterated her statement that Louis was very well informed—'it is he himself who has allowed me to give you this warning, which is a striking mark of his consideration for you'.

1702 gives us some significant glimpses of the unreality of Louis' pretence that Philippe V was a national King, standing on his own feet:

> Versailles, 26 February 1702. You express your desire to serve on the Italian front with too much eagerness for me to doubt the joy which my consent to your doing so has afforded you.

> Marly, 3 March 1702. I was considering only your own satis-faction when I sanctioned your plan of taking the Queen with you

to Naples; but my friendship does not permit me to keep silent about the inconveniences which I foresee in the plan . . .

10 September . . . No one else can tell you what I can . . . I will admit the sorrow with which I see that you lack the courage to fight a vice so odious (as sloth). I know that it drags you down, and that you give in to it whenever there is a question of listening to business discussions and applying yourself to them. I am sorry to say it, but I am assured that the letters which I get from you, and even those which you send to the Queen, are dictated by Louville . . . Do not imagine that the public remains ignorant of the fact; it was known to your subjects earlier than it was to me . . .

5 May, 1703 . . . I do not know why you ask my advice on your fear of making your own decisions. I have often urged you to over-come this. I shall be glad to hear that you speak as the master, and no longer to hear that you have to have your mind made up for you, even in trifles. It would be almost better that you should make mistakes by acting on your own decisions than to avoid them by remaining in leading strings.

It was a bad year for Louis in the field. In February Villeroi, who was a better hand at leading a cotillon than an army, was surprised and taken prisoner at Cremona; and all France poured ridicule on him. To the great annoyance of Louis, who spoke in the tenderest and most obliging way of his old friend. He told his courtiers that he was aston-ished and indignant at those who exulted in Villeroi's misfortunes; adding that he thought that the friendship with which he had honoured him had brought part of this hatred on the Maréchal. He even used the word 'favourite', which had never escaped his lips before in speaking of anyone; and he continued to talk for some time like a man determined to support a friend who had been unfortunate. It was very human that he should have come to the aid of the man who had shared his schoolroom at the Louvre and had been the confidant of his early love affairs; but it was more creditable to Louis' heart than to his head.

On 15 May England and Holland declared war on France, in October an unsatisfactory campaign closed with the loss of Liège and most of Guelderland, and at Court there was nothing but gloom and recrimination. A junior officer back from the front, tells us that at

Versailles all the Generals were muttering about the reproaches with which the King had received them on their return. Maréchal Catinat was thought to have forgotten his trade; Maréchal de Boufflers, usually a prime favourite, was reproached; Tallard was told that he had been imprudent; and officers visiting Mme de Maintenon found her 'very uneasy and out of temper, and felt the effects of her resentment'.

On the credit side of the ledger the only really important item was the death of William III, which took place on 19 March. And even that event was of less significance than had at first been thought; for William's lifework was done when he had built up his great coalition against Louis in 1701; and had built so firmly that the Grand Alliance was to resist all the strains put upon it until it had brought France to the edge of ruin. Militarily too, Louis lost by William's death, for with it his enemies were disembarrassed of the worst General in Europe.

For respite from the cares of this depressing summer Louis turned more and more to his pet, the Duchess of Burgundy, who had fallen in love with Trianon where she anticipated Marie Antoinette by playing at dairy-farming; and to Trianon Louis and his Court often went of an evening. Nothing, we are told, could be more magnificent than those evenings at Trianon; magnificent by the standards of the XVIIth century perhaps, but a magnificence which to us seems a trifle vulgar. For instance, in those immense gardens the bedded flowers were all changed every day; with the result that the scent of the tuberoses was often so strong that the whole Court was driven indoors.

Charmer though the Duchess was, we share the astonishment of the Court at the liberties she allowed herself towards the King; take for instance her doings on a July night in 1702. First she drove to a private ball in Paris —conduct frowned upon by Louis in anyone else—and there danced until five in the morning; after that she paid a surprise visit to the Halles, the central Paris market, then heard Mass, drove back to Versailles, and woke the King up to tell him all about it; a thing that a Minister of State, charged with the gravest of news, would have thought twice before doing. And Louis was delighted to see her.

1703 brought the King no relief. In January a Huguenot rebellion, fomented by the Allies, broke out in the Cévennes; in the summer

Villars' plan to take a French army down the Danube was ruined by his quarrels with the Elector of Bavaria; Marlborough drove the French out of Cologne; and in September Savoy and Portugal deserted Louis' cause. Not the least of these troubles was the revolt in the Cévennes, which Louis' advisers had told him was 'a fire of straw'. Montrevel, a man whose birth was his only claim to distinction, was sent to quell the trouble, and adopted the simple plan of giving his troops entire liberty to kill anyone whom they thought looked like a rebel; but the only result of this jack-boot policy had been to goad the Camisards, as the rebels were called, into selling their lives more dearly and liquidating horribly every priest they could lay their hands upon. In 1704 Montrevel was replaced by Villars, who was at the moment unemployed, being no favourite with Louis; and with good reason, for this plump, brilliant, jovial, swaggering Gascon was a man born before his time, a sceptic, and worse still, completely unimpressed by the divinity of Kings or the splendour of Courts. Caring nothing for the underlying religious question, Villars adopted a policy of conciliation, and by midsummer had not only stamped out the revolt but had actually negotiated a meeting between its leader, Cavalier, and the King. It was an astonishing feat; that Louis, with his pride and iron bigotry, should have been brought to give an audience to a rebellious heretical baker of twenty-two speaks volumes for the diplomatic skill of Villars. This interview was the high-light of the baker's life, and consequently his conversation with the King is much too long to quote; 'Be wiser in the future and it will be the better for you', said Louis in dismissing him after having made an unsuccessful attempt to convert him. After which Chamillard, the King's incompetent War Minister, who had been present throughout the interview, took Cavalier off to his office to try what he could do with him. Even, said Chamillard, if he did not believe in what the Church taught, he could pretend that he did. He might pray to the Devil if he pleased whilst at Mass, but he only had to go to it a few times to make his fortune. Let him only attend Mass, and he could reckon on a pension of £125 a year and a regular commission as a Brigadier. Chamillard's missionary effort gives us an illuminating glimpse of the corrupt cynicism at the back of those 'conversions' which for the last twenty years had so edified Louis and the pious ladies of his Court.

On 2 August a crippling disaster overtook Louis; at sunrise his army of the Rhine, Tallard commanding, had deployed for battle with its right flank resting on the Danube village of Blenheim; across the tributary Nebel were the Allies under Marlborough and Eugène; and when darkness fell, Tallard was a prisoner who had lost half his army, including nine thousand of the best infantry in France, trapped in Blenheim village. Well might the twelve hundred officer prisoners say to each other, 'Oh, que dira le Roi!' For Blenheim was more than a lost battle, it was the close of an epoch. Since Condé's victory at Rocroi more than half a century earlier, France had been indisputably the first military power in the world, and that position she was not to recapture until the coming of Napoleon. Bourbon armies were to fight bravely again, and never more courageously than in the next few years, but the old confidence in victory, which is an army's greatest asset, had vanished.

And what did the King say? Unable for once to conceal his grief and indignation, he complained openly 'of the little regard his Generals had had for his glory'; and he cashiered two Quartermaster-Generals and fourteen Brigadiers. And his heart must have stood still when he realized the full magnitude of the calamity; he had gone to bed on 1 August master of a victorious army thrusting deep into the Empire, and before the next sunset his vital problem had become how to defend the western bank of the Rhine; and even to do that would involve the creation of a new army in the middle of an exhausting campaign. He can have had but small pleasure in the pompous rejoicings at Marly on 12 August to celebrate the birth of a son to the Duchess of Burgundy though the collation, the drums, trumpets, hautboys, and triumphal arches might have momentarily cheated him into the belief that all was well, had he not heard of the incident of the fireworks. Rain had threatened on the previous day, and labourers had been employed in sheeting the set piece:

PASSER BY: What are you doing there?
LABOURER: Packing up this *feu de joie* to send it to the Emperor; we have no use for it now.

So even the *canaille* already grasped the full extent of his humiliation; this must have been Louis' bitter thought.

Even at St Cyr he no longer found his former comfort; instead of being welcomed by his child-friends with flowers in their hair, divided into groups dancing to the music of their own songs, it was now his task to offer futile consolation to tear-stained girls whose fathers and brothers had died in battle; well might his face at Vespers be 'filled with a grave sadness and the most humble resignation'.

And, constantly tormenting him, Louis had the well-nigh hopeless problem of making expenditure approximate to revenue; a problem aggravated by his own theory, which he imagined to be economic but which was really a political hangover from the Fronde, namely that revenue by loan was dangerous. And as taxation could be made to yield no more, he fell back on raising the deficit by the multiplication and sale of unnecessary offices; which produced a vicious circle, for the inducement held out to the buyers was tax-exemption. A situation no better realized by the Controller-General, Pontchartrain, than it was by Louis himself; for Pontchartrain's gleeful comment was, 'Every time Your Majesty creates an office, God sends a fool to buy it'. But nothing showed more clearly the economic naiveté of Louis and his advisers than the astonishing action taken in December 1706; when they discovered that there was 'too much corn in the Kingdom', and sold their surplus to the enemy to 'bring back a lot of money into France'.

On the expenditure side Louis was forced into hateful petty econ-omies which cut his pride to the quick. At Marly for example, he was forced to cut off his guests' tea, coffee, candles, and stationery; and the result of this war-time austerity was that the visitors 'sat at table in the silence of the refectory of a convent; no one dreamt of talking or laughing'. Like any Victorian bourgeois, Louis had to try to couple rigid economy with the weary struggle to keep up appearances for the benefit of his neighbours. Rightly or wrongly he thought that it was wise policy to devote the winters to pleasures and amusements, in order to hearten his subjects, and to show his enemies how little uneasiness their victories caused him. There were balls at Marly on every visit, often fancy dress ones; and at these Louis, though long past such diversions, would appear with a gauze robe thrown over his ordinary clothes, so that no one might feel that the host had not had the civility to assume a disguise himself. And the traditional Royal generosity must still flow, both in hard cash and by expenses incurred to stimulate the circulation of money. In February 1706 for instance, we notice that he gave £2,500 to an eight year old girl from Brittany who was being brought up by Mme de Maintenon; and in September of the same year the Court visited Fontainebleau, out of charity to the townsfolk to whom the cancellation of the Royal visit would have been disastrous.

At last under the scourge of misfortune we detect some signs in Louis of a real penitence for his own past sins; when the Duchess of Burgundy's child, the little Duke of Brittany, died in April 1705, he said that they had offered many prayers for the health of this infant, but they had not known what they were doing; by his death he had become an angel in Heaven. Great Princes were exposed to so many temptations that one should rather fear than hope that they would live.

The year 1705 brought Louis a curious reminder of his vanished youth; Marie Mancini, Connétable de Colonna, landed in Provence. How Louis' heart would have leapt at the news in the old days, and how differently he would have reacted to it. But now, poor Marie had difficulty in obtaining leave to visit her family, and it was granted only on condition that she kept away from Versailles and Paris; probably because Mme de Maintenon viewed with strong disfavour any idea of a sentimental meeting between Marie and the King. Marie would have been wiser to have stayed in Italy, for everything had completely changed since she had left France. There was no one now whom she could contact except her own relations, and practically the only house open to her was that of her brother, the Duc de Nevers. She speedily became disgusted at her cold reception and returned to Italy.

For Louis the darkness of those days was shot with gleams of sunlight; he still had the company of the Duchess of Burgundy, his garden at Marly, his friends at St Cyr; and he could still relish the tonic effect of an adroit compliment. Chatting one day with Boileau, he expressed his disapproval of the current habit of using the words *grand* and *gros* as if they were synonyms, and asked the great critic for his opinion. 'Sire', replied Boileau, 'I can see all the difference in the world between Louis Le *Grand* and Louis Le *Gros*'. But in spite of such remarks as this, Boileau had taken the measure of his master's foot; a year or two earlier he told a friend that he had always noticed that when the conversation did not turn round Louis' acts, the King was at once bored and was ready to yawn or to retire.

On 30 March 1706 died one of the few remaining great men of Louis' early and middle period, Maréchal Vauban; he had been the foremost military engineer of his day, and it was to him that the King owed no small part of such soldierly reputation as he had acquired at his annual siege. We mention his death here in order to refute the charge of ingratitude brought against Louis, who is alleged to have let Vauban languish in disgrace for publishing his *Dixme Royale* in 1700. The fact is that when Louis heard that Vauban's condition was despaired of, he ordered Boudin, his own Physician-in-Ordinary, to go at once to the Maréchal, and spoke of him with great esteem and friendship, saying that he looked like losing a man who loved his King and his country.

1706 was another disastrous year for France; on 11 May Villeroi was beaten at Ramillies, and the debacle entailed the loss of the Netherlands; in June the Allies proclaimed the Archduke Charles King of Spain; the lost battle of Turin resulted in Louis' expulsion from Piedmont in September; and in October the French peace proposals were brusquely rejected by the enemy. The most serious of these blows was of course Ramillies, which reduced Louis to a complicated state of misery; there was terror at the desperate situation in which he found himself; sorrow that it should have been the bungling incompetence of his old friend Villeroi which had brought him to such a pass; and mortification at the sinister news that at Ramillies even the Household troops 'had behaved very ill'. But though Louis' sufferings were acute, he managed to retain his outward tranquillity over every aspect of the matter except the behaviour of his Guards; and on that subject he expressed himself with bitterness. But he still defended Villeroi, though the outcry against his continued employment was unanimous in the army, and expressed without reserve. It is ironical that as the only exception to his own rule of never having a favourite, Louis should have selected the man who very nearly lost him his Crown; and we watch with a mixture of sympathy and exasperation his obstinate determination to see in Villeroi a competent soldier dogged by misfortune. And with an exasperation untempered by sympathy, Villeroi's stupidity in rejecting the olive branch extended to him by Louis when, in obedience to the public clamour, he was compelled to dismiss him. Whatever may be thought of Louis' conduct in the Villeroi affair as King, there can be no two opinions about the tolerance and kindliness of Louis the man. In June he asked Villeroi to resign, promising him that it would be published that the Maréchal had been allowed to quit the Flanders

Command at his own urgent request; and, Louis went on to say, he personally would always be grateful for a sacrifice more painful to himself than to Villeroi; to which the Maréchal was fool enough to reply that as he was neither sick nor wounded, he could not dishonour himself by resigning without any plausible excuse. Even after this, Louis wrote to him three or four times more, always in the same affectionate tone as that of his first letter. But when to the last of his appeals the Maréchal replied arrogantly that the King could deprive him of his command, but must not expect that he was going to meet him half-way, Louis lost his temper and dismissed him. 'I have never,' wrote Mme de Maintenon, 'seen the King more moved than he was at the action he was compelled to take', and as for M de Villeroi, she added, he was now in despair, and with only too much reason; for it was the dry and bitter despair of one who had deliberately incurred a disgrace which his King had done his utmost to spare him.

1707 was ushered in with further austerities. The Sons and Daughters of France did not receive the usual New Year gifts, the King refused his own of £35,000 in new minted gold, and Montespan's pension was reduced from £10,000 a year to £7,200; a drop in the ocean, but these economies were favourably viewed by the public.

All eyes were now fixed on Louis who, at a cost known only to himself, continued to act his part to perfection. Firm, tranquil, level-headed, kindly, he was meticulous in carrying out his usual routine, and even so close an observer as Mme de Maintenon said that if she did not know better, she would have thought that he had no anxieties. But not even the King's example could dispel the gloom which now hung over his Court, where sadness, boredom, and distrust reigned, and where libels circulated, which increased daily in number and in venom. And cruellest blow of all for Louis must have been the knowledge that the worst of them were written by his own daughter, 'Mme La Duchesse'.

Militarily, it was a rather better year than 1706. On 25th April Berwick, commanding in Spain, won the victory of Almanza, which settled the question of who was to be King of that country—a battle which sticks in one's memory owning to the odd fact that the victorious French were commanded by an Englishman, and the beaten English by a Frenchman. In Flanders Vendôme conducted a not unsuccessful defensive; and Villars, having forced the lines of Stolhofen, invaded

Germany. But against this, Eugène and the Duke of Savoy had invaded Provence; Louis had been forced to evacuate Italy to reinforce his vital fronts; and in March occurred an incident which made him the laughing stock of Europe. A Dutch Colonel, one Guetem, with fifteen troopers, got through the French lines and, incredible though it may sound, finished his raid by capturing Beringhen, Louis' First Equerry, on the road from Paris to Versailles. Greatly annoyed though Louis was, he had the good sense to conceal the fact, and when Guetem was captured and Beringhen released a few days later, he showed up at his best; the Dutch Colonel was brought to Marly, thanked politely by the King for his kindness to Beringhen, and then taken to see the spring review of the Guard Cavalry as a preliminary to a twelve day visit to Paris as Beringhen's guest, where he saw the city, the theatres, and the Opera. He was run after by everyone, then went as a prisoner on parole to Rheims to rejoin such of his comrades as had been taken.

On Friday 27 May Mme de Montespan died at Bourbon, aged sixty-six, and a Mortemart to the end. Up to the last moment of her life, said Saint Simon, she was perfectly beautiful, and the best company in the world; her charm of manner caused her haughty airs to be overlooked and even combined well with them. There was never anything like her conversation which was, according to Saint Simon, an incomparable mixture of wit, elegance, and the most delicate politeness. She had an odd way of putting everything, and seemed to have a language peculiar to herself, but it was the language natural to her family; her brother (the Duc de Vivonne) and her sisters (the Abbess of Fontevrault and Mme de Thianges) all shared it. Then the memoirist goes on to belabour Louis for his insensibility on hearing of his ex-mistress's death. And perhaps we must not blame Saint Simon, for he was a child of five when the Poisoning Scandal broke, and was ignorant of the horror and disgust with which Louis had greeted the revelations of Athénaïs' traffic with the Devil. Louis' insensibility was fully justified, but not his resentment at his bastards for mourning their mother; for they were as ignorant as was Saint Simon of her real character.

One result of her death was that d'Antin, her legitimate son, whom she had always kept in the background, became a considerable personage at Court; twenty-five years of diligent servility had so far brought him nothing except the Government of Orléans, but now Louis visited his country house, Petit Bourg, and in June made him

Director-General of Buildings. 'I now had', says d'Antin, 'what I had been striving for all my life, the privilege of access to the King whenever he was not in Council or with Mme de Maintenon'. And in his newly acquired position he displayed an ignoble cleverness; one of Louis' foibles was a pride in the straightness of his eye; and d'Antin tells us complacently how he used to wedge stones under the statues at Versailles to throw them off the true, in order that Louis might call his attention to the fact, and d'Antin praise His Majesty's exquisite nicety of observation. And so well did d'Antin play his cards that he was to die in 1736 a notable entertainer of Royalty, enormously rich, and a Duke and Peer.

In 1708 Louis thought seriously of taking the Flanders Command in person, and was probably deterred from so doing only by the reflection that it was impossible to leave Chamillard in charge of the War Office; for here was a case, unlike that of Villeroi, where Louis retained an incompetent man out of personal affection, knowing him to be incompetent; 'Chamillard', said the King to Berwick this year, 'thinks he knows more than any General, whereas in fact he knows nothing about anything'. Whatever the reason, it was fortunate for Louis that he gave up the scheme; for had he not done so, he would have been in nominal command at Oudenarde on 11 July, and would have been held personally responsible for the disaster.

Oudenarde seemed at first to be the coup de grâce for France; except for Vendôme's beaten rabble the road to Paris lay open, and had Marlborough been allowed to mask the fortress of Lille and race for the French capital, there does not seem to have been any reason why he should not have taken it; but providentially for Louis, Vienna refused to countenance anything so unorthodox, and insisted that Lille must be taken before any further advance was attempted. The city, invested in October, was magnificently defended by Boufflers, who held out until mid-December; and when he at last surrendered, their prize had cost the Allies fifteen thousand men. In fact, one may say that in 1708 Boufflers and Vienna, between them, saved France.

Even Oudenarde was unable to reduce Louis to despair. On 14th August Mme de Maintenon wrote a pessimistic letter to Mme des Ursins, the King of Spain's French monitress at Madrid, which she ended by saying that Ursins knew Louis XIV too well to judge his feelings by those of his Mme de Maintenon; and that the King could no more instil a fragment of his courage into her than she could infect him with the least portion of her alarm.

But the fall of Lille in December was a different matter, and Mantenon, in giving the sad news to Mme des Ursins, said that the King was stricken to the heart to see one of his own first conquests in enemy hands; this beautiful town, so French, pillaged by all the nations which had entered it. And he was not less sensible of the disgrace of having been unable to attempt its relief. And, she added, she was all the more afraid of the impression which this would make on the King because of his efforts to hide it. One of the results of the Oudenarde disaster was that Villars, who to put it mildly, was not one of the most bashful Generals in the French service, and who was tired of the 'small war' role assigned to him, wrote thus to Mme de Maintenon on 23 August:

> I have the honour to tell you, Madame, that in taking leave of the King I took the liberty to say that if there was a major action in Flanders, I dared to flatter myself that the troops would see my arrival on the morning of the battle with joy . . . Truly, Madame, I flatter myself that when this campaign ends, I shall receive a courier from His Majesty ordering me to Flanders.

And lest Maintenon should not blow his trumpet loudly enough, he sounded a blast himself when he returned to Versailles in the winter; having listened to the King's account of the calamity in Flanders, he remarked with a shrug of his shoulders, 'Sire, Villars cannot be everywhere'.

The only consolation which Louis could give himself in the universal darkness was that of rewarding Boufflers, which he did royally; thinking of every possible thing which could please the hero of the day. Boufflers was given the *entrées*, created a Duke and Peer, and, against all precedent, his twelve-year old son was given the succession of his father's Government of Flanders. And Boufflers deserved it all, for when he volunteered to defend Lille he was an old, sick man, hazarding on a single throw the reputation which he had acquired during a lifetime of toilsome service.

Tired and hag-ridden though Louis was, suffering constantly from insomnia, his wonderful constitution still stood the burden thrown upon it, and at seventy he looked ten years younger than his age; and he was still the open air man he had always been. Writing about this time to Madrid, Maintenon says how she envied the King those Spanish gardens, full of breeze and sunshine; for these were the two things which Louis delighted in; he had, she continued, planted more trees than any man she knew, but he had always insisted on cutting back the branches so that there should be no shade. And, racked by anxiety, he could still remember those little courtesies which endeared him to so many, and did so much to blind them to his selfishness. Coming in from a shoot in September with a good bag of pheasants, he remembered that there were four fast days in the coming week, and distributed the birds amongst those courtiers who had a dispensation from fasting on account of ill-health. And in January 1709 we find him cancelling a visit to Trianon because when going to Marly on the previous day, he had noticed that the Life Guard escort was suffering from the intensely cold weather.

Finance had become a nightmare, and in this spring Louis, still adamant about State Loans, and unable to borrow, was reduced to begging. One afternoon about five o'clock he was walking slowly along the row of 'pavilions' in which he housed his guests at Marly, and as he passed that allotted to Desmarets, his Controllor-General of Finance, the minister came out in the company of Samuel Bernard, the richest banker in Europe. The King greeted them, and turning to Bernard said that as he had never seen Marly, he would be pleased to show him round. Bernard of course expressed his intense delight at such an honour, and during the whole walk the King showed him everything worth looking at, and talked to the man of money with his own inimitable gracious charm. The King got his loan, and Bernard never learnt that his 'accidental' meeting with Louis had been carefully contrived by the King and Desmarets.

Bankruptcy was thus momentarily staved off, but gloom reigned everywhere; in the Ministries, in the King's Cabinet, and at Court, where it produced mass neurosis. For nerves were strained to breaking point, and the continual demand was for news from the front, the only sedative which could afford momentary relief; even bad news, which was preferable to the torture of no news at all. The Prayers of Forty-Eight Hours were offered up everywhere; the Duchess of Burgundy spent whole nights in the chapel, and wore out her ladies with watching. All card playing ceased, even conversation languished, and courtiers were ashamed of the alarm painted on each other's faces; and if a horse was heard passing, all ran to the nearest window without knowing why they did so. And this psychological climate produced a flood of ill-informed criticism which drove the King nearly to the limit of his self-control. The courtiers, wrote Mme de Maintenon, were unbearable, criticising everything that was done, yet unable to offer a single constructive idea themselves; and, she went on to say that if the decision rested with her, all these carpers would be either in the army or in their governments. The women, she added, should also be sent packing, for they were if anything worse than the men; there was hardly one of them who did not give military decisions, criticise those the Generals took, and blame the King's every move. And when poor Louis tried to put some heart into his Court, or escaped from its intolerable atmosphere for an hour or two, it was imputed to him for unrighteousness. He had, said an habitual grumbler, passing fits of cheerfulness and firmness which were more surprising than edifying. At moments when his whole Court was anxiously expecting a battle he would drive people wild by going out shooting or walking. Perhaps, adds our authority, he wished to show that his anxiety was insufficient to make him change his usual habits, or perhaps he actually did not feel enough to give up his usual routine.

Then as a crowning disaster for Louis came an appalling winter which reluctantly gave place to the worst spring which Europe had known for a hundred and six years.

XI

IN 1709 the hand of God was heavy on France, and Louis began to pay in misery and humiliation some part of the debt which he had incurred by his arrogant pride during the previous forty years. The situation at the front was terrifying, but the Allied peace terms were so intolerable that even now Louis could not bring himself to accept them. And that nothing might be wanting to the people's sufferings, the year began with one of the hardest and most prolonged frosts on record. All along the Channel coast the shallow water was coated with ice thick enough to bear loaded wagons; seed and root died in the ground, colleges and theatres closed, and all outdoor work ceased; water mills would not run, travellers were found dead on the highways, and birds in the fields; bread and wine froze in heated dining rooms. Nearly all the children born that spring perished, and between 5 January and 2 February the number of deaths from cold and starvation in Paris and its environs alone, was estimated at twenty-four thousand. The people were dying like flies in autumn, said 'Madame' in March, and by April scurvy was rife in the capital, with plague impending. No money was available for the import of grain, and ill-conceived panic legislation to conserve stocks had the usual result of establishing a black market which forced prices still higher; between February and October the price of corn rose from $\frac{1}{2}$d. per pound to $11\frac{1}{2}$d., with no corresponding increase in wages; which no doubt had the effect of checking inflation, but at the price of killing off thousands who were unable to subsist on boiled grass and tree bark.

Even Louis admitted that the weather was exceptional, and on 9 January he did not go out all day, saying that so long as this horrible cold spell continued, he would not leave the house. Nearly a month later he was still forced to stay indoors; and was in a very bad humour, said Mme de Maintenon, suffering from continual headaches owing to lack of exercise. And as he now cared for no indoor amusements, she found the task of entertaining him almost beyond her powers. By the end of April even the courtiers realized the appalling state to which France was reduced, and at Marly nothing was spoken of but the public misery. No labourer, we are told, was more concerned about the prospect of the crops and the rising cost of living than were the courtiers; who indeed had a very direct interest in the matter, for those of them who had any incomes at all, drew them from their farms. And every day news of food riots reached even to Marly.

And there was worse to come. July brought with it prodigious hailstorms and inundations, which ruined the vintage and such crops as had survived the great frost; by August the country was on the verge of a revolution, and, ominous portent for the dynasty, there was a hunger march to Versailles. The King himself heard the mob from his window, shouting in the streets. Very bold speeches were made, containing the most outspoken complaints against his government, and against himself personally; people going so far as to exhort each other to bear it no longer, for nothing worse could happen to them than had happened already. In Paris things were even more critical; bread could not be moved without a Lifeguard escort, and there was a dangerous attempt to sack the house of the Chief of Police; 'Monseigneur', the most popular member of the Royal family, dared no longer drive through the streets; and as for Mme de Maintenon, she could not venture to show her face outside Versailles; and by September we learn that even the wealthiest were feeling the pinch.

In the provinces the situation was as bad as in the capital, and in July came startling news from Languedoc; one of the now common bread riots had shown signs of developing into something more serious, and a Swiss regiment, ordered to fire on the mob, had flatly refused to obey. And Louis, so far from being able to punish, had to issue a paternal edict reducing the Languedoc taxes by £85,000; a gesture which was less benevolent than it seemed, for in fact revenue by taxation had now dried up almost entirely, and the King was reduced to extraordinary measures to keep his last army in the field. By June he was endeavouring without success to pawn the Crown jewels, and three months earlier he had appealed to his subjects to send their plate to the Mint; and though he himself set the example, the response was poor. Saint Simon's conduct on this occasion was typical of the selfishness displayed by his caste. Among those who gave up the use of silver plate, the majority, he tells us, kept it locked up, to turn into money if necessary, or to bring it into use again if better times came. And the memoirist himself 'brought up the rear'. It was not until he found himself almost the only man of his rank still dining off plate that he sent 'some plain old-fashioned stuff' to the Mint and hid the remainder.

It is to Mme de Maintenon that we turn to see how Louis reacted to the terrible position in which he now found himself; noting first however that she was under no illusions as to the King's share of responsibility for the disaster which had overwhelmed France. We must, she wrote, regard all that has happened as coming from God; the King had been too proud, and God had humiliated him to save his soul; his frontiers had been too widely and perhaps unjustly extended, and God had decided to confine him within narrower bounds. And she went on to describe her own trials in living with the King in his present state; he was, she said, always calling her away from what she had to do, and she had always to be ready for him, in good health and spirits. He would come in, express astonishment at finding her windows shut, and open them all, leaving her to freeze. Nor would he allow her to arrange her furniture as she liked it. On his bad days it was her task to soothe his grief, his depression, his vapours, and to wipe away the tears which he could no longer control. And worst of all were the exertions she had to make to prevent awkward silences; for Louis himself now had no conversation. And though he strove desperately to command himself in public, he was not always successful; his face, we are told, looked 'ravaged', and at a Council meeting Torcy, his Foreign Secretary, described him as 'completely overwhelmed and grief-smitten'. Yet with it all, in this terrible year he never quite lost that courage and dignity which forced even Saint Simon to admit that now at last he had earned the title of 'Louis Le Grand' which had been so prematurely bestowed upon him.

Terrible though conditions were in the interior, they did not constitute the sole, or even the major problem which confronted Louis and his ministers; there was the state of the Army of Flanders, the last army which Louis could muster. As long ago as the autumn of 1708 Boufflers on his return from the front had told the King plainly that peace must be made on any terms which could be had, and since then the situation had markedly deteriorated. The magazines were empty, and corn was apparently not to be had at any price; the officers were eating black bread, and many of them were wearing nothing under their uniform coats, having sold their linen to buy food; and all, officers and men alike, 'were ready to take off their hats at the name of

Marlborough'. In fact it was an army which was already beaten before a shot had been fired and to this desperate situation Louis applied the remedy for which all France was clamouring; he sent for Villars and gave him the Flanders command.

It was Villar's hour. Perhaps he alone realized the terrifying responsibility of the task confided to him, and the pitiful resources available for its accomplishment; and understood too that nothing but cheerful confidence must be read in his face, racked with anxiety though he was. His only asset was his unbounded popularity with the troops, and upon this he traded up to the limit; and, even by modern democratic ideas, beyond the limit. What was Louis' France to make of a Commander-in-Chief who day and night moved among his men, joking with private soldiers and slapping them on the back? And who made it a practice to pass part of the night in the men's billets, drinking a tot of brandy with them and telling them stories? And one has only to study Rigaud's portrait of Villars to understand the type of stories he was given to telling; and how well he must have told them.

Even the famine did not come entirely amiss to Villars, for the rumour in the provinces that there was bread with the army caused a rush to enlist, so at least he could take the field with his regiments up to strength. That was, assuming that he could take the field at all. Maintenon, writing to her confidante at Madrid, said that she had just seen Villars, who had told her that owing to lack of provisions, munitions, money, and indeed of everything, he did not think that he would be able to enter upon a campaign; and, she went on to say, when Villars, always chockful of confidence, courage, and expedients, talked thus, things must be as bad as they could possibly be. From the front Villars wrote to her on 25 June saying, 'I need all my resolution to seem gay and tranquil after such nights as I pass'. But it was only to Mme de Maintenon that he showed himself so unreservedly, and to the War Minister he wrote in a vein of flippant irony which one imagines the King cannot have found to his taste:

27 July. One grows accustomed to anything, but the habit of not eating is difficult to acquire.

12 August. As we cannot have peace, we must implore the intercession of Our Lady of Hit-Hard.

An admirable tonic was administered to army morale in September,

198

when Boufflers, with rare self-effacement, left for Flanders to serve as a 'Volunteer' under Villars; that is to say that, dropping his rank and seniority, he was coming to make himself useful in any capacity which the Commander-in-Chief might direct. So it was with a good heart that the last hope of France faced up to Marlborough and Eugène at Malplaquet on 11 September. Louis had hoped to avoid a battle, but it was welcomed by Villars whose confidence in his new Army of Flanders was justified. Admittedly Malplaquet was, technically speaking, a French defeat, for the Allies were left in possession of the battlefield; but they gained precious little else. In killed alone they lost 20,000 men, whilst France retired fighting, in good order, and with a total casualty list of 8,000 killed and wounded. Best of all, Villars had shown his countrymen that Marlborough was not invincible; and in future no French army would go into action against 'Malbrouk' certain of its own defeat, as had been the case in Villeroi's time.

But Villars, who was himself badly wounded in the battle, had no illusions about the worth of his own achievement; he saw clearly that final victory was impossible, and when he reached Versailles in a litter, his first words to Mme de Maintenon were that France must have peace at whatever price. Of Villar's reception by Louis we need say no more than that it satisfied Villars himself; and that the King's compliments to him—as recorded by Villars—take up rather more than a page of print. But Louis was no more the dupe of the half-victory of Malplaquet than was his Marshal; and he allowed himself to be influenced by it no further than to reject his ministers' advice, that in view of the probable Allied plan for 1710, the seat of government should be moved to the south of France.

1710 opened with further attempts at economy on Louis' part; there were no New Year Gifts, and he handed his own £20,000 over to the Army of Flanders; work on Marly was discontinued and hospitality curtailed. And it is interesting to note that the latter economies were instituted out of deference to that public opinion to which Louis was accused of being so indifferent. He had been informed that his people were complaining bitterly of the waste of money at Marly, and this made him so angry that Maintenon had the greatest difficulty in dissuading him from leaving the place instantly.

Small wonder that Louis was grasping so eagerly at the most petty economies, for in this year two startling facts reveal the condition of his finances by 1710; Maintenon told a friend that her credit with the Treasury was not good for an advance of £40; and in May a Parisian draper refused to supply Louis himself with bed-sheets unless he got cash with the order.

But if the King could not afford to let his Maintenon have £40, he could still find a trifle when it was a question of giving pleasure to children. On 25 January all the youngsters about the palace were invited by Louis to a puppet show at which the guest of honour was the three-year old Duc de Bretagne, Burgundy's eldest son; and a day or two later he told Mme de Maintenon's little Breton girl that he was looking out for a husband for her, and that when he had found the right man he would give him the Government of Gérande and the Colonelcy of the first infantry regiment which fell vacant.

But for Louis such things were ephemeral palliatives to days which began in gloom and ended in despair. After the Council meeting of 19 February, Torcy noted in his diary that the state of affairs was frightful. There was neither money nor credit; officers and soldiers were dying of misery; there were no magazines, and no way of making any. And he did not see how the army could take the field, much less hold out for a campaign. And the meeting of 30 April disclosed the fact that matters were in an even worse state than had been thought. The infantry was more unfit than when it had gone into winter quarters, and all, cavalry and infantry alike, looked more like ghosts than living men; whilst the few horses the cavalry still had were dying of starvation. By 21 May there had been some improvement in material conditions, but the officers' morale was low; they could talk of nothing but the weakness of their battalions, of which the strongest was down to three hundred and fifty men. 'And', concluded Torcy, 'it is under such circumstances that we have to envisage a decisive battle within a hundred miles of Paris'.

Even the news that the Peace Conference had actually begun to sit at Gertruydenburg brought no comfort to Louis, who well knew that, situated as France now was, his delegates' role would be limited to receiving such conditions as the Allies might please to impose upon them. And even Torcy could offer his master no better consolation than to assure him that any terms agreed to in the present state of things, could be regarded as similar to those promises which one made to a would-be assassin in a dark wood. One might have imagined that the unfortunate Louis' cup was now full; but in June came a theological crisis. This, luckily, is not the place to explore 'The affair of the Constitution', a development of the interminable Jansenist controversy; and we mention it only to show the bewildered and exasperated King's approach to a complicated and well-nigh insoluble problem. In those days, said Torcy, there was nothing easier than to discredit an enemy with the King. All that was needed was a charge of having an inclination towards Jansenism, or a distant acquaintance with some Oratorian. By this means a man who had never heard Grace spoken of, became not only a heretic but a personal enemy of the King and a disturber of the public peace. And it was clemency to limit the Royal indignation to excluding him and his family from all favour. It is Louis at his worst, the bigoted, intolerant product of that formalized substitute for Christianity which was now offered at Versailles; and to what extent religion had degenerated into mere ceremony can be seen in an interesting letter of 'Madame's', written this year. No one, she tells her correspondent, except Grand-Daughters of France could have a Clerk of the Chapel to say their responses for them at Mass, and hold a candle beside them from the *Sanctus* to the *Domine non dignus sum*. Princesses of the Blood had neither Clerk nor candle, and had to have their responses said by their pages. At the end of Mass the priest brought the Corporal to be kissed; but it did not travel lower down the ranks than the Children of France, and likewise with the chalice.

Throughout the summer Villars stood cautiously on the defensive in Flanders, and as Torcy remarked bitterly, it was regarded as good news that an army eighty thousand strong had succeeded in avoiding a battle.

Then on 24 August occurred an event in London which was to save Louis and his hard-pressed country; the Whig Ministry fell.

Anne and her new Tory government were scarcely less anxious for peace at any price than was Louis, and they set about obtaining it in a way which went far to justify sneers at *perfide Albion*; for though officially England did not drop out of the war until July 1712, she became virtually the secret ally of France from the moment the Tories assumed power; descending even to the incredible baseness of communicating Anne's orders to her Commander-in-Chief in the field to his opponent Villars, and in January 1711 opening secret negotiations with Louis behind the backs of her allies.

In April Louis had a further piece of good fortune; the Emperor died on the 17th, and was succeeded by the Archduke Charles, the allied candidate for the Spanish Crown. An event which demolished the last Whig argument for continuing the war; for why should England exhaust herself further in order to have Spain governed from Vienna instead of from Versailles?

The news of the Emperor's death aroused no regrets in Louis who, when it arrived, was absorbed in his own loss, that of 'Monseigneur' who died of small-pox at Meudun on 17 April also; and Louis' behaviour was such as to give the lie to the rumour, even then current, that he disliked his heir and kept him at arm's length. As 'Monseigneur' lay unconscious and dying, the King was in his son's room, 'seated on a day bed, trembling from head to foot', and when all was over, he went to Marly, where on his arrival he spent three and a half hours in the most violent transports of grief. 'Madame', who was one of the few people allowed to accompany him, tells us that she saw the King the next morning, and that he was so afflicted that it would have 'softened a stone'; but that he did not repine, and spoke to all with resignation and sadness; but tears were constantly in his eyes, and from time to time he stifled a sob. And 'Madame' says that she was terrified lest the King fall ill himself, 'for he looked very bad'.

Though England could now be regarded almost as an ally, the war dragged on, but under rather more favourable conditions for Louis; on 28 July Villars reported that his infantry was fairly strong, and without question stronger than he had seen it for the past three years; and a month later everyone was cheered by the news that the enemy officers were no longer paid, their credit notes were cashable only at thirty-five per cent discount, and their regimental agents were going bankrupt.

Villars succeeded in manoeuvering his way through the campaigning season without disaster, and in September Prior arrived at Versailles to discuss peace terms; incidentally making a personal hit with Louis, who took a great fancy to him.

Needless to say the restless, inquisitive little Duchess of Burgundy soon got wind of what was going on, and favoured Grandpa Louis and 'Aunt' Maintenon with her views on the situation:

Hearing them one evening speak in friendly terms of the English Government, she broke in, 'Aunt, it cannot be denied that England is better governed under a Queen than under a King; and, Aunt, do you know why?', fluttering and frisking about the room as she spoke; 'it is because under a King the country is really governed by women, and under a Queen by men'. The odd part is that they both laughed, and quite agreed with her.

It is our farewell glimpse of the charming Duchess, whose unexpected death on 12 February 1712 inflicted the keenest sorrow on Louis which he had known since the death of his mother in 1666. Ever since the girl's arrival at Court she had been indispensable to him, and to her he had always shown a rare unselfishness; insisting on her leaving him to attend balls and parties, though he admitted that he found everything dull while she was absent. Even if for some reason she missed the family supper, Louis would be graver and more silent than usual. And the Duchess, unlike Louis' daughters, always showed him every consideration, making a discreet use of her privilege of leaving the Court circle; and when she did go off to a party, she always saw him before she left and when she returned. Or if she got back too late, made a point of going to him first thing in the morning to give him all the gossip which she had collected on the previous night. She was his only pleasure, for her humour was so gay that she could always distract him, and she always had some titbit of information with which to amuse him, however sorrowful he was. And with her death, night fell upon the old King.

At half past eight on the morning of the 18 February, while his wife's body lay in state in the next room, the Duke of Burgundy died also; and the same coach took 'the hope of France' and his Duchess on their last journey to St Denis; and on 11 March their elder son, the Duke of Brittany, was laid beside them in the Royal vault.

Louis, stunned with grief at the loss of the Duchess, seemed to have no emotion left for the further tragedies which followed so swiftly upon her death; but he had to arouse himself to control the panic which swept through the Court world. All three victims had exhibited the same symptoms, and in each case the doctors had had to confess themselves baffled as to the cause of death; which seems in fact to have been scarlet fever. And in a society whose automatic reaction to any form of undiagnosed illness was to cry poison, mass hysteria broke out.

The Duc d'Orléans was chosen as society's scapegoat; he was an amateur chemist; he was systematically poisoning his way to the Throne; he had dealt with 'Monseigneur', the heir, first; now with the Duke of Burgundy and the Duke's eldest son; next it would be the turn of the late Duke's remaining child; then Louis XIV's; and thus at last Philippe would become the lawful King of France. In this universal panic only a few of the levellest heads realized the absurdity of thinking that lazy, good-natured Philippe even wanted the Crown, much less was capable of seeking it by such horrible methods. For to Orléans, already a typical libertine Prince of the Eighteenth Century, the divinity of Royalty was merely a convenient piece of humbug which enabled such men as himself to enjoy a life of privilege divorced from duty; he was perfectly comfortable on the steps of the Throne, but to have found himself its occupant would have filled him with dismay. Louis, with his usual penetration, had divined his nephew's reprehensible views with fair accuracy. He disliked him, but he was a fair-minded man, and, convinced that Orléans was no poisoner, he steadily refused to countenance slanders on his nephew's conduct. But even Louis could not stop people's mouths, and this absurd suspicion was to cling to the unlucky Philippe for the rest of his days.

With the arrival of Prior, Louis felt that he was entering port at last; and despite his sorrows the knowledge that France had escaped from deadly peril, seems to have rejuvenated him. Even Mme de Maintenon recognized the fact, and her letters began to show unwonted gleams of optimism. Louis, she reported in the summer, no longer had disturbed nights, but woke like a baby after seven solid hours sleep; and at seventy-four he was going out at Fontainebleau in the heat of the day, dashing through the sands of the forest surrounded by horses and dogs. And, she concluded, he now enjoyed better health than he did when he was forty. November found the Court at Marly, and once more Mme de Maintenon is writing; by candle light she tells us, whilst Louis was strolling about his garden in a heavy downpour of rain. And a day or two later he shot for two hours.

But his lynx-eyed courtiers regarded the King's health with less confidence than did Mme de Maintenon. On 27 October at Versailles, the King dined early, then drove to Marly to take a walk; and it was noticed on the way that for the first time in his life he fell asleep in the coach. Also, that at a musical party in Maintenon's rooms that evening, he looked tired out. And already far-seeing courtiers were quietly preparing for the time when Versailles would cease to be the hub of France. The Comte de Toulouse and and also d'Antin both bought magnificent houses in the Place des Victoires that winter, and the fact that these two men, who were necessarily so much about the King's person, should have acquired town residences, caused a good deal of speculation at Court.

Though the general Peace Conference opened at Utrecht on 12 January 1712, and secret articles of truce between France and England were signed in May, Louis still had the Imperialists and the Dutch to reckon with; and he was only too well aware that if he sustained a significant reverse in Flanders all his enemies would be at his throat again. So on 12 April he sent for Villars:

LOUIS: The confidence I have in you is clearly shown by my entrusting you with the safety of my Kingdom. But after all, luck may turn against you. If you meet with disaster, how would you advise that I personally should act?

VILLARS (hesitates).

LOUIS: Very well then, here is my opinion. Everyone wants me to go to Blois and not to await the enemy march on Paris which would follow on your defeat. But I know very well that armies the size of yours are never so completely routed that most of the regiments cannot be reassembled behind the Somme. I should then go to Peronne or St Quentin, collect what troops I could scrape together, join you, and make a last effort in which you and I would either die together or save the State; for I will never consent to let the enemy approach my capital.

To which Villars, always more of a soldier than a courtier, replied gravely that he was glad to hear it; and that a nobler death could not be chosen by a great King.

On 24 July, at Denain, Villars attacked the Austro-Dutch army under Eugène and defeated it; the first indisputable large-scale victory won by France in a major theatre since the outbreak of a disastrous war. But now that it had come at last, it was decisive; the Dutch accepted the terms already agreed upon between Anne and Louis as a basis for further negotiations; and though the Empire was to fight on with incompetent doggedness until 1714, Louis had the feeling that he was now almost at peace. In October Villars concluded a triumphant campaign by taking Douai, Bouchain, and Le Quesnoy. Even Mme de Maintenon allowed herself a glimmer of optimism. Never she said, had a miracle been clearer, nor a revelation more sudden. In July France, without courage, munitions, artillery, or wagons, had been forced to be the helpless spectator of any enterprise which Prince Eugène had seen fit to undertake; and now the Prince lay inactive at Mons, himself reduced to the role of onlooker.

One crumb of comfort Louis obtained in this year of domestic affliction, namely a reconciliation with his old friend Villeroi; ardently but proudly desired by both men, for the two had reached the age at which there was no future, and the past, brighter than the present, demanded an old and tried companion in whose company each could relive it. And Villeroi was now the only man left of that brilliant company which had encircled the King in 'the beautiful years'; he was full of old stories of their younger days, said St Simon, in which the King always took great delight; he knew all the gossip of the Town and Court, he could talk of music and hunting; in short, his memory was a sort of general warehouse.

It was Mme de Maintenon, knowing that Villeroi could amuse the King better than anyone, who brought about the reconciliation, presumably a day or two before Burgundy's death. Anyway, on the day of the death the guests at Marly were astonished at seeing Maréchal de Villeroi appear amongst them, and the King received him with as much kindness and familiarity as he could show to anyone in that moment of anguish and depression. Villeroi never left Court again, and he was the only man who enjoyed the entrée of Mme de Maintenon's room for the rest of her life.

But Villeroi's company could do little to dispel the gloom which now hung over the vast palace of Versailles; and indeed the whole structure of the Court began to collapse after the Duchess of Burgundy's death. The palace became solitary, and attendance there was now a duty, not a pleasure; it became the fashion for every Princess and great lady to maintain a little 'pleasure house', and amongst these was now the social life which had formerly been concentrated at Versailles.

Even Louis was tiring of the icy ritual in which he had entombed himself, and it was noticed that he, who had formerly so enjoyed the pomp of Kingship, now disliked ceremonial receptions; and it was now a constraint to him to be obliged to do the honours of his Court, though when it was unavoidable, he could still perform his task with grace and dignity. More and more of his time was spent either in Maintenon's rooms, where he had taken to dining with her privately, waited on by a single servant, or else in the company of the two-year old Dauphin, the future Louis XV. Whom we notice in July at Marly, whither his governess had taken him so that the King could have the pleasure of seeing him walk.

Louis at seventy-five was still in many respects the same man that he had been fifty years earlier; stag-hunting six or seven hours on end, said Mme de Maintenon, then coming home to eat too much, and spend too long at table. And she, now seventy-eight, was more sensible than ever to the fact that the honour of Louis' company could be enjoyed only at the price of freezing—freezing contentedly, for everything that contributed to the King's health or pleasure had to be found good. From Marly in August she wrote complaining to Mme des Ursins that when with the King, one must not pay any attention to discomfort; to him nothing mattered but grandeur, magnificence, and symmetry; draughts did not count when compared with the aesthetic satisfaction of having two doors exactly opposite each other. And, she added, she had known him to relish a room with four huge doors and two enormous windows. They were having an ungenial August, she continued, and everybody except the King was frozen; for he insisted on all the women wearing summer frocks; 'and', she says in conclusion, 'there is not one of us of any age who is not padded with cotton wool underneath her dress'. Nor were things any better at Fontainebleau, to which palace Louis moved his Court in September. Mme des Ursins must not imagine, said Maintenon, that she could have a screen in front of her big window, because Louis held that screens destroyed the symmetry of a room—'and so I must perish symmetrically'.

We all know of course that Mme de Maintenon was right when she said that Louis ate too much; but she might have mentioned that, unlike the rest of the family, he never ate between meals, and that in the matter of drinking he was exceptionally temperate. For the greater part of his life he drank only Burgundy and water, and never at any time had he drunk unmixed wine; nor did he ever take liqueurs, tea, coffee, or chocolate. All that he was ever seen to take between his meals were a few cinnamon pastilles which he used to slip in his pocket at dessert when he was collecting biscuits for his dogs.

The war still continued; but languidly, for all the combatants were exhausted, and the Generals realized that the struggle had passed out of their hands into those of the diplomatists. In March Louis agreed to procure from the Ducs de Berri and d'Orléans a public renunciation of their contingent rights to the Spanish Throne; which, coupled with Philippe V's renunciation of his rights in France, published in the preceeding July, satisfied the Allies. But even now, Louis' bigotry led him to endanger the peace which he so badly needed; between March and May the rival statesmen fought a battle over the exiled Huguenots. Louis stuck out for no concessions to his heretic subjects, and won his point; though after the signing of the Peace of Utrecht on 11 April he as a personal courtesy to Queen Anne, released all Huguenots serving in the galleys. For by this time his relations with Anne were almost tender; in April she offered him the Garter, which Louis gracefully evaded, out of consideration for the feelings of the unhappy 'James III' at St Germain; but, not to be outdone in politeness, he sent the English Queen a bath chair.

Freed of his other burdens, Louis was now able to put a little more drive into his war with the Empire. Before the end of the year Villars had taken Landau and Freiburg, and by the spring of 1714 the Emperor realized that he was engaged in a hopeless struggle; and peace between France and the Empire was signed at Rastadt on 6 March.

But if it was peace abroad, Louis found things far from peaceable at home, where he had entered upon the weary struggle to secure the acceptance of the Bull *Unigenitus*—a coil into which we will not follow him, though we may perhaps allow ourselves one snapshot:

LOUIS: If one could bring over the nine Bishops who oppose its acceptance, we could at least avoid the danger of a schism; but it will not be easy to do.

MME LA DUCHESSE: Well then, tell the forty other Bishops to come over to the side of the nine; they will not refuse you.

An airy solution which at least gives us a clever woman's estimate of the moral integrity of the French Episcopate.

Only one more blow remained for Louis to endure, and that was the death of his youngest grandson, the Duc de Berri, which occurred on 11 May 1714 as the result of a hunting accident; and as if that had been the signal for which the King was waiting, he withdrew from Court life almost completely after this event. Withdrew mentally as well as physically; 'when I was King . . .', he would now say in beginning some story of the old days to Maintenon and Villeroi. But habit and self-discipline still kept him at his desk, and in his office he was to remain King of France until the end. Nor did his refusal to go on playing the 'Grand Monarque' for the benefit of his Court imply that at seventy-six there was any diminution in his remarkable bodily energy. On a typical day this spring he hunted for seven hours, then went to a concert in Maintenon's rooms, as fresh as if he had done nothing. And he was, she tells us still hunting regularly twice a week, and on the other days either shooting or walking; on four evenings he would have his music, or else a performance of one of Molière's more serious plays; and all this in addition to his normal allowance of office work, Councils, and audiences. She could not, continued Maintenon, accustom herself to the King's continuing good health; his vigour, eyesight, and skill showed no deterioration; and on the day before this letter was written, he had brought down thirty-two pheasants in thirty-four shots.

Old age exaggerates the ruling qualities, and in Louis there had always been nothing stronger than his love for children; particularly his own bastards, a love which in this summer betrayed him into the most indefensible act of his life. He made a will in which he declared that the bastards and their male issue were eligible to succeed to the Crown in default of an heir of the legitimate Bourbon line. We do not know if it was Louis himself who wrote into the preamble the excuse that the King was moved so to decree by his anxiety to spare his people the horrors of a disputed succession; but whoever the author, the attempted justification for the act was mere sophistry. Even the most zealous supporter of absolutism would allow that a Kingdom is an entailed estate, not personal property to be disposed of by a will. Had Louis' will stood, its logical result would have been to convert an absolute monarchy into an Oriental despotism; for once the King's right to choose his successor was admitted, of what value was the proviso safeguarding the prior rights of his legitimate descendants? The specious arguments put forward in the will deceived nobody, not even the rank and file of Louis' subjects, whose common-sense produced the unanswerable retort that a King of France could not create Sons of France without the co-operation of his Queen. Louis of course had no difficulty in compelling his Parlement to confirm the legality of his decision, but this was done with many mental reservations; and no one thought for a moment that the King had had the final say in a matter of such far-reaching importance. Not even Louis himself, who remembered how his father's will had become spoiled parchment within four days of Louis XIII's death. His final words on the subject to his dearly loved Duc du Maine, show how well the King understood both France and his own son:

> You know that however great I make you, you will be nothing after my death, and it will be your business to turn all that I have done for you to account—*if you can.*

The first days of 1715 brought with them a hint that Louis was at last beginning to feel his age. Whilst going to bed on 17 January, he told his courtiers that never in his life had he experienced such cold as that which he had felt that day during his walk at Marly; and it was the first time that anyone except Mme de Maintenon had ever heard him complain of the weather.

Both his pious hatred of Jansenism and his detailed knowledge of what was going on are apparent in April, when he called the attention of his Lieutenant of Police to the fact that there were three preachers in Paris whose sermons smelt of Jansenism—'and His Majesty is astonished to learn of such important matters from others than his Chief of Police'. The most fatiguing duties of his office he still performed unflinchingly; on June 28 for instance we notice that after Mass he touched two thousand sick, saying to each one of them, 'The King touches you; may God heal you'.

But he now realized that he was an old man, and that he could no longer afford to waste energy on those trifles into which he used to enter so as keenly as if they were matters of State. In this summer, fashion had decreed new styles of Court dress for the women, and 'Mme La Duchesse' and her half-sister the Princesse de Conti, clad in two of the new models, went to the King's room after supper to ask which he preferred. Louis replied absently that they might dress as they pleased, for it was a matter of indifference to him; then, thinking they might be hurt by his lack of interest, he roused himself to say that he must admit that he did not care for the aprons and scarves.

But what did ladies' dresses matter to him now? Or indeed anything about the Court from which he had fled to escape the boredom which he, with his phobia about cliques, had himself created. Conversation, said 'Madame', was no longer the thing at Court; the men were so afraid to speak that each communicated his fear to the rest. So 'Madame' lived alone, finding that company in which the only possible topics of conversation were the rain, the fine weather, clothes, and gambling, fatigued her, and that she preferred her solitude.

By the end of July Louis' health was causing anxiety to his intimate friends; there was no definite illness, but within a matter of weeks he had sunk into old age, and by 10 August even men like Saint Simon, dependent on valet's gossip for their information, realized that the King could not last much longer. On the previous day he had had what proved to be his last hunt, and on the 10th had visited Marly, where he gave directions for the siting of some statuary; and at six in the evening he left his beloved Marly for ever. When he got back to Versailles he was so worn out that it was only with a painful effort that he could drag himself to his Prie-Dieu. But by the following morning he had recovered sufficiently to hold the usual Council meeting and to drive to Trianon after dinner; it was his farewell to that wind and sunshine in which he had so delighted, for he was never to go out of doors again. On the 12th, though he admitted that he was suffering from pain in his left leg, he insisted on walking to Mme de Maintenon's rooms in the evening. He never walked again; and on this day Maintenon, seeing him so beaten down, knew that this was death, whatever the doctors might say to the contrary. Louis himself probably suspected it, but he struggled on with that dogged courage which he had inherited from Anne of Austria; and on the 13th he had himself carried to the Throne Room to give a farewell audience to the Persian Ambassador—actually standing unsupported throughout the whole ceremony. But on the 14th he could no longer conceal his condition either from himself or his entourage, and after a bad night he heard Mass, and dined in bed, where he stayed until five o'clock when he had himself carried to Mme de Maintenon's room. On the 18th he reluctantly agreed that Fagon, his First Physician, should sleep in his room; and only because Maintenon was at the end of her tether. Ill herself, and now eighty years of age, she had been spending her days in comforting Louis and her nights in dozing on a mattress by the side of his bed. Certainly whatever may have been her real feelings towards the King—and these we shall never know—her conduct to him in his last days was irreproachable. Tuesday 20 August was the beginning of the end, for after that day Louis never left his room again; on the 21st he was too ill to review the Household Troops, even from his balcony, and delegated the duty to the Duc du Maine; and by the 24th, gangrene had developed in his leg. On that day Maintenon helped him to destroy some old papers, amongst which they found a rosary—'Keep it', said Louis, 'not as a relic but to remind you of me always'.

By this time there was no doubt left that Louis was dying. Even Dangeau dreaded it, and there is something rather pathetic about his inability to confide such a blasphemous suspicion even to his secret journal. The utmost he could bring himself to admit was that he began to fear that this illness was more serious than was at first thought. On the 25th Louis was much worse; but it was the feast of St Louis, and the fact that he was dying did not strike the King as an adequate excuse for departing from the ritual of the day. He insisted that the usual ceremonies should be observed, that the drums and hautboys should play as usual in front of his window as soon as he was awake, and that his band of four and twenty violins should perform in the adjoining room during his dinner. During the course of the day Louis, Maintenon, Mareschal, his First Surgeon, and Fagon met to consider whether the last desperate expedient of amputating the gangrened leg should be attempted; and it was the King who settled the matter.

LOUIS: Do you think you can save my life by this operation?
MARESCHAL: Sire, there is little hope of it.
LOUIS: Well, then there is no use in my suffering it. (Turning to Villeroi). Goodbye, my old friend, we must part.

And this matter settled, he sent for the Duc d'Orléans, to whom he said,

My dear nephew, in my will I have assured you all the rights to which your birth entitles you. To you I commend the Dauphin; serve him as faithfully as you have served me . . . and I recommend all my servants, upper and lower, to your kindness . . . do not, I beg of you, abandon them in their necessities ... and remember me. I have made the wisest and most just provisions I could for the good of the State, but one cannot foresee everything, and if anything (in my will) needs altering, you will act as you think best.

At seven in the evening Mme de Maintenon and her ladies came to the King's room, where his band was assembling for a concert, but the guests had hardly entered when Louis fell asleep. When he awoke his mind was wandering, but he pulled himself together, apologized for his impoliteness, and said that the time had come for him to receive the last Sacraments. The ladies were dismissed, Cardinal de Rohan and Father Le Tellier then came in, and he had a long talk with them, whilst Maintenon withdrew in order to shed the tears she was unable to restrain; when she came back, she was in time to hear Louis say, ' ... and you two will answer for it before God.' The Sacraments were then administered by Rohan, to whom Louis said, 'I have had a long life but how little of it has been lived for God'.

On the 26th Louis said farewell to his courtiers in these words:

Gentlemen, I have to ask your pardon for setting you so bad an example. I thank you for the manner in which you have served me, and for the loyal attachment you have always shown. I am sorry that it has not been in my power to do as much for you as I could have wished; the bad times must be my excuse ... I feel that my emotions are becoming too strong for me; I see that you too are moved. Farewell, Gentlemen. I hope you will sometimes think of me when I am gone.

Then came a last interview with Villeroi, at which he appointed him Governor to the Dauphin, or 'the young King' as he had begun to call him; giving instructions that the child should be taken to the purer air of Vincennes as soon as he himself was dead, and kept there until Versailles had been thoroughly disinfected. It is touching to notice that even thus late in the day Louis' passion for detail had not abandoned him. When Villeroi had left the room it occurred to the King that as the Court had not been to Vincennes during the past fifty years, Cavoye, his Quartermaster-General, had never arranged the billets there; and he pointed out a box which contained a plan of the château, and ordered it to be sent to Cavoye. Having done this, he called for his servants, with whom the room was instantly crowded; and all of them dropped to their knees, 'filled with sorrow at losing so good a master', as one of them tells us. The curtains of the bed were then pulled open, and Louis tenderly expressed his thanks for their goodness to him at all times, adding that if he had given any of them cause for chagrin, he begged their pardons. And before wishing them goodbye he urged the upper servants to treat the lower kindly and fairly, 'as I myself have done to the best of my ability'.

On the 27th he interviewed his troublesome family, appearing for the last time in that role of domestic peace-maker which he had always played with such common-sense and patience; urged them to live in unity and concord, and said to 'Madame' with a laugh, 'I do not say this on your account, for you need no such exhortations; it is for the benefit of the other Princesses that I speak'.

Though sinking fast, Louis was conscious throughout the day, which Mme de Maintenon spent by his bedside. And some of their conversation she preserved for the Dames de St Cyr:

LOUIS: I have always heard it said that it is difficult to make up one's mind to die; now that I am at that formidable moment I do not find the resolution a painful one.

MAINTENON: It is difficult to resolve to die when one has inordinate attachments to the living, or hatred in one's heart, or is leaving restitution unmade.

LOUIS: Oh, as regards restitution, I owe it to no private person; and as for that which I owe my Kingdom, I trust in the mercy of God.

After telling the Dames this, Maintenon went on to say that the King had said goodbye to her three times; assuring her on the first occasion that death brought him no sorrow except that of leaving her, then remarking with a sigh that they would soon be reunited. The second time he asked her forgiveness for not having made her happy; and added that nevertheless he had always loved and esteemed her. The third time he expressed anxiety for her worldly position after his death, and sent for the Duc d'Orléans to whose keeping he entrusted her, and whom he begged to do all that she might ask for herself, her relations, and her friends; saying that he was very sure that she would not abuse the Regent's kindness.

During the night the King slept a little, but was more often awake, and the watchers saw him constantly join his hands in prayer. He said all the prayers he was accustomed to use when in good health, but it was observed that he struck his chest at the *Confiteor*.

Mme de Maintenon's detractors are fond of saying that she callously deserted her husband as soon as he lost consciousness on 28 August; and it is true that she spent that night at St Cyr. But she had not left Versailles until she was assured by the physicians that the King would not recover his senses, and when on the 29th he did in fact do so, she hastened back to her post. During the day Louis had gleams of consciousness in which he recognized her; and once he said, 'Madame, you show great courage in remaining here for such a spectacle as this'. On the 30th Dangeau wrote of him that he was now a mere machine; most of the day he was unconscious, and when he was awake his mind wandered. On Saturday the 31st, the last day of his life, he remained insensible until eleven at night when he was aroused by the Prayers for the Dying, which he repeated so loudly that his voice was heard above those of the priests and attendants; and he even recognized Cardinal de Rohan, to whom he said, 'This is the Church's last favour'. These were Louis' last words to a fellow mortal, though not the last he uttered; for during the night he was several times heard to say, *Nunc et in hora mortis*; and a few minutes before the end, 'Help me, oh my God! Haste Thee to help me!'

He died at a quarter to eight on the morning of Sunday, 1 September, three days before his seventy-seventh birthday, having been King of France for seventy-two years, three months, and eighteen days, the longest reign in European history.

★ ★ ★

Almost two hundred and fifty years have passed since Louis XIV died, yet even today he remains a controversial figure, of whose character no definitive assessment has been made; not even by those who have concerned themselves mainly or exclusively with Louis the King. Whilst on Louis the man such verdicts as have been given are bewildering in their variety and divergence. A just, kindly man, striving to do what he thought was right? A pompous mediocrity? A brutal and selfish tyrant? Not one of these opinions but leaves us with a feeling that no handy dogmatisation can sum up adequately his complex character.

Louis was fatally handicapped by coming into a world in which everyone from his mother downwards regarded him not so much as a Dauphin but as tangible evidence of a miracle performed to save France. One does not discipline a demi-god, and for Louis there were few of those checks on interior malformation which operate on ordinary mortals. To a large extent he had to improvise his own character empirically, and it is not his failures in so doing which strike us, but his successes. Often proud, selfish, and arrogant, the remarkable thing is that he could so often show himself unselfish and modest.

With his pride we are less concerned than with his other vices, for pride was in him an attribute of the King rather than of the man. And his selfishness stems from the divinity which hedged his nursery; is indeed often merely a prolongation into maturity of the naïf childish conviction that what pleases us must please all our circle.

And then, consider that the evidence for his selfishness is largely drawn from the letters of Mme de Maintenon. No man, says Johnson, is willing to live under the eye of perpetual disapprobation; and if Maintenon's attitude towards Louis was not one of perpetual dis-approbation, it was at least that of frequent disapproval. And what man would wish to have his character fixed for posterity by his wife's letters to a female confidante, in which were reflected the transient irritations of the day? 'One must perish in symmetry', cries Mme de Maintenon; does it mean much more than that she had a headache when she sat down to write to Mme des Ursins? Selfish Louis could be, as in despoiling 'Mademoiselle' for the benefit of the Duc du Maine; but even there, Louis drew no personal advantages from a transaction which was the only one of its kind in the reign. And this selfish man invariably used his casting vote against himself in Council when he came into monetary collision with his subjects.

His arrogance we may perhaps omit from the reckoning, for this again was a quality of the King, and with his Kingship we are but incidentally concerned. Unless the reader insists on counting as arrogance his flaunting of his mistresses before the eyes of his Queen; but that I think should rather be called the selfishness of insensibility.

His charity, said Spanheim, was vanity. Possibly so, but it was as unceasing as it was discriminating; and if Spanheim always gave alms without feeling a glow of self-satisfaction, he was a better man than most of us.

No one now thinks of Louis as a great, or a good, or perhaps even as a genial man; yet he had in him more of all three qualities than had many who have been more leniently assessed by posterity. He had standards and values to which he adhered unflinchingly; as *père de famille* to twenty million children he struggled valiantly with the impossible task of keeping them all fed with the outmoded economic machinery at his disposal. And as father to the House of Bourbon he showed a kindliness and generosity to his family such as was then very uncommon in the heads of great Houses. Of his innate justice there is ample evidence; of his almost invariable good temper; and in his magnanimity to the traducers of his regime there is something of real greatness. If he aroused some hatred, he also inspired much affection. And let us remember that the whole of his private life was spent under a microscope, through which peered a crowd of jealous, often ungrateful men and women, who have recorded their impressions for our benefit. To me it seems that few historical figures emerge better from so searching a test; and that this Louis, warped but not broken by upbringing, absolutism, and flattery, need not fear comparison with any other man whose life has been so minutely preserved for us.

INDEX

(Louis XIV, being mentioned on every page, is necessarily omitted from the Index)

exposes Fouquet, 1661, 51; economics, 1663, 62; Louis' confidant in love affairs, *ibid.*; work, 80; and La Vallière, 1671, 90; flatters Louis, 1673, 97; convinced of Montespan's guilt, 1680, 120; death, 151

Colonna, Marie Mancini, Connétable de, 1640–1715, Louis attracted by, 1656, 29; he falls in love with, 1657, 30–1; and Louis' illness, 1658, 32–3; and Savoy marriage, 34–5; alienates Queen, 1659, 34; exiled, 1659, 35–6; meeting with Louis, 37; breaks with Louis, 1659, 37; defamed by Mazarin, 39; marries Colonna, 1661, 40; revisits France, 1705, 187

Condé, Louis II de Bourbon, Prince de, called 'M. Le Prince', 1621–1686, wins Rocroi, 1643, 15; and Lens, 1648, 19; and Fronde, 1649, 19–21; released from prison, 1651, starts fresh rebellion, 23–4; defeated by Turenne, 1652, 25; flees to Netherlands, 26; commands in Ardennes, 1672, 94; under-valued by Louis, 1673, 96

Conti, L. A. de Bourbon, 3rd Prince de, 1661–1685, in disgrace, 1685, 134–5

Conti, F. L. de Bourbon, 4th Prince de, 1664–1709, 'Mme La Duchesse' his mistress, 1694, 159; refused command, 1695, 160

Conti, M. A. de Bourbon, Princesse de, 1666–1739, 76, in disgrace, 1685, 134–5; and her sisters, 1694, 159; plays fashion model for Louis, 1715, 210–11

Court life, boredom of, 65–6, 73, 119; in 1681, 123; in 1686, 139; economy campaign, 1693, 156; in 1695, 162; in 1707, 189

Créqui, C. de Blanchefort, Duc de, *ob.* 1687, Ambassador to Vatican, 1662, 53–4

D

Dangeau, P. de Courçillon, Marquis de, 1638–1720, welcomes Princess of Savoy, 1696, 164; and Louis' death, 1715, 212

Dauphine, M. A. C. V., of Bavaria, 1660–1690, marries 'Monseigneur', 1680, 121; has a son, 1682, 127; death, 149

Desmarets, N., Controllor-General of Finances, and Bernard, 1709, 193

E

Enghien, H. J. de Bourbon, Duc d', 1643–1709, on Court life, 1665, 65–6; corresponds with Louis, 1670, 86

England, Henrietta of France, Queen of, 1609–1669, and her daughter, 1661, 48

England, Mary of Modena, Queen of, 1658–1718, arrives in France, 1688, 144

England, Anne, Queen of, 1665–1714, dishonesty of, 1710, 201–2 and Louis, 1713, 208

Estrades, G., Maréchal d', and London riots, 1661, 53; and 'the flag', 1662, 55

Eugène of Savoy, Prince, 1663–1736, at Blenheim, 1704, 185; invades Provence, 1707, 190; and Malplaquet, 1709, 199; and Denain, 1712, 205.

F

Fagon, First Physician to Louis, 211–2

Felix, C. F., 1642?–1702, operates on Louis, 1686, 138

Fénelon, F. de S. de la Motte, Archbishop of Cambrai, 1651–1715, Louis' opinion of, 148; and Maintenon, 148–9; attacks Louis, 1695, 162–3; and Burgundy 167–8; banished, 167–9; his brother cashiered, 1698, 170; significance of 'Télémaque', 174

Fontanges, M. A. S. de Roussilles, Duchesse de, 1661–1681, becomes Louis' mistress, 1678, 116–8; created Duchess, and abandoned, 1680, 121; death, 122–3

Fouquet, N., 1615–1680, Superintendant of Finances, explanation of Louis' treatment of, 22; Mazarin warns Louis against, 1661, 40; crimes and downfall, 1661, 50–52

France, Anne of Austria, Queen of, 1600–1666, birth of first child, 13; character, 14–16; sons' education, 16–18; Louis' love for, 18–19; in 1650, 21; humiliated by rebels, 1651, 22; hands over Regency, 1651, 23; scolds Louis, 1655, 28; anxiety over Marie Mancini, 1658,

32-3; journey to Lyons, 33-4; quarrel with Louis, 1659, 35; relief at Mazarin's death, 1661, 40-41; her difficulties, 1661, 48; exposes Houdancourt to Louis, 1662, 57; Louis' tenderness to, 1663, 61; estranged from Louis, 1664, 64, illness, 1665, 66; death, 1666, 67-8

France, Marie Thérèse of Austria, Queen of, 1638-1683, sees Louis for first time, 1660, 38; wedding night, 39; bears a son, 1661, 41, 54; jealous of 'Madame', 1661, 47-8; Louis' tenderness to, 51-2, 54; and 'Spanish Letter Plot', 1662, 56-8; hears of Louis' infidelity, 1663, 60-1; he promises reformation, 64; forced to recognize La Vallière, 1664, 65; and Louis, 1666, 73; made pretext for 'War of Devolution', 1667, 74; anger with La Vallière, 1667, 76; en route to Dunkirk, 1670, 85-6; her life, 1673, 100-1; forgives La Vallière, 1674, 101; receives Louis' mistresses and bastards, 1678, 118; rapprochement with Louis, 122; last illness and death, 1683, 127-8

Fronde, The, 1648-53, origin of, 19

Frontenac, Mme de, Louis' childish passion for, 1650, 21-2

Furstembourg, W. E., Prince-Cardinal von, 1629-1704, Elector of Cologne, 1688, 142

G

Gembloux, 1693, Louis' conduct at, 155-6

Gramont, P., Chevalier de, 1621-1707, boldness of, to Louis, 100

Gramont, Antoine III, Duc de, 1604-1678, cheated in Louis' room, 1666, 70

Guetem, Dutch Colonel, exploit of, 1707, 190

Guiche, A de Gramont, Cte de, 1637-1673, falls in love with 'Madame', 1661, 50

H

Harlay de Chanvallon, Archbishop of Paris, 1625-1695, witnesses Louis' marriage, 1684, 129-30

Heurtebise, 1676, Louis' conduct at, 106-7

J

James II, King of England, 1633-1701, ineptitude of, 1688, 141-2; reaches France, 1689, 144-5; Louis' consideration for, 1697, 168; death, 1701, 179

'James III, King of England', 1688-1766, recognized by Louis, 1701, 179-80

L

La Chaise, F. d'Aix, Fr., S. J., 1624-1709, Louis' confessor, 129; and Louis, 1694, 161; Louis' opinion of, 1696, 163; loses influence, 1701, 181

La Feuillade, F. d'Aubusson, Maréchal-Duc de, 1623-1691, flattery of Louis, 116, 138

La Motte-Argencourt, Mlle de, Louis in love with, 1657, 29

La Motte-Houdancourt, Mlle de, ob. 1689, and Louis, 1662, 57

La Porte, P., 1603-1680, Louis' valet, 17; reproves Louis, 1649, 20-21; dismissed, 1653, 26

Lauzun, A. N. de Caumont, Duc de, 1633-1723, imprisoned, 1665, 66; his audacity, 1669, 81-2; and 'Mademoiselle', 1670, 88-9; his fall, 1671, 91; released 1681, 123; rescues English Royal family, 1689, 144

La Vallière, Louise Le Blanc La Baume, Mlle de, 1644-1710, history, appearance, character, 49-50; attracts Louis, 49; becomes his mistress, 1661, 50; quarrels with Louis, 1662, 55-6; and 'Spanish Letter Plot', 1662, 56-8; Queen discovers her position, 1663, 60; bears a son, 1663, 62-3; position, 1664, 65, 67; Louis cools towards, 1666, 71-2; and Montespan, 1666, 72-3; created Duchess, 1667, 76; follows Louis uninvited to Flanders, ibid.; Louis' treatment of, 1668, 79-80; flees to Chaillot, 1671, 89-90; bids farewell to Court and enters convent, 1674, 101-2

La Vallière, M. H. Le B. La B., Chevalier de, imprisoned for hooliganism, 1693, 156-7

Le Nôtre, A., 1613-1700, Louis' gardener, 125-6

Leopold I, Emperor, 1658-1705, and Partition Treaties, 1700, 174-5

35–6; irritation with Louis, 36–7; victory over Louis, 37; negotiations for Marie's marriage, *ibid.*; defames her, 1660, 39–40; political education of Louis by, 1660, 40; death, 40–1

Mercœur, L. V. Mancini, Duchesse de, 1636–1657, admired by Louis, 1655, 27; her marriage, 1655, 29

Mesmes, Jean Jacques II, President de, 1630–1698, reprimanded by Louis, 1688, 143–4

Molière, J. B. Poquelin, 1622–1673, in high favour with Louis, 1661, 44; 'Impromptu de Versailles' produced, 1663, 62; 'L'Amour Medecin' produced, 1665, 67

Monaco, C. de Gramont, Princesse de, 1639–1678, seduced by Louis, 1665, 66

Montalais, Mlle de, 1662, 55–6

Montausier, C. de St Maure, Duc de, 1610–1690, warns 'Mademoiselle' to hasten her marriage, 1670, 89; Louis' forbearance to, 1672, 93; plots to keep Scarron at Court, 1674, 102; boldness to Louis, 1676, 108

Montchevreuil, H. de Mornay, Marquis de, 1622–1706, witness at Maintenon's marriage, 1684, 130

Montespan, Louise Athénaïs de Rochechouart-Mortemart, Marquise de, 1641–1707, confidante of La Vallière, 72; accompanies Court to Flanders, 1667, 74; hypocrisy of, 76; becomes Louis' mistress, 1667, 77–8; he attempts to conceal the fact, 1668, 79–80; terrified by Lauzun, 1669, 81–2; bears a child, 82; engages Scarron as governess, 82–3; and La Vallière, 1671, 90; growing suspicions of Scarron, 1674, 102–4; Louis separates from, 1676, 105; his regret and relapse, 105–6; fight with Maintenon, 108–10; recapture of Louis, 1677, 113; in 1678, 116; final quarrel with Louis, 118; implicated in Poisoning Scandal, 1680, 120; relations with Maintenon, 121; rebuffed by Louis, 1686, 138; retires from Court, 1691, 150; pension reduced, 1707, 189; death, 190

Montpensier, A. M. L. de Bourbon, Duchesse de, called 'Mademoiselle', 1627–1693, reprimanded by Louis,

1649, 20; helps Condé, 1652, 25; and Montespan's surrender, 1667, 77; en route for Dunkirk, 1670, 85–6; projected marriage, 88–9; her sacrifice for Lauzun, 1681, 123–4

Montrevel, N. A. de La Baume, Maréchal de, 1645–1716, and Cévennes rebellion, 1703, 184

Mortemart, G. de Rochechouart, Duc de, *ob.* 1675, hears his daughter is Louis' mistress, 1667, 77

N

Navailles, S. de Baudéan, Duchesse de, 1627?–1700, bars Louis from Maids' bedroom, 1662, 57; exiled, 1664, 60

Noailles, L. A. de, Cardinal-Archbishop of Paris, 1651–1729, warned of Louis' distrust, 1701, 181

O

Orange, William, of, 1650–1702, in 1673, 96; at Heurtebise, 1676, 106; and Cassel, 1677, 112; lands in England, 1688, 144, *mot* on Louis, 1691, 152; loses Namur, 1692, 153; at Gembloux, 1693, 155–6; plot to murder, 1696, 163; France recognizes as King of England, 1697, 168; opposes English recognition of Philippe V, 1701, 179; death, 183

Orléans, Gaston de France, Duc d', called 'Monsieur', 1608–1660, insolence to Louis, 1651, 22; ceases to be Lieut.-General, 1651, 23

Orléans, Philippe de France, Duc d', called 'Monsieur', 1640–1701, love for his mother, 14; and flight from Paris, 1649, 19; Louis' affection for, 1652, 24; childish quarrel with Louis, 24–5; in 1658, 32; marriage, 1661, 45; character, *ibid.*; jealousy of Louis, 48; tires of ornamental role, 1666, 71; scandalous quarrel with 'Madame', 1670, 84–5; second marriage 1671, 91–2; Louis' goodnature to, 93; commands an army, 1676, 106; victory at Cassel, 1677, 112; public rejoicing at, 113; rebuked by Louis, 1684, 133; a babbler, 1690, 148; practical joke on, 1696, 160; bored by Court gloom, 1696, 160; is snubbed by Louis, 1698, 169, death, 180

222

224